Taste of Home

SOUPS & BREADS

TASTE OF HOME BOOKS • RDA ENTHUSIAST BRANDS, LLC • MILWAUKEE, WI

1610 N. 2nd St., Suite 102,
Milwaukee WI 53212-3906

Visit us at **tasteofhome.com** for other Taste of Home books and products.

International Standard Book Number:
979-8-88977-158-6

Content Director: Mark Hagen
Creative Director: Raeann Thompson
Associate Creative Director: Jami Geittmann
Senior Editor: Christine Rukavena
Senior Art Director: Courtney Lovetere
Assistant Art Director: Carrie Peterson
Manager, Production Design: Satyandra Raghav
Senior Print Publication Designer: Bipin Balakrishnan
Print Production Artist: Nandini Mittal
Deputy Editor, Copy Desk: Ann M. Walter
Senior Copy Editor: Suchismita Ukil
Associate Copy Editor: Rachana Rana

Cover Photography:
Photographer: Mark Derse
Set Stylist: Stephanie Marchese
Food Stylist: Sue Draheim

Pictured on front cover:
Cheese Chicken Soup, p. 172; Copycat Cheesecake Factory Brown Bread, p. 225; Buttermilk Biscuits, p. 288; Ravioli Soup, p. 140

Pictured on back cover:
Parmesan Scones, p. 302; Chicken Tortilla Soup, p. 42; Cheeseburger Soup, p. 166; Bacon Walnut Bread with Honey Butter, p. 242; Olive Bread, p. 237; Chinese Beef Noodle Soup, p.129; Chipotle Pumpkin Butternut Soup, p. 118; No-Knead Harvest Bread, p. 238

Printed in China
3 5 7 9 10 8 6 4 2

Pumpkin & Bean Soup, p. 109

P. 301

P. 122
P. 310

TWO BOOKS IN ONE!

The perfect mealtime pairing is at your fingertips with this collection of heartwarming specialties. With ***Taste of Home Soups & Breads***, settling in for a simply comforting feast has never been easier ... or more delicious!

The first half of this cookbook features the hearty soul-soothing soups you love, from all-time standbys to new tastes featuring ramen noodles, shrimp and more. You'll even discover stews, chili and meatless soups sure to become favorites.

The second half serves up golden breads, biscuits and other buttery delights. The easy-to-follow recipes, step-by-step directions and bread-baking tips in this cookbook guarantee success, whether you're an experienced baker or simply starting out.

Best of all, slow-cooker and Dutch oven icons, as well as "Pair It With" boxes, make menu planning as simple as can be!

Warm spirits, make memories and get cozy with the 200+ recipes in ***Soups & Breads***. Page through this keepsake cookbook and set your table with everyone's favorite mealtime pairing tonight.

CONTENTS

SOUPS

Soup Making 101 6
All-Time Classics 14
Beef & Poultry 44
Seafood, Meatless & More 72
Beans & Lentils 98
Ramen & Pasta 120
Creamy & Cheesy 148
Stews & Chili 174

BREADS

Bread Basics 200
Yeast & Rising 208
Quick & Easy 240
Rolls, Biscuits & More 264
Special & Savory 290

INDEXES

Soups Index 316
Breads Index 319

SOUPS

Soup Making 101 6
All-Time Classics 14
Beef & Poultry 44
Seafood, Meatless & More 72
Beans & Lentils 98
Ramen & Pasta 120
Creamy & Cheesy 148
Stews & Chili 174

SOUP MAKING 101

Whether you're new to preparing soup or a regular pro, you'll find that the tips and hints here promise to make the most of your time in the kitchen, amp up flavor and keep family and friends asking for more.

TYPES OF SOUP

There are numerous varieties of soup and countless recipes for each. Understand the different types of soup, and menu planning becomes a breeze. Below are just a few of the more popular types—all of which appear in this handy cookbook.

BISQUE

A thick, pureed soup often prepared with seafood. It may also be made with poultry or vegetables.

CHILI

A satisfying stewlike soup, typically seasoned with chili peppers or chili powder. It usually includes meat (often ground beef), beans and tomatoes, as well as onion, garlic and spices.

CHOWDER

A chunky soup of many variations that typically includes milk, potatoes, and some kind of pork, such as bacon or ham. Many chowders include fish, clams or other seafood.

CREAMED SOUP

A pureed soup that has a creamy, silky texture. Most cream soups focus on a single vegetable with smaller pieces of the main ingredient. It may be thickened with flour or potatoes and can be made with or without cream.

CURRY

Curry refers to an array of dishes primarily originating from India and Southeast Asia. Curries range from being a basic curry-seasoned sauce to specialty dishes involving meats and vegetables.

GUMBO

A hearty stewlike soup that's usually served with white rice. It's known for its flavorful broth, often thickened with a roux. It may contain shellfish, chicken, sausage, ham, tomatoes, onions, garlic, sweet peppers and/or celery.

HOW TO FREEZE SOUP

Keep this expert advice in mind so your soup tastes just as good as it did the day you made it.

1 WATCH PORTION SIZE.

Freezing your soup in one- or two-person portions makes for easy meal planning and helps the soup freeze faster.

2 CHOOSE THE RIGHT CONTAINER.

Opt for freezer-safe containers and leave about 1½ in. of headspace. Soup expands as it freezes, and you don't want your container to crack or break. When you're ready to eat, run cold water over the outside of the container to loosen the soup. It will pop out right into your pot. If you want to maximize freezer space, ladle cooled soup into freezer-safe quart- or gallon-sized plastic bags. Freeze flat and stack once the soup is fully frozen.

3 NEVER FREEZE HOT SOUP.

Hot soup put directly in the freezer will develop large ice crystals and freeze unevenly, resulting in mushy soup when thawed. For the best results, first cool your soup to at least room temperature (but, preferably, below 40° in the refrigerator).

4 AVOID FREEZER BURN.

If you're particularly concerned about freezer burn, cover the surface of the liquid with plastic wrap, smooth the plastic so that it makes contact over the surface of the food, then put the lid on the container.

SOUPS TO AVOID FREEZING

Soups with starches. Starches soak up liquid and get soggy when reheated. That's why we avoid freezing soups that contain pasta, rice and cubed potatoes.

That said, there are a few exceptions to the rule. Pureed potatoes end up just fine. And interestingly enough, barley keeps its texture and shape when frozen. If freezing one of these soups, hold pasta, rice or potato pieces. Add them after you've thawed the soup.

Dairy-based soups. A freezer does odd things to milk's texture, and the soup will be grainy when it thaws. Add milk and other dairy products when you're reheating thawed soup.

HOW TO REHEAT FROZEN SOUP

For the quickest cook time, thaw your soup overnight in the fridge. That way, when you get home from work, it's as easy as bringing the soup to a slow simmer on the stovetop. Stir regularly so that nothing sticks to the bottom as it reheats.

You can also pop your frozen soup cube right into a stockpot and let it melt over low heat. This can take quite a bit of time for larger portions of soup, but it's a good way to defrost and reheat individual portions.

For best quality, soups last about 3 months in the freezer, though certain vegetable-based broth soups can be safely frozen for 6 months or more.

PUT LABELS ON THE SOUP.

Before placing soup in the freezer, label the outside of the container with the name of the recipe, date and reheating instructions.

For Example: *White chili; January 9; reheat on stovetop and top with shredded cheese.*

This will help you remember what the food is, how long it's good for and if there are any extra steps to finish up the recipe.

Pro Tip: Set a freezer-safe storage bag into a glass, folding the top edge of the bag over the rim. You can then easily ladle the soup into the bag.

STOCK UP!

Making your own broth from scratch is much easier than you might think. It is the simplest way to take your soups and stews (and other dishes) to the next level, and save a little bit of money at the same time. Best of all, stocks freeze great!

USE IT WITH
The Best Beef Stew, p. 195

HOW TO MAKE

BONE BROTH

This rich broth is worth the effort. Use some in your favorite soup recipes that call for beef stock or broth, then freeze the rest for up to six months.

PREP: 1½ hours + cooling • **COOK:** 8-24 hours • **MAKES:** about 2½ qt.

- 4 lbs. meaty beef soup bones (beef shanks or short ribs)
- 2 medium onions, quartered
- 3 chopped medium carrots, optional
- 3 chopped celery ribs, optional
- ½ cup warm water (110°-115°)
- ½ tsp. salt
- 3 bay leaves
- 3 garlic cloves, peeled
- 8 to 10 whole peppercorns
- Cold water

1. Place the bones in a large stockpot or Dutch oven and add enough water to cover. Bring to a boil over medium-high heat; reduce heat and simmer for 15 minutes. Drain, discarding liquid. Rinse bones; drain.

2. In a large roasting pan, roast boiled bones at 450°, uncovered, for 30 minutes. Add onions and, if desired, carrots. Roast until the bones and vegetables are dark brown, 30-45 minutes longer; drain fat.

3. Transfer bones and vegetables to a large stockpot or Dutch oven.

4. Add ½ cup warm water to the roasting pan; stir to loosen browned bits. Transfer pan juices to pot. Add salt, bay leaves, garlic, peppercorns and enough cold water just to cover. Slowly bring to a boil, about 30 minutes. Reduce heat; simmer, covered with the lid slightly ajar, 8-24 hours, skimming foam. If necessary, add water as needed to keep ingredients covered.

5. Remove beef bones; cool. Strain the broth through a cheesecloth-lined colander, discarding vegetables and seasonings.

6. If using immediately, skim fat. Or refrigerate broth 8 hours or overnight; remove fat from surface before using.

1 CUP 30 cal., 0 fat (0 sat. fat), 0 chol., 75mg sod., 0 carb. (0 sugars, 0 fiber), 6g pro.

SIMMER DOWN

The longer you simmer this broth, the more collagen will be extracted from the bones, leading to broth with a silky texture and body. Don't worry if the bones start to fall apart. This is a sign you've extracted as much as you can from them.

HOW TO MAKE

VEGETABLE BROTH

Use this homemade broth in any recipe that calls for vegetable broth. It's an easy alternative to store-bought versions, and it'll be lower in sodium as well. Cover and refrigerate the broth up to three days or freeze up to six months.

PREP: 45 min. • **COOK:** 1¾ hours • **MAKES:** 5½ cups

- 2 Tbsp. olive oil
- 2 medium onions, cut into wedges
- 2 celery ribs, cut into 1-in. pieces
- 1 whole garlic bulb, separated into cloves and peeled
- 3 medium leeks, white and light green parts only, cleaned and cut into 1-in. pieces
- 3 medium carrots, cut into 1-in. pieces
- 8 cups water
- ½ lb. fresh mushrooms, quartered
- 1 cup packed fresh parsley sprigs
- 4 sprigs fresh thyme
- 1 tsp. salt
- ½ tsp. whole peppercorns
- 1 bay leaf

1. Heat oil in a stockpot or a Dutch oven over medium heat. Add onions, celery and garlic. Cook and stir for 5 minutes or until the vegetables are tender. Add leeks and carrots; cook and stir 5 minutes longer.

2. Add water, mushrooms, parsley, thyme, salt, peppercorns and bay leaf. Bring to a boil. Reduce heat; simmer, uncovered, for 1 hour.

3. Remove from the heat. Strain through a cheesecloth-lined colander; discard vegetables. If using immediately, skim fat. Or refrigerate 8 hours or overnight; remove fat from surface before using.

1 CUP 15 cal., 0 fat (0 sat. fat), 0 chol., 105mg sod., 3g carb. (2g sugars, 1g fiber), 1g pro.

1

2

3

USE IT WITH

Pumpkin & Bean Soup, p. 109

USE IT WITH

Copycat Olive Garden Chicken Gnocchi Soup, p. 130

HOW TO MAKE

TURKEY STOCK

Turn Thanksgiving leftovers into a savory stock that freezes wonderfully. Use the turkey stock in any recipe calling for chicken stock or chicken broth.

PREP: 10 min. • **COOK:** 1 hour 50 min. • **MAKES:** 3½ qt.

- 1 leftover turkey carcass (from a 12- to 14-lb. turkey)
- 4 qt. water
- 2 medium carrots, sliced
- 2 celery ribs, sliced
- 1 medium onion, sliced
- 3 fresh thyme sprigs
- 2 tsp. minced fresh basil
- 1 sprig fresh parsley
- 1 bay leaf
- 1 garlic clove, minced

1. Place all ingredients in a stockpot. Bring to a boil. Reduce heat; cover and simmer for 1½ hours.

2. Discard turkey carcass. Cool broth for 1 hour. Strain through a cheesecloth-lined colander; discard vegetables and herbs.

3. If using immediately, skim fat from broth; or refrigerate 8 hours or overnight, then remove fat from surface. Broth can be frozen for up to 3 months.

1 CUP 33 cal., 1g fat (0 sat. fat), 1mg chol., 89mg sod., 1g carb. (0 sugars, 0 fiber), 2g pro.

HOW TO MAKE

CHICKEN BROTH

Collagen-rich and laced with veggies and herbs, homemade broth is healthier than commercial versions, which can be laden with preservatives and salt. This chicken broth will keep in the fridge, tightly covered, for four to five days. Or seal it tightly in a freezer-safe container and freeze it for up to a year.

PREP: 10 min. • **COOK:** 3¼ hours • **MAKES:** about 6 cups

- 2½ lbs. bony chicken pieces (legs, wings, necks or back bones)
- 2 celery ribs with leaves, cut into chunks
- 2 medium carrots, cut into chunks
- 2 medium onions, quartered
- 2 bay leaves
- ½ tsp. dried rosemary, crushed
- ½ tsp. dried thyme
- 8 to 10 whole peppercorns
- 2 qt. cold water

1. Place all ingredients in a stockpot or Dutch oven. Slowly bring to a boil; reduce the heat until mixture is just at a simmer.

2. Simmer, uncovered, for 3-4 hours, skimming foam as necessary. Remove chicken.

3. Set chicken aside until cool enough to handle. Remove meat from bones. Discard bones; save meat for another use. Strain broth; discard vegetables and seasonings. If using immediately, skim fat from broth; or refrigerate for 8 hours or overnight. Remove fat from surface before using.

1 CUP 25 cal., 0 fat (0 sat. fat), 0 chol., 130mg sod., 2g carb. (0 sugars, 0 fiber), 4g pro.

CHICKEN STOCK SUCCESS

- Keep the liquid at a bare and steady simmer (not a full rolling boil). This helps impurities rise to the top, which you can skim off as foam. Skimming the foam ensures a clear and well-flavored—not cloudy—broth.
- The terms "stock" and "broth" are often interchanged by chefs and home cooks. To be 100% accurate, the term stock refers to liquid made from bones, fat, meat and vegetables. Broth is made with just meat and vegetables. Stock is what most people are preparing when they make this flavorful liquid at home.
- Most stocks and broths can be frozen for up to a year in sealed containers.

1

2

3

CHICKEN SOUP GLITCHES & FIXES

Taste of Home *readers told us their biggest mishaps making chicken noodle soup at home. Here are our top solutions:*

MUSHY NOODLES

To prevent soggy noodles, let the uncooked egg noodles stand in the hot soup, covered, for 20 minutes before serving. Cooking the noodles off heat ensures they plump gently; doing so in the soup means they absorb the delicious broth instead of absorbing the plain water.

DRY, TASTELESS CHICKEN

Say "buh-bye" to blah chicken by using bone-in thighs instead. They stay juicy and moist and have a richer, more robust flavor than boneless skinless chicken breasts.

BLAND BROTH

The thighs are key here. Give a homey boost to store-bought broth by searing meaty, skin-on chicken thighs first. This builds those irresistible brown bits on the bottom of the pan before you add the broth. A little spritz of lemon juice is the finishing touch. The subtle contrast brightens and balances the herby, savory broth.

USE IT WITH

Hearty Homemade Chicken Noodle Soup, p. 20

SOUPS

ALL-TIME CLASSICS

OLD-FASHIONED SPLIT PEA SOUP WITH HAM BONE

The old-fashioned favorite is a snap to make, and it's economical too. Carrots, celery and onion accent the subtle flavor of the split peas, while a ham bone adds a meaty touch to this hearty soup. It's sure to chase away autumn's chill.

—Laurie Todd, Columbus, MS

PREP: 15 min. + standing • **COOK:** 2¼ hours • **MAKES:** 10 servings (about 2½ qt.)

- 1 pkg. (16 oz.) dried green split peas
- 1 meaty ham bone
- 1 large onion, chopped
- 1 tsp. salt
- ½ tsp. pepper
- ½ tsp. dried thyme
- 1 bay leaf
- 1 cup chopped carrot
- 1 cup chopped celery

1. Sort peas and rinse with cold water. Place peas in a Dutch oven; add water to cover by 2 in. Bring to a boil; boil for 2 minutes. Remove from heat; cover and let stand for 1-4 hours or until peas are softened. Drain and rinse peas, discarding liquid.

2. Return peas to Dutch oven. Add 2½ qt. water, ham bone, onion, salt, pepper, thyme and bay leaf. Bring to a boil. Reduce the heat; cover and simmer for 1½ hours, stirring occasionally.

3. Remove ham bone; when cool enough to handle, remove meat from bone. Discard bone; dice meat and return to soup. Add carrot and celery. Simmer, uncovered, for 45-60 minutes or until soup reaches desired thickness and vegetables are tender. Discard bay leaf.

1 CUP 202 cal., 3g fat (1g sat. fat), 11mg chol., 267mg sod., 31g carb. (6g sugars, 12g fiber), 14g pro. **DIABETIC EXCHANGES** 2 starch, 1 lean meat.

"This was excellent! Hearty, flavorful and satisfying. This recipe is going in my family's laminated recipe binder!"

—DAWN0728, TASTEOFHOME.COM

STAUB
STAUB

BEEF VEGETABLE SOUP

Convenient frozen veggies and hash browns make this meaty soup easy to prepare. Simply brown the ground beef, then stir everything together to simmer all day. It's wonderful when served with bread and a salad.

—Carol Calhoun, Sioux Falls, SD

PREP: 10 min. • **COOK:** 8 hours • **MAKES:** 10 servings (2½ qt.)

- 1 lb. ground beef
- 1 can (46 oz.) tomato juice
- 1 pkg. (16 oz.) frozen mixed vegetables, thawed
- 2 cups frozen cubed hash brown potatoes, thawed
- 1 envelope onion soup mix

1. In a large skillet, cook beef over medium heat until no longer pink, 5-7 minutes, crumbling meat; drain. Transfer to a 5-qt. slow cooker. Stir in juice, vegetables, potatoes and soup mix.

2. Cover and cook on low for 8-10 hours.

1 CUP 139 cal., 4g fat (2g sat. fat), 22mg chol., 766mg sod., 16g carb. (6g sugars, 3g fiber), 11g pro.

CLAM CHOWDER

You simply cannot beat a bowl of thick and creamy clam chowder on a chilly day. This one comes together easily, even if you've never made the popular dish before.

—Rosemary Peterson, Archie, MO

TAKES: 30 min. • **MAKES:** 12 servings (3 qt.)

- 2 cans (6½ oz. each) minced clams
- 6 medium potatoes, peeled and diced
- 6 medium carrots, diced
- ½ cup chopped onion
- ½ cup butter, cubed
- 1½ cups water
- 2 cans (12 oz. each) evaporated milk
- 2 cans (10¾ oz. each) condensed cream of mushroom soup, undiluted
- 1 tsp. salt
- ½ tsp. pepper

1. Drain clams, reserving liquid; set clams aside.

2. In a large kettle, combine potatoes, carrots, onion, butter, water and reserved clam juice. Cook over medium heat for 15 minutes or until the vegetables are tender. Stir in milk, soup, salt and pepper. Simmer, uncovered, until heated through. Stir in clams.

1 CUP 230 cal., 11g fat (7g sat. fat), 33mg chol., 560mg sod., 28g carb. (7g sugars, 3g fiber), 6g pro.

MINESTRONE MADE EASY

This recipe is special to me because it's one of the few dinners my entire family loves. And I can feel good about serving it because it's full of nutrition and low in fat.

—Lauren Brennan, Hood River, OR

PREP: 25 min. • **COOK:** 40 min. • **MAKES:** 11 servings (2¾ qt.)

- 2 large carrots, diced
- 2 celery ribs, chopped
- 1 medium onion, chopped
- 1 Tbsp. olive oil
- 1 Tbsp. butter
- 2 garlic cloves, minced
- 2 cans (14½ oz. each) reduced-sodium chicken broth
- 2 cans (8 oz. each) no-salt-added tomato sauce
- 1 can (16 oz.) kidney beans, rinsed and drained
- 1 can (15 oz.) garbanzo beans or chickpeas, rinsed and drained
- 1 can (14½ oz.) diced tomatoes, undrained
- 1½ cups shredded cabbage
- 1 Tbsp. dried basil
- 1½ tsp. dried parsley flakes
- 1 tsp. dried oregano
- ½ tsp. pepper
- 1 cup uncooked whole wheat elbow macaroni
- 11 tsp. grated Parmesan cheese

1. In a large saucepan, saute carrots, celery and onion in oil and butter until tender. Add garlic; cook 1 minute longer.

2. Stir in broth, tomato sauce, kidney beans, garbanzo beans, tomatoes, cabbage, basil, parsley, oregano and pepper. Bring to a boil. Reduce heat; cover and simmer for 15 minutes. Add macaroni; cook, uncovered, 6-8 minutes or until macaroni and vegetables are tender.

3. Ladle soup into bowls. Sprinkle with cheese.

FREEZE OPTION Before adding cheese, freeze cooled soup in freezer containers. To use, partially thaw in refrigerator overnight. Heat through in a saucepan, stirring occasionally; add broth or water if necessary.

1 CUP 180 cal., 4g fat (1g sat. fat), 4mg chol., 443mg sod., 29g carb. (7g sugars, 7g fiber), 8g pro. **DIABETIC EXCHANGES** 2 starch, 1 lean meat.

THICK OR THIN ... YOUR CHOICE

The easiest way to thicken minestrone soup is to add 2-4 Tbsp. of tomato paste. You can also add additional beans and vegetables or stir in extra cheese. Cheese thickens the soup's texture while making it even more delicious.

HEARTY HOMEMADE CHICKEN NOODLE SOUP

This satisfying soup with a hint of cayenne is brimming with vegetables, chicken and noodles. The recipe originally came from my father-in-law, but I made some changes to give it my own spin.

—Norma Reynolds, Overland Park, KS

PREP: 20 min. • **COOK:** 5½ hours • **MAKES:** 12 servings (3 qt.)

- 12 fresh baby carrots, cut into ½-in. pieces
- 4 celery ribs, cut into ½-in. pieces
- ¾ cup finely chopped onion
- 1 Tbsp. minced fresh parsley
- ½ tsp. pepper
- ¼ tsp. cayenne pepper
- 1½ tsp. mustard seed
- 2 garlic cloves, peeled and halved
- 1¼ lbs. boneless skinless chicken breast halves
- 1¼ lbs. boneless skinless chicken thighs
- 4 cans (14½ oz. each) chicken broth
- 1 pkg. (9 oz.) refrigerated linguine
- Optional: Coarsely ground pepper and additional minced fresh parsley

1. In a 5-qt. slow cooker, combine first 6 ingredients. Place mustard seed and garlic on a double thickness of cheesecloth; bring up corners of cloth and tie with kitchen string to form a bag. Place in slow cooker. Add chicken and broth. Cover and cook on low for 5-6 hours or until meat is tender.

2. Discard spice bag. Remove chicken; cool slightly. Stir linguine into soup; cover and cook on high about 30 minutes longer or until pasta is tender. Cut chicken into pieces and return to soup; heat through. Sprinkle with ground pepper and additional parsley if desired.

1 CUP 199 cal., 6g fat (2g sat. fat), 73mg chol., 663mg sod., 14g carb. (2g sugars, 1g fiber), 22g pro. **DIABETIC EXCHANGES** 3 lean meat, 1 starch.

"This is the best chicken soup that I have ever made! I wouldn't change a thing. You need to make it!"

—AMYDOO, TASTEOFHOME.COM

PAIR IT WITH
Savory Stuffing
Bread, p. 210

LOADED BROCCOLI-CHEESE SOUP

LOADED BROCCOLI-CHEESE SOUP

For anyone who loves baked potatoes or broccoli cheese soup, this is the best of both worlds. If you have bacon lovers, offer crumbled, cooked bacon as a topping. Then everyone is happy—carnivore or not!

—Vivi Taylor, Middleburg, FL

PREP: 15 min. • **COOK:** 6 hours 10 min. • **MAKES:** 8 servings (2 qt.)

- 1 pkg. (20 oz.) refrigerated O'Brien hash brown potatoes
- 1 garlic clove, minced
- 2 cups reduced-fat sour cream
- ¼ cup all-purpose flour
- ½ tsp. pepper
- ⅛ tsp. ground nutmeg
- 3 cups vegetable stock
- 1 pkg. (12 oz.) frozen broccoli florets, thawed
- 4 cups shredded cheddar cheese
- ½ cup finely chopped green onions

1. Combine the hash browns and garlic in a 5- or 6-qt. slow cooker. In a large bowl, whisk sour cream, flour, pepper and nutmeg until smooth; stir in stock. Pour into slow cooker; stir to combine. Cook, covered, on low for 6-8 hours or until the hash browns are tender.

2. Add broccoli and 3 cups cheese; cover and cook 10 minutes longer or until cheese is melted. Serve with green onion and remaining 1 cup cheese.

1 CUP 386 cal., 23g fat (13g sat. fat), 62mg chol., 921mg sod., 26g carb. (6g sugars, 2g fiber), 20g pro.

ALPHABET SOUP

Instead of opening a can of alphabet soup, why not make some from scratch? Kids love this traditional soup with a tomato base, ground beef and alphabet pasta.

—Sharon Brockman, Appleton, WI

TAKES: 30 min. • **MAKES:** 11 servings (2¾ qt.)

- 1 lb. ground beef
- 1 medium onion, chopped
- 2 qt. tomato juice
- 1 can (15 oz.) mixed vegetables, undrained
- 1 cup water
- 2 beef bouillon cubes
- 1 cup uncooked alphabet pasta
- Salt and pepper to taste

In a large saucepan, cook beef and onion over medium heat for 5-7 minutes or until meat is no longer pink, crumbling beef; drain. Add tomato juice, vegetables, water and bouillon; bring to a boil. Add pasta. Cook, uncovered, until the pasta is tender, 6-8 minutes, stirring frequently. Add salt and pepper.

1 CUP 148 cal., 4g fat (2g sat. fat), 19mg chol., 858mg sod., 19g carb. (7g sugars, 2g fiber), 10g pro.

YUMMY CHICKEN & DUMPLING SOUP

Like a security blanket for the soul, this soup is a true classic. My husband is not very fond of leftovers, but he says he could eat this every day of the week.

—Morgan Byers, Berkley, MI

PREP: 25 min. • **COOK:** 40 min. • **MAKES:** 4 servings

- ¾ lb. boneless skinless chicken breasts, cut into 1-in. cubes
- ¼ tsp. salt
- ⅛ tsp. pepper
- 2 tsp. olive oil
- ¼ cup all-purpose flour
- 4 cups reduced-sodium chicken broth, divided
- 1 cup water
- 2 cups frozen french-cut green beans
- 1½ cups sliced onions
- 1 cup shredded carrots
- ¼ tsp. dried marjoram
- ⅔ cup reduced-fat biscuit/baking mix
- ⅓ cup cornmeal
- ¼ cup shredded reduced-fat cheddar cheese
- ⅓ cup fat-free milk

1. Sprinkle chicken with salt and pepper. In a large nonstick skillet, heat oil over medium-high heat. Add the chicken; cook and stir until no longer pink. Remove from heat.

2. In a large saucepan, whisk flour and ½ cup broth until smooth. Stir in water and remaining broth. Add beans, onions, carrots and marjoram. Bring to a boil. Reduce heat; simmer, uncovered, 10 minutes. Add chicken; return to a simmer.

3. Meanwhile, in a small bowl, mix biscuit mix, cornmeal and cheese. Stir in milk just until moistened. Drop batter in 12 portions on top of simmering soup. Reduce heat to low; cover and cook for 15 minutes or until a toothpick inserted in center of dumpling comes out clean.

1¼ CUPS 353 cal., 8g fat (2g sat. fat), 52mg chol., 1111mg sod., 44g carb. (10g sugars, 5g fiber), 28g pro. **DIABETIC EXCHANGES** 3 lean meat, 2 starch, 2 vegetable, 1 fat.

PAIR IT WITH

Copycat Cheesecake Factory Brown Bread, p. 225

QUICK CREAM OF MUSHROOM SOUP

My daughter-in-law, a gourmet cook, served this soup as the first course for a holiday dinner. She received the recipe from her mother and graciously shared it with me. Now I'm happy to share it with my own friends and family.

—Anne Kulick, Phillipsburg, NJ

TAKES: 30 min. • **MAKES:** 6 servings

- 2 Tbsp. butter
- ½ lb. sliced fresh mushrooms
- ¼ cup chopped onion
- 6 Tbsp. all-purpose flour
- ½ tsp. salt
- ⅛ tsp. pepper
- 2 cans (14½ oz. each) chicken broth
- 1 cup half-and-half cream
- Chopped chives, optional

1. In a large saucepan, heat butter over medium-high heat; saute mushrooms and onion until tender.

2. Mix flour, salt, pepper and 1 can broth until smooth; stir into mushroom mixture. Stir in remaining can of broth. Bring to a boil; cook and stir until thickened, about 2 minutes. Reduce heat; stir in half-and-half. Simmer, uncovered, until flavors are blended, about 15 minutes, stirring occasionally. If desired, top with chives.

1 CUP 136 cal., 8g fat (5g sat. fat), 33mg chol., 842mg sod., 10g carb. (3g sugars, 1g fiber), 4g pro.

CAN I FREEZE IT?

We don't recommend freezing most dairy-based soups, such as this cream of mushroom soup. Cream soups can often taste—and look—grainy once reheated.

BEEF BARLEY LENTIL SOUP

BEEF BARLEY LENTIL SOUP

I serve this soup often to family and friends on cold nights, along with homemade rolls and a green salad. For variety, you can substitute jicama for the potatoes.

—Judy Metzentine, The Dalles, OR

PREP: 20 min. • **COOK:** 8 hours • **MAKES:** 10 servings (about 3¾ qt.)

- 1 lb. lean ground beef (90% lean)
- 1 medium onion, chopped
- 2 cups cubed red potatoes (¼-in. pieces)
- 1 cup chopped celery
- 1 cup chopped carrots
- 1 cup dried lentils, rinsed
- ½ cup medium pearl barley
- 8 cups water
- 2 tsp. beef bouillon granules
- ½ tsp. lemon-pepper seasoning
- 2 cans (14½ oz. each) stewed tomatoes, coarsely chopped
- 1 tsp. salt

1. In a nonstick skillet, cook beef and onion over medium heat until meat is no longer pink, 6-8 minutes, breaking up beef into crumbles; drain.

2. Transfer beef to a 5-qt. slow cooker. Layer with potatoes, celery, carrots, lentils and barley. Combine water, bouillon and lemon pepper; pour over vegetables. Cook, covered, on low for 6 hours or until vegetables and barley are tender.

3. Add tomatoes and salt; cook 2 hours longer.

1½ CUPS 232 cal., 4g fat (2g sat. fat), 28mg chol., 603mg sod., 33g carb. (6g sugars, 6g fiber), 16g pro. **DIABETIC EXCHANGES** 2 lean meat, 1½ starch, 1 vegetable.

EGG DROP SOUP

We start many stir-fry meals with this easy soup, which cooks in just minutes. I got the recipe from my grandma's old cookbook.

—Amy Beth Corlew-Sherlock, Lapeer, MI

TAKES: 15 min. • **MAKES:** 4 servings

- 3 cups chicken broth
- 1 Tbsp. cornstarch
- 2 Tbsp. cold water
- 1 large egg, lightly beaten
- 1 green onion, sliced

1. In a large saucepan, bring broth to a boil over medium heat. Combine cornstarch and water until smooth; gradually stir into broth. Bring to a boil; cook and stir until thickened, about 2 minutes.

2. Reduce heat. Drizzle beaten egg into hot broth, stirring constantly. Remove from heat; stir in onion.

¾ CUP 39 cal., 2g fat (0 sat. fat), 53mg chol., 714mg sod., 3g carb. (1g sugars, 0 fiber), 3g pro.

THE BEST EVER CHILI

My dad and my father-in-law are the cooking gurus in our chili-loving clan. But after my honeymoon to New Mexico, inspired by the fresh and fragrant chile peppers at the Santa Fe farmers market, I felt it was time to introduce them to my spicy, meaty version of this chili with a touch of masa harina.

—Sarah Farmer, Waukesha, WI

PREP: 20 min. + standing • **COOK:** 1 hour 20 min. • **MAKES:** 8 servings (3½ qt.)

- 3 dried ancho or guajillo chiles
- 1 to 2 cups boiling water
- 2 Tbsp. tomato paste
- 3 garlic cloves
- ¼ cup chili powder
- 1½ tsp. smoked paprika
- 2 tsp. ground cumin
- 1 lb. ground beef
- 1½ tsp. Montreal steak seasoning
- 2 lbs. beef tri-tip roast, cut into ½-in. cubes
- 2 tsp. salt, divided
- 2 tsp. coarsely ground pepper, divided
- 2 Tbsp. canola oil, divided
- 1 large onion, chopped (about 2 cups)
- 1 poblano pepper, seeded and chopped
- 1 tsp. dried oregano
- 1½ tsp. crushed red pepper flakes
- 3 cups beef stock
- 1 bottle (12 oz.) beer
- 2 cans (14½ oz. each) fire-roasted diced tomatoes, undrained
- 1 can (16 oz.) kidney beans, drained
- 3 Tbsp. masa harina
- Optional: American cheese slices, sour cream, shredded cheddar cheese, diced red onion, sliced jalapenos, cilantro and corn chips

1. Combine chiles and enough boiling water to cover; let stand until softened, about 15 minutes. Drain, reserving ⅓ cup of the soaking liquid. Discard stems and seeds. Process chiles, tomato paste, garlic and reserved liquid until smooth.

2. In a small skillet, toast the chili powder, paprika and cumin over medium heat until aromatic, 3-4 minutes; remove and set aside. In a Dutch oven, cook and stir ground beef and steak seasoning over medium-high heat until beef is no longer pink, about 5 minutes; remove and drain.

3. Sprinkle steak cubes with 1 tsp. each salt and pepper. In same Dutch oven, brown beef in batches in 1 Tbsp. oil over medium-high heat; remove and set aside. Saute onion and poblano pepper in remaining 1 Tbsp. oil until tender, about 5 minutes. Stir in the toasted spices, oregano and pepper flakes. Add cooked meats along with beef stock, beer, tomatoes, beans, remaining 1 tsp. salt and 1 tsp. pepper, and chile paste mixture. Cook over medium heat for 20 minutes; reduce heat to low. Stir in masa harina and simmer 30-45 minutes longer. Serve with desired toppings.

FREEZE OPTION Freeze cooled chili in freezer containers. To use, partially thaw in refrigerator overnight. Heat through in a saucepan, stirring occasionally; add broth or water if necessary.

1¾ CUPS 473 cal., 20g fat (6g sat. fat), 103mg chol., 1554mg sod., 29g carb. (8g sugars, 7g fiber), 41g pro.

FROM-SCRATCH SEASONING

Montreal steak seasoning is a delicious flavor booster. It's a handy seasoning to stock in your pantry, but it's also easy to make. In a bowl, mix together 2 Tbsp. each kosher salt and coarsely ground pepper, and 2 tsp. each onion powder, dried minced garlic, paprika, crushed coriander seeds and crushed red pepper flakes. Store in an airtight container.

LOBSTER BISQUE

My grandmother would make lobster bisque all the time, so I always thought of it as comfort food. If you don't care to cook live lobsters, they can usually cook it where you buy them. Just be sure to tell them you want to keep the shells; they are key to the most delicious soup!

—James Schend, Pleasant Prairie, WI

PREP: 35 min. • **COOK:** 1¾ hours • **MAKES:** 8 servings (2 qt.)

- 2 live lobsters (about 1 lb. each)
- 2 medium carrots, peeled and chopped
- 1 medium onion, chopped
- 3 Tbsp. butter
- 2 Tbsp. tomato paste
- 2 garlic cloves, minced
- ¾ cup white wine or sherry
- 1 carton (32 oz.) seafood stock
- ⅔ cup uncooked long grain rice
- 2 cups heavy whipping cream
- 1 tsp. minced fresh thyme
- 1½ tsp. salt
- 1 tsp. coarsely ground pepper
- Minced fresh parsley, optional

1. In a Dutch oven, add 2 in. water; bring to a rolling boil. Add the lobsters; cover and steam for 8 minutes. Remove lobsters, reserving liquid. When cool enough to handle, remove meat from claws and tail, reserving any juices; refrigerate meat and juices.

2. In the same Dutch oven, cook carrots and onion in butter over medium-high heat until tender, 5-8 minutes. Stir in tomato paste and cook until it starts to caramelize, about 5 minutes. Add garlic; cook 1 minute. Stir in wine and simmer until reduced by half. Add lobster shells, bodies, reserved cooking liquid, reserved lobster juices and stock. Bring mixture to a simmer; cook 1 hour. Strain mixture, pressing to extract as much liquid as possible; discard shells and solids.

3. Return liquid to Dutch oven. Add rice and cook until extremely soft, 25-30 minutes. Puree in a blender until smooth. Add cream, thyme, salt and pepper. Bring mixture to very low simmer; add reserved lobster meat and cook until heated through. Sprinkle with additional ground pepper and parsley if desired.

1 CUP 373 cal., 26g fat (17g sat. fat), 127mg chol., 942mg sod., 20g carb. (4g sugars, 1g fiber), 10g pro.

PAIR IT WITH

Easy Cheesy Biscuits, p. 278

FRENCH ONION SOUP

This satisfying soup is fantastic on any autumn or winter day. The blend of Swiss, Parmesan and mozzarella gives it a richness that onion soup lovers will enjoy.

—Gina Bergamino, Chanhassen, MN

TAKES: 30 min. • **MAKES:** 7 servings

- 2 large red onions, thinly sliced
- ¼ cup butter, cubed
- 2 cans (14½ oz. each) chicken broth
- 3 cups water
- 1 envelope onion soup mix
- 1 tsp. pepper
- 1 tsp. Worcestershire sauce
- ½ tsp. garlic powder
- 7 slices French bread (¾ in. thick)
- ½ cup shredded Swiss cheese
- ½ cup shredded part-skim mozzarella cheese
- ¼ cup grated Parmesan cheese

1. In a Dutch oven, saute onions in butter until tender. Add the broth, water, soup mix, pepper, Worcestershire sauce and garlic powder. Bring to a boil. Reduce heat; cover and simmer for 5 minutes.

2. Meanwhile, place bread slices on an ungreased baking sheet. Sprinkle with Swiss and mozzarella cheeses. Broil 4 in. from the heat for 1-2 minutes or until cheese is melted.

3. Ladle soup into serving bowls; top each with a toast slice. Sprinkle with Parmesan cheese.

1 SERVING 205 cal., 12g fat (7g sat. fat), 34mg chol., 1120mg sod., 17g carb. (3g sugars, 2g fiber), 8g pro.

GRANDMA'S TOMATO SOUP

Gram had this delicious soup cooking on the stove every time I visited her. She enjoyed making this and other wonderful dishes for family and friends, and she made everything with love.

—Gerri Sysun, Narragansett, RI

TAKES: 15 min. • **MAKES:** 2 servings

- 2 Tbsp. butter
- 1 Tbsp. all-purpose flour
- 2 cups tomato juice
- ½ cup water
- 2 Tbsp. sugar
- ⅛ tsp. salt
- ¾ cup cooked wide egg noodles
- Chopped fresh parsley, optional

In a saucepan over medium heat, melt butter. Add flour; stir to form a smooth paste. Gradually add tomato juice and water, stirring constantly; bring to a boil. Cook and stir until thickened, about 2 minutes. Add sugar and salt. Stir in egg noodles and heat through. If desired, sprinkle with parsley.

1 CUP 259 cal., 12g fat (7g sat. fat), 44mg chol., 1144mg sod., 36g carb. (20g sugars, 1g fiber), 4g pro.

MATZO BALL SOUP

This traditional matzo ball soup is worth the extra effort. If you prefer, you can add egg noodles instead of matzo balls.

—Julia Sherman, New Market, TN

PREP: 25 min. + chilling • **COOK:** 1½ hours • **MAKES:** 12 servings (4½ qt.)

- 1 broiler/fryer chicken (3 to 4 lbs.)
- 1 can (14½ oz.) chicken broth
- 1¾ tsp. kosher salt, divided
- 1 lb. carrots, coarsely chopped
- 6 celery ribs, coarsely chopped
- ½ cup coarsely chopped sweet onion
- 2 garlic cloves, minced
- ¼ tsp. pepper
- ¼ cup minced fresh parsley

MATZO BALLS

- 2 large eggs
- 2 Tbsp. canola oil
- 1 pkg. (5 oz.) matzo ball mix
- ¼ cup finely chopped onion

1. Place chicken in a large soup kettle; add broth, 1 tsp. kosher salt and enough water to cover the chicken. Bring to a boil. Reduce heat; simmer for 55-65 minutes or until meat is tender, skimming surface as foam rises.

2. Remove chicken and set aside until cool enough to handle. Strain broth and skim fat; if needed, add additional water to make 10 cups broth. Return broth to kettle; add carrots, celery, onion, garlic, pepper and remaining salt. Bring to a boil. Reduce heat; simmer for 15 minutes or until carrots are tender.

3. Meanwhile, for matzo balls, in a small bowl, whisk eggs and oil. Add matzo ball mix and onion; toss with a fork until combined. Cover and refrigerate for 15 minutes.

4. Remove and discard skin and bones from chicken; shred chicken and add to soup. Stir in parsley. Bring to a boil. Drop matzo ball dough by tablespoonfuls into boiling soup. Reduce heat; cover and simmer for 20-25 minutes or until a toothpick inserted into a matzo ball comes out clean (do not lift cover while simmering).

5. With a slotted spoon, carefully remove matzo balls and divide among soup bowls. Ladle soup over top. If desired, top with additional parsley and pepper.

1½ CUPS 160 cal., 6g fat (1g sat. fat), 73mg chol., 509mg sod., 11g carb. (3g sugars, 2g fiber), 15g pro. **DIABETIC EXCHANGES** 2 lean meat, 1 vegetable, ½ fat.

MAKING MATZO

The longer you cook matzo balls, the denser they become. It's a matter of preference. Some people like heavy, dense matzo balls, known as sinkers. Other people prefer light, fluffy floaters. Mixing also plays a role in matzo ball consistency, as with dumplings or quick bread. To make light, floating balls, use a gentle touch and avoid overhandling the dough. If you crave dense sinkers, mix the dough more thoroughly.

HEARTY NAVY BEAN SOUP

Use thrifty dried beans and a ham hock to create this comfort-food classic. Bean soup is a family favorite that I make often.

—Mildred Lewis, Temple, TX

PREP: 30 min. + soaking • **COOK:** 1¾ hours • **MAKES:** 10 servings (2½ qt.)

- 3 cups (1½ lbs.) dried navy beans
- 1 can (14½ oz.) diced tomatoes, undrained
- 1 large onion, chopped
- 1 meaty ham hock or 1 cup diced cooked ham
- 2 cups chicken broth
- 2½ cups water
- Salt and pepper to taste
- Minced fresh parsley, optional

1. Rinse and sort beans; soak according to package directions.

2. Drain and rinse beans, discarding liquid. Place in a Dutch oven. Add tomatoes with juice, onion, ham hock, broth, water, salt and pepper. Bring to a boil. Reduce the heat; cover and simmer until beans are tender, about 1½ hours.

3. Add more water if necessary. Remove ham hock and let it stand until cool enough to handle. Remove meat from bone; discard the bone. Cut meat into bite-sized pieces; set aside. (For a thicker soup, cool slightly, then puree beans in a food processor or blender and return to pan.) Return ham to soup and heat through. Garnish with fresh parsley if desired.

1 CUP 244 cal., 2g fat (0 sat. fat), 8mg chol., 410mg sod., 42g carb. (5g sugars, 10g fiber), 18g pro. **DIABETIC EXCHANGES** 3 starch, 2 lean meat, 1 vegetable.

"Very simple. Loved it. This was my first time making navy bean soup, and it was so easy!"

—ACLEVEL, TASTEOFHOME.COM

PAIR IT WITH
Grandma's Onion Squares, p. 262

FAVORITE BAKED POTATO SOUP

My husband and I enjoyed a delicious potato soup at a restaurant while on vacation and I came home determined to duplicate it. It took me five years to get the taste right!

—Joann Goetz, Genoa, OH

PREP: 20 min. • **BAKE:** 65 min. + cooling • **MAKES:** 10 servings (2½ qt.)

- 4 large baking potatoes (about 12 oz. each)
- ⅔ cup butter, cubed
- ⅔ cup all-purpose flour
- ¾ tsp. salt
- ¼ tsp. white pepper
- 6 cups 2% milk
- 1 cup sour cream
- ¼ cup thinly sliced green onions
- 1 cup shredded cheddar cheese
- 10 bacon strips, cooked and crumbled

1. Preheat oven to 350°. Pierce potatoes several times with a fork; place on a baking sheet. Bake until tender, 65-75 minutes. Cool completely.

2. Peel and cube potatoes. In a large saucepan, melt butter over medium heat. Stir in flour, salt and pepper until smooth; gradually whisk in milk. Bring to a boil, stirring constantly; cook and stir until thickened, about 2 minutes. Stir in the potatoes; heat through.

3. Remove from heat; stir in sour cream and green onion. Top servings with cheese and bacon.

1 CUP 469 cal., 28g fat (17g sat. fat), 86mg chol., 563mg sod., 41g carb. (10g sugars, 3g fiber), 14g pro.

STARCHY SITUATION

A gummy, gluey texture can happen in potato soup when the potatoes are mashed or worked in too vigorously and too much of their starch is released into the broth. To prevent this, stir the cooked potato cubes gently into the soup. If you're breaking down the potatoes for a thicker soup or a soup with an all-creamy texture, mash the cooked potatoes lightly with a fork or masher—don't use a food processor or potato ricer.

GAZPACHO

My daughter got this recipe from a friend a few years ago. Now I serve it often as an appetizer, and it certainly is the talk of any party!

—Lorna Sirtoli, Cortland, NY

PREP: 15 min. + chilling • **MAKES:** 5 servings

- 2 cups tomato juice
- 4 medium tomatoes, peeled and finely chopped
- ½ cup chopped seeded peeled cucumber
- ⅓ cup finely chopped onion
- ¼ cup olive oil
- ¼ cup cider vinegar
- 1 tsp. sugar
- 1 garlic clove, minced
- ¼ tsp. salt
- ¼ tsp. pepper

In a large bowl, combine all ingredients. Cover and refrigerate until chilled, at least 4 hours.

1 CUP 146 cal., 11g fat (2g sat. fat), 0 chol., 387mg sod., 11g carb. (8g sugars, 2g fiber), 2g pro. **DIABETIC EXCHANGES** 2 vegetable, 2 fat.

BLACK BEAN ZUCCHINI GAZPACHO Substitute 2 large tomatoes for 4 medium. Add 1 can (15 oz.) drained rinsed black beans, 2 chopped medium zucchini and ¼ tsp. cayenne.

REFRESHING GAZPACHO Increase tomato juice to 4½ cups. Add 2 chopped celery ribs, 1 finely chopped red onion, 1 each chopped medium sweet red pepper and green pepper, ¼ minced fresh cilantro, 2 Tbsp. lime juice, 2 tsp. sugar and 1 tsp. Worcestershire sauce. Serve with cubed avocado if desired.

FARMERS MARKET FIND

Like most fresh tomato recipes, the most important factor when choosing tomatoes for gazpacho is using juicy, fully ripe tomatoes. Many people use vine-ripe tomatoes, plum tomatoes or heirloom tomatoes for gazpacho. Your best bet is to find them at a farmers market or try growing your own.

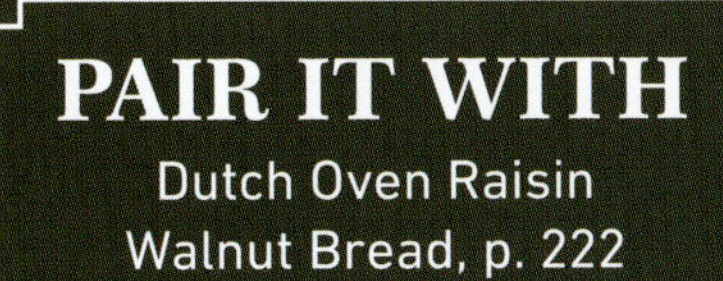

PAIR IT WITH

Dutch Oven Raisin Walnut Bread, p. 222

BUTTERNUT SQUASH SOUP

Much of the work for this soup can be done in advance, and it keeps all day in the slow cooker. The recipe can easily be doubled if you're feeding a crowd. Once you've tried it, consider mixing it up—add sage or savory with the thyme, or replace the thyme with nutmeg. For a vegan version, replace the chicken broth with vegetable broth.

—Jennifer Machado, Alta, CA

PREP: 30 min. • **COOK:** 6 hours • **MAKES:** 12 servings (3 qt.)

- 1 Tbsp. olive oil
- 1 large onion, chopped
- 2 garlic cloves, minced
- 1 medium butternut squash (about 4 lbs.), peeled and cut into 1-in. pieces
- 1 lb. Yukon Gold potatoes (about 2 medium), cut into ¾-in. pieces
- 2 tsp. minced fresh thyme or ¾ tsp. dried thyme
- 1 tsp. salt
- ¼ tsp. pepper
- 5 to 6 cups chicken or vegetable broth
- Sour cream, optional

1. In a large skillet, heat oil over medium heat. Add onion; saute for 4-5 minutes or until tender. Add garlic; cook 1 minute longer. Transfer to a 6-qt. slow cooker. Add next 5 ingredients and 5 cups broth to the slow cooker. Cook, covered, on low until vegetables are soft, 6-8 hours.

2. Puree soup using an immersion blender. Or cool slightly and puree the soup in batches in a blender; return to slow cooker. Stir in additional broth to reach desired consistency; heat through. If desired, top servings with sour cream.

FREEZE OPTION Freeze cooled soup in freezer containers. To use, partially thaw in refrigerator overnight. Heat through in a saucepan, stirring occasionally; add broth if necessary.

1 CUP 124 cal., 2g fat (0 sat. fat), 2mg chol., 616mg sod., 27g carb. (6g sugars, 6g fiber), 3g pro. **DIABETIC EXCHANGES** 2 starch.

ITALIAN WEDDING SOUP

You don't have to be Italian to love this easy-to-make soup with tiny round pasta! Homemade meatballs pair beautifully with ready-made stock and rotisserie chicken.

—Mary Sheetz, Carmel, IN

PREP: 30 min. • **COOK:** 40 min. • **MAKES:** 9 servings (2¼ qt.)

- 2 large eggs, lightly beaten
- ½ cup dry bread crumbs
- ¼ cup minced fresh parsley
- 2 Tbsp. grated Parmesan cheese
- 1 Tbsp. raisins, finely chopped
- 3 garlic cloves, minced
- ¼ tsp. crushed red pepper flakes
- ½ lb. lean ground beef (90% lean)
- ½ lb. bulk spicy pork sausage
- 2 cartons (32 oz. each) reduced-sodium chicken broth
- ½ tsp. pepper
- 1½ cups cubed rotisserie chicken
- ⅔ cup uncooked acini di pepe pasta
- ½ cup fresh baby spinach, cut into thin strips
- Shredded Parmesan cheese, optional

1. In a large bowl, combine the first 7 ingredients. Crumble beef and sausage over mixture and mix lightly but thoroughly. Shape into ½-in. balls.

2. In a Dutch oven, brown meatballs in small batches; drain. Add broth and pepper; bring to a boil. Reduce heat; simmer, uncovered, for 10 minutes. Stir in chicken and pasta; cook 5-7 minutes longer or until the pasta is tender. Stir in spinach; cook until wilted. Sprinkle with shredded Parmesan cheese if desired.

FREEZE OPTION Before adding cheese, cool soup. Freeze soup in freezer containers. To use, partially thaw in refrigerator overnight. Heat through in a saucepan, stirring occasionally; add broth or water if necessary. Sprinkle each serving with cheese.

1 CUP 253 cal., 10g fat (4g sat. fat), 94mg chol., 797mg sod., 18g carb. (3g sugars, 1g fiber), 21g pro.

"My family loved this recipe. I made some extra meatballs, as that's their favorite part. Very easy and very good."

—LORIMARKLE, TASTEOFHOME.COM

CHICKEN TORTILLA SOUP

This soup is as good as (if not better than) any I've had in a restaurant. I get so many compliments when I serve it; you will too.

—Laura Black Johnson, Largo, FL

TAKES: 30 min. • **MAKES:** 8 servings (2½ qt.)

- 2 Tbsp. olive oil
- 1 large onion, chopped
- 1 can (4 oz.) chopped green chiles
- 2 garlic cloves, minced
- 1 jalapeno pepper, seeded and chopped
- 1 tsp. ground cumin
- 1 can (15 oz.) tomato sauce
- 1 can (14½ oz.) diced tomatoes with garlic and onion, undrained
- 5 cups reduced-sodium chicken broth
- 1 rotisserie chicken, shredded, skin removed
- ¼ cup minced fresh cilantro
- 2 tsp. lime juice
- ¼ tsp. salt
- ¼ tsp. pepper
- Crushed tortilla chips
- Optional: Shredded Monterey Jack and/or cheddar cheese, avocado, sliced jalapeno and lime wedges

1. In a Dutch oven, heat the oil over medium heat; saute onion for 5 minutes or until tender. Add chiles, garlic, jalapeno and cumin; cook for 1 minute. Stir in tomato sauce, tomatoes and broth. Bring to a boil; reduce heat. Stir in chicken.

2. Simmer, uncovered, 10 minutes. Add cilantro, lime juice, salt and pepper. Serve with chips and desired toppings.

NOTE Wear disposable gloves when cutting hot peppers; the oils can burn skin. Avoid touching your face.

1¼ CUPS 200 cal., 8g fat (2g sat. fat), 55mg chol., 941mg sod., 9g carb. (4g sugars, 2g fiber), 22g pro.

FREEZER FACTS

Like most broth-based soups, Chicken Tortilla Soup is great to store in the freezer for later! Skip freezing the chips, cheese or any other toppings. We suggest freezing the soup in small containers so it's easier to defrost leftovers. And don't forget to label each container with the recipe name and the date prepared. Frozen Chicken Tortilla Soup lasts for 4-6 months in the freezer.

PAIR IT WITH
Quick Jalapeno
Hush Puppies, p. 297

SOUPS

BEEF & POULTRY

PRESSURE-COOKER JALAPENO POPPER CHICKEN CHILI

This quick and comforting chili tastes like jalapeno poppers! You can't have just one bowl.

—Natasha Galbreath, Spanaway, WA

PREP: 30 min. • **COOK:** 10 min. • **MAKES:** 7 servings

- 2 Tbsp. butter
- 1 lb. ground chicken
- 1 large onion, chopped
- 2 to 4 jalapeno peppers, seeded and finely chopped
- 4 garlic cloves, minced
- 1 can (15¼ oz.) whole kernel corn, undrained
- 1 can (15 oz.) black beans, rinsed and drained
- 1 can (10 oz.) diced tomatoes and green chiles, undrained
- 1 pkg. (8 oz.) cream cheese, cubed
- ¼ cup water or chicken broth
- 2 Tbsp. ranch salad dressing mix
- 1 Tbsp. chili powder
- 1 tsp. onion powder
- 1 tsp. ground cumin
- ¼ tsp. crushed red pepper flakes
- Shredded cheddar cheese, sour cream and crumbled cooked bacon

1. Select saute setting on a 6-qt. electric pressure cooker and adjust for medium heat; add butter. When butter is hot, add the chicken, onion, jalapenos and garlic; cook and stir until chicken is no longer pink and vegetables are tender, 6-8 minutes, breaking up chicken into crumbles. Stir in corn, beans, diced tomatoes and chiles, cream cheese, water, dressing mix and seasonings. Press cancel.

2. Lock lid; close pressure-release valve. Adjust to pressure-cook on high for 8 minutes. Quick-release pressure. Stir before serving. Garnish with shredded cheddar cheese, sour cream, bacon and additional jalapenos.

FREEZE OPTION Before adding toppings, cool chili. Freeze chili in freezer containers. To use, partially thaw in refrigerator overnight. Heat through in a saucepan, stirring occasionally; add water or broth if necessary. Sprinkle with toppings.

NOTE Wear disposable gloves when cutting hot peppers; the oils can burn skin. Avoid touching your face.

1 CUP 344 cal., 20g fat (10g sat. fat), 84mg chol., 1141mg sod., 25g carb. (6g sugars, 5g fiber), 17g pro.

"Really tasty, and easy and economical to make. This will be a staple in my home. Thank you!"

—SHAWNA753, TASTEOFHOME.COM

PAIR IT WITH
Crusty Homemade Bread, p. 219

STEAK SOUP

The nice thing about this thick soup is you can make it in an afternoon without too much fuss. It's perfect for soccer-practice night.

—Mary Dice, Chemainus, BC

PREP: 20 min. • **COOK:** 1¾ hours • **MAKES:** 6 servings

- 2 Tbsp. butter
- 2 Tbsp. canola oil
- 1½ to 2 lbs. beef eye round roast, cut into ½-in. cubes
- ¼ cup chopped onion
- 3 Tbsp. all-purpose flour
- 1 Tbsp. paprika
- 1 tsp. salt
- ¼ tsp. pepper
- 4 cups beef stock or broth
- 2 cups water
- 1 bay leaf
- 4 sprigs fresh parsley, chopped
- 2 sprigs celery leaves, chopped
- ½ tsp. dried marjoram
- 1½ cups chopped celery
- 1½ cups cubed peeled potatoes
- 1½ cups sliced carrots
- 1 can (6 oz.) tomato paste

1. In a Dutch oven, melt butter over medium heat; add oil. Brown the beef and onion. Combine flour, paprika, salt and pepper; sprinkle over beef and mix well. Stir in stock and water. Add bay leaf, parsley, celery leaves and marjoram. Bring to a boil; reduce heat and simmer, covered, about 1 hour or until tender.

2. Add the celery, potatoes and carrots. Simmer, covered, for 30-45 minutes or until vegetables are tender and soup begins to thicken. Stir in tomato paste; simmer, uncovered, 15 minutes or until heated through. Discard bay leaf.

1 CUP 319 cal., 13g fat (4g sat. fat), 56mg chol., 1112mg sod., 21g carb. (5g sugars, 4g fiber), 30g pro.

BEEF-SOUP BASICS

- Any lean cut of beef like rump roast or chuck roast will work as a great substitute for eye round roast in this soup recipe. You may need to adjust the cooking time as needed for tenderness.
- Browning beef in batches helps get an even sear and prevents overcrowding, which is one of the main reasons why meat steams instead of browns when cooking.
- For an even richer soup, use only beef stock instead of both stock and water.

FLAVORFUL MEATBALL SOUP

My husband and I are both diabetics and like to find tasty recipes like this one that are in line with our dietary requirements. I like to serve the soup with baked wheat tortilla triangles, fresh fruit and a variety of cubed cheeses.

—Rebecca Phipps, Rural Hall, NC

PREP: 30 min. • **COOK:** 40 min. • **MAKES:** 6 servings

- 1 lb. lean ground turkey
- 2½ tsp. Italian seasoning, divided
- ¼ tsp. paprika
- ¼ tsp. salt, divided
- ¼ tsp. coarsely ground pepper, divided
- 4 tsp. olive oil, divided
- 2 celery ribs, chopped
- 15 fresh baby carrots, chopped
- 1 small onion, chopped
- 1 can (15 oz.) cannellini beans, rinsed and drained
- 1 can (14½ oz.) Italian diced tomatoes, undrained
- 1 can (14½ oz.) reduced-sodium chicken broth
- ¾ cup chopped cabbage
- ¾ cup cut fresh green beans
- 3 Tbsp. shredded part-skim mozzarella cheese

1. In a large bowl, lightly but thoroughly combine the turkey, 1½ tsp. Italian seasoning, paprika, ⅛ tsp. salt and ⅛ tsp. pepper. Shape into 36 meatballs.

2. In a large skillet coated with cooking spray, brown meatballs in batches in 2 tsp. oil until no longer pink. Remove and keep warm.

3. In a large saucepan coated with cooking spray, saute the celery, carrots and onion in remaining oil until tender. Stir in the cannellini beans, tomatoes, broth, cabbage, green beans and remaining Italian seasoning, salt and pepper.

4. Bring to a boil. Reduce heat; stir in meatballs. Simmer, uncovered, until green beans are tender, 15-20 minutes. Sprinkle with cheese.

1 CUP 254 cal., 10g fat (2g sat. fat), 62mg chol., 748mg sod., 21g carb. (7g sugars, 5g fiber), 19g pro. **DIABETIC EXCHANGES** 2 lean meat, 1 starch, 1 vegetable, 1 fat.

TURKEY DUMPLING SOUP

Simmering up a big pot of this soup is one of my favorite holiday traditions. The recipe is a variation of one my mom made when I was growing up, and my family can't get enough of the tender dumplings.

—Debbie Wolf, Mission Viejo, CA

PREP: 20 min. • **COOK:** 20 min. + simmering • **MAKES:** 16 servings (4 qt.)

- 1 meaty leftover turkey carcass (from an 11-lb. turkey)
- 6 cups chicken broth
- 6 cups water
- 2 celery ribs, cut into 1-in. slices
- 1 medium carrot, cut into 1-in. slices
- 1 Tbsp. poultry seasoning
- 1 bay leaf
- ½ tsp. salt
- ½ tsp. pepper

SOUP INGREDIENTS

- 1 medium onion, chopped
- 2 celery ribs, chopped
- 2 medium carrots, sliced
- 1 cup fresh or frozen cut green beans
- 1 pkg. (10 oz.) frozen corn
- 1 pkg. (10 oz.) frozen peas
- 2 cups biscuit/baking mix
- ⅔ cup 2% milk

1. In a stockpot, combine the first 9 ingredients. Bring to a boil. Reduce heat; cover and simmer for 3 hours.

2. Remove carcass and allow to cool. Remove meat and set aside 4 cups for soup (refrigerate any remaining meat for another use); discard bones. Cut meat into bite-sized pieces. Strain broth, discarding vegetables and bay leaf.

3. Return broth to pan; add the onion, celery, carrots and beans. Bring to a boil. Reduce heat; cover and simmer for 10 minutes or until vegetables are tender. Add corn, peas and reserved turkey. Bring to a boil; reduce heat.

4. Combine biscuit mix and milk. Drop by teaspoonfuls into simmering broth. Cover and simmer for 10 minutes or until a toothpick inserted in a dumpling comes out clean (do not lift the cover while simmering).

1 CUP 185 cal., 5g fat (1g sat. fat), 30mg chol., 724mg sod., 19g carb. (4g sugars, 2g fiber), 14g pro.

CHICKEN FLORENTINE SOUP

Simmer orzo and cubed cooked chicken in a light and mildly spicy broth, then add a healthy amount of spinach, a little half-and-half and a squeeze of lemon. It's a quick-cook soup with bright and beautiful flavors.

—*Taste of Home* Test Kitchen

PREP: 15 min. • **COOK:** 25 min. • **MAKES:** 6 servings (2 qt.)

- 2 Tbsp. olive oil
- 1 medium onion, chopped
- 1 medium carrot, chopped
- 1 celery rib, chopped
- 4 garlic cloves, minced
- 2 tsp. Italian seasoning
- 1½ tsp. salt
- ½ tsp. pepper
- ¼ tsp. crushed red pepper flakes
- 6 cups reduced-sodium vegetable broth
- 1 cup uncooked orzo pasta
- 2 cups cubed cooked chicken breast
- 2 cups fresh baby spinach
- ¼ cup half-and-half cream
- 2 Tbsp. lemon juice
- ¼ cup grated Parmesan cheese

1. In a Dutch oven or large sauce pan, heat oil over medium heat. Add onion, carrot and celery; cook and stir until tender, 3-4 minutes. Add garlic; cook 1 minute longer. Stir in Italian seasoning, salt, pepper and red pepper flakes.

2. Add broth; bring to a boil. Stir in orzo and cooked chicken. Reduce heat; simmer, covered, until orzo is al dente, 8-10 minutes. Stir in spinach, half-and-half and lemon juice. Serve soup in bowls topped with Parmesan cheese.

1⅓ CUPS 300 cal., 9g fat (2g sat. fat), 44mg chol., 848mg sod., 34g carb. (5g sugars, 3g fiber), 21g pro.

EASY PASTA OPTIONS

There are plenty of small pasta shapes meant specifically for soup. Consider anelli, ditalini, ancini di pepe or similar options. In a pinch, you could even break up fine noodles like spaghettini or angel hair pasta into very short lengths and use those in soup recipes such as this one.

COWBOY SOUP

This soup is a hearty main dish perfect for when the weather turns cold. Mix and match ingredients that you have on hand in your pantry.

—*Taste of Home* Test Kitchen

PREP: 15 min. • **COOK:** 20 min. • **MAKES:** 12 servings (4½ qt.)

- 2 lbs. ground beef
- 2 medium onions, chopped
- 2 garlic cloves, minced
- 4 cups beef broth
- 2 cans (15 oz. each) Ranch Style beans (pinto beans in seasoned tomato sauce), undrained
- 2 cans (14½ oz. each) diced tomatoes, drained
- 2 large potatoes, peeled and chopped
- 2 cans (10 oz. each) diced tomatoes with green chilies, undrained
- 2 cups frozen corn
- 1 can (15 oz.) mixed vegetables, drained
- 1 Tbsp. chili powder
- 1 tsp. ground cumin
- ½ tsp. salt
- ¼ tsp. pepper
- Sliced jalapeno pepper, optional

1. In a Dutch oven, cook beef and onion over medium heat until meat is no longer pink, breaking meat into crumbles. Add garlic; cook 1 minute longer. Drain. Stir in next 11 ingredients.

2. Bring to a boil. Reduce heat; cover and simmer until the potatoes are tender, 10-15 minutes. Serve with sliced jalapeno if desired.

1½ CUPS 324 cal., 11g fat (4g sat. fat), 47mg chol., 1150mg sod., 37g carb. (6g sugars, 8g fiber), 21g pro.

WHAT IS COWBOY SOUP?

Some say Cowboy Soup is similar to a chili, and while it does have a comparable spice profile, Cowboy Soup is not typically as spicy as most chili recipes. It also contains extra ingredients that make the soup more filling, like chunks of potatoes, sweet corn and canned mixed vegetables.

PAIR IT WITH
Honey Beer Bread, p. 246

TURKEY-SWEET
POTATO SOUP

TURKEY-SWEET POTATO SOUP

A batch of this soup brings the nostalgic flavors and heartwarming feel of the holidays at any time of year.

—Radine Kellogg, Fairview, IL

PREP: 20 min. • **COOK:** 30 min. • **MAKES:** 4 servings

- 2 medium sweet potatoes, peeled and cubed
- 2 cups water
- 2 tsp. sodium-free chicken bouillon granules
- 1 can (14¾ oz.) cream-style corn
- 1 Tbsp. minced fresh sage
- ¼ tsp. pepper
- 1 Tbsp. cornstarch
- 1 cup 2% milk
- 2 cups cubed cooked turkey breast

1. In a large saucepan, combine potatoes, water and bouillon; bring to a boil. Reduce heat; cook, covered, until potatoes are tender, 10-15 minutes.

2. Stir in corn, sage and pepper; heat through. In a small bowl, mix cornstarch and milk until smooth; stir into soup. Bring to a boil; cook and stir until thickened, 1-2 minutes. Stir in turkey; heat through.

1½ CUPS 275 cal., 3g fat (1g sat. fat), 65mg chol., 374mg sod., 39g carb. (13g sugars, 3g fiber), 26g pro. **DIABETIC EXCHANGES** 3 lean meat, 2½ starch.

TURKEY & NOODLE TOMATO SOUP

Turn V8 juice, ramen and frozen veggies into a wonderful soup that really satisfies. I like to serve it with biscuits.

—Jennifer Bridges, Los Angeles, CA

TAKES: 30 min. • **MAKES:** 6 servings (2 qt.)

- 1 lb. ground turkey
- 1 envelope reduced-sodium onion soup mix
- 1 pkg. (3 oz.) beef ramen noodles
- 1½ tsp. sugar
- ¾ tsp. pepper
- ¼ tsp. salt
- 1 bottle (46 oz.) reduced-sodium V8 juice
- 1 pkg. (16 oz.) frozen mixed vegetables

1. In a Dutch oven, cook turkey over medium heat 6-8 minutes or until no longer pink, breaking into crumbles; drain. Stir in soup mix, 1½ tsp. seasoning from the noodles, sugar, pepper and salt. Add V8 juice and vegetables; bring to a boil. Reduce heat; simmer, uncovered, 5 minutes.

2. Break noodles into small pieces; add to soup (discard remaining seasoning or save for another use). Cook 3-5 minutes longer or until noodles are tender, stirring occasionally.

1⅓ CUPS 331 cal., 14g fat (5g sat. fat), 52mg chol., 1247mg sod., 33g carb. (11g sugars, 6g fiber), 18g pro.

GREEN CHILE CHICKEN SOUP

Very little beats a warm, zesty bowl of this soup, especially when you're craving some comforting spice. The recipe is loaded with smoky green chiles and tender chicken, all simmered in a savory and spicy broth. The corn adds a touch of sweetness, and salsa verde ties everything together with its tangy, vibrant taste.

—*Taste of Home* Test Kitchen

TAKES: 40 min. • **MAKES:** 8 servings (2 qt.)

- 2 Tbsp. olive oil, divided
- 1 lb. boneless skinless chicken thighs, cubed
- 1 medium onion, chopped
- 4 garlic cloves, minced
- 2 tsp. chili powder
- 1 tsp. ground cumin
- ¾ tsp. paprika
- ½ tsp. dried oregano
- ½ tsp. pepper
- 1 can (14½ oz.) white kidney or cannellini beans, rinsed and drained
- 1 cup frozen corn
- 2 cans (4 oz. each) chopped green chiles
- 1 jar (16 oz.) salsa verde
- 4 cups reduced-sodium chicken broth
- ½ cup fresh cilantro leaves, chopped

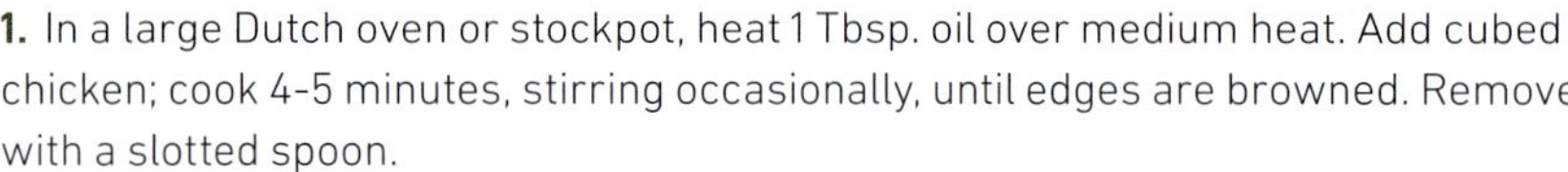

1. In a large Dutch oven or stockpot, heat 1 Tbsp. oil over medium heat. Add cubed chicken; cook 4-5 minutes, stirring occasionally, until edges are browned. Remove with a slotted spoon.

2. In the same pot, add remaining 1 Tbsp. oil. Add onion; cook 3-4 minutes or until tender. Stir in garlic, chili powder, cumin, paprika, oregano and pepper; cook until fragrant, 1-2 minutes. Stir in chicken, beans, corn, green chiles, salsa verde and broth. Bring to a simmer; cook until chicken is tender, 15-20 minutes. Before serving, stir in cilantro.

1 CUP 211 cal., 8g fat (2g sat. fat), 38mg chol., 827mg sod., 19g carb. (4g sugars, 6g fiber), 16g pro.

PAIR IT WITH
Tender Whole Wheat Rolls, p. 281

TURKEY SAUSAGE & LENTIL SOUP

My son, Chris, gave me the recipe for this filling Mediterranean-inspired soup. We warm up with a big bowl of it several times during cooler months.

—Kathy Mazur, Sarasota, FL

PREP: 25 min. • **COOK:** 45 min. • **MAKES:** 12 servings (3¾ qt.)

- 1 pkg. (19½ oz.) Italian turkey sausage links, casings removed
- 1 large onion, chopped
- 2 celery ribs, chopped
- 1 medium carrot, chopped
- 2 garlic cloves, minced
- 1 bay leaf
- ½ tsp. fennel seed
- ½ tsp. dried oregano
- ½ tsp. dried thyme
- ½ tsp. pepper
- ⅛ tsp. crushed red pepper flakes, optional
- 2 cups dried brown lentils, rinsed
- 2 cans (14½ oz. each) no-salt-added diced tomatoes, undrained
- 2 cartons (32 oz. each) reduced-sodium chicken broth
- Optional: Fat-free plain Greek yogurt and minced fresh parsley

1. In a 6-qt. stockpot, cook and crumble sausage over medium-high heat until no longer pink, 5-7 minutes; remove with a slotted spoon.

2. In same pot, saute onion, celery and carrot until tender, 4-6 minutes. Add garlic and seasonings; cook and stir 1 minute. Stir in sausage, lentils, tomatoes and broth; bring to a boil. Reduce heat; simmer, covered, until lentils are tender, 30-40 minutes, stirring occasionally. Remove bay leaf.

3. Transfer 5 cups soup to a blender; cool slightly. Cover; process until smooth. Return to pot; heat through. If desired, top servings with yogurt and parsley.

FREEZE OPTION Freeze cooled soup in freezer containers. To use, partially thaw in refrigerator overnight. Heat through in a saucepan, stirring occasionally; add broth or water if necessary.

1¼ CUPS 187 cal., 3g fat (1g sat. fat), 17mg chol., 639mg sod., 25g carb. (4g sugars, 5g fiber), 15g pro. **DIABETIC EXCHANGES** 1½ starch, 1 lean meat.

BURGOO

A Kentucky Derby favorite, this hearty, comforting meat-and-vegetable stew will feed a large crowd. It takes a bit of effort but is worth it.

—*Taste of Home* Test Kitchen

PREP: 30 min. • **COOK:** 2½ hours • **MAKES:** 24 servings (7½ qt.)

- 3 Tbsp. olive oil, divided
- 2 lbs. boneless pork shoulder butt roast, cut into 1½-in. cubes
- 2 lbs. boneless beef chuck roast, cut into 1½-in. cubes
- 2 lbs. bone-in chicken thighs
- 3 medium carrots, cut into 1-in. pieces
- 2 celery ribs, cut into 1-in. pieces
- 1 large onion, chopped
- 1 large green pepper, chopped
- 3 garlic cloves, minced
- 2 cartons (32 oz. each) reduced-sodium beef broth
- 1 can (28 oz.) crushed tomatoes
- 3 bay leaves
- 2 tsp. salt
- 2 tsp. dried thyme
- 1 tsp. pepper
- 2 medium potatoes, peeled and cubed
- 2½ cups frozen lima beans (about 12 oz.)
- 2½ cups frozen corn (about 12 oz.)
- 2 cups finely chopped cabbage
- ¼ cup Worcestershire sauce
- 3 Tbsp. cider vinegar
- Hot pepper sauce, optional

1. In a large stockpot, heat 2 Tbsp. oil over medium heat. Brown pork in batches; remove and set aside. Repeat with beef and chicken. In same pan, heat remaining 1 Tbsp. oil over medium heat. Add carrots, celery, onion and green pepper; cook and stir until tender, 5-7 minutes. Add garlic; cook 1 minute longer.

2. Add broth, stirring to loosen browned bits from pan. Add tomatoes, bay leaves, salt, thyme and pepper. Return pork, beef and chicken to pan. Bring to a boil. Reduce heat; cover and simmer until meat is very tender, about 2 hours.

3. Remove chicken to a plate. When cool enough to handle, remove meat from bones; discard skin and bones. Using 2 forks, shred the meat into bite-sized pieces. Return meat to stockpot.

4. Add the potatoes, lima beans, corn and cabbage; cover and cook for 30 minutes. Discard bay leaves. Stir in Worcestershire sauce and vinegar. If desired, serve with hot sauce.

1¼ CUPS 265 cal., 13g fat (4g sat. fat), 67mg chol., 404mg sod., 15g carb. (4g sugars, 3g fiber), 22g pro.

SLOW-COOKER CHICKEN POTPIE

This slow-cooker version of a comfort food favorite takes just minutes of prep. No need to make a crust; just bake refrigerated biscuits to top portions of the tasty chicken-vegetable mixture.

—*Taste of Home* Test Kitchen

PREP: 15 min. • **COOK:** 5 hours • **MAKES:** 8 servings (2 qt.)

- 2 lbs. boneless skinless chicken breasts, cubed
- 1 can (10½ oz.) condensed cream of chicken soup, undiluted
- 1 cup 2% milk
- 2 medium potatoes, peeled and cubed
- 1 medium onion, chopped
- 1 celery rib, sliced
- 1½ tsp. garlic powder
- 1 tsp. poultry seasoning
- 1 tsp. salt
- ½ tsp. pepper
- 2½ cups frozen mixed vegetables (about 12 oz.), thawed
- 1 tube (16.3 oz.) large refrigerated buttermilk biscuits

1. Combine first 10 ingredients in a greased 4- or 5-qt. slow cooker. Cook, covered, on low until chicken is no longer pink, 4½-5 hours. Stir in mixed vegetables; cook 30 minutes longer.

2. Meanwhile, bake biscuits according to package directions. Spoon chicken mixture into bowls; top with biscuits.

1 CUP STEW WITH 1 BISCUIT 420 cal., 13g fat (4g sat. fat), 68mg chol., 914mg sod., 47g carb. (8g sugars, 4g fiber), 30g pro.

"My husband loves chicken potpie, but I don't always have time to make it. This recipe lets it cook all day, and all I have to do is bake the biscuits. Adding them to the bowls instead of the top of the potpie keeps them from getting soggy."

—NH-RESCUE, TASTEOFHOME.COM

RIBOLLITA

Also known as bread soup, this is a hearty and flavorful Italian dish that uses up stale bread. If you'd like the bread to have more texture, toast it before stirring it into the soup.

—*Taste of Home* Test Kitchen

PREP: 15 min. • **COOK:** 25 min. • **MAKES:** 8 cups (2 qt.)

- 2 Tbsp. olive oil
- 3 medium carrot, sliced
- 1 medium onion, chopped
- 1 celery rib, chopped
- 2 garlic cloves, minced
- 6 cups chicken stock
- 1 can (14½ oz.) diced tomatoes
- ¼ tsp. salt
- ¼ tsp. pepper
- ⅛ tsp. crushed red pepper flakes
- 1 can (15 oz.) white kidney or cannellini beans, rinsed and drained
- 8 cups coarsely chopped fresh kale
- 3 cups torn day-old Italian bread
- Shredded Parmesan cheese

1. In a Dutch oven, heat olive oil over medium heat. Add carrot, onion and celery; cook until crisp-tender, 5-7 minutes. Stir in garlic; cook 1 minute longer. Add next 7 ingredients; bring to a boil. Reduce heat; simmer, covered, until vegetables are tender, 15-20 minutes.

2. Add bread; cook and stir until bread is softened. Serve with Parmesan cheese.

1 CUP 206 cal., 5g fat (1g sat. fat), 0 chol., 806mg sod., 32g carb. (5g sugars, 5g fiber), 9g pro.

AMP IT UP

Feel free to stir some cooked chicken, turkey or pork into this soup. You could even add chopped bacon left from breakfast.

ITALIAN SAUSAGE PIZZA SOUP

My mom's friend shared this recipe with her more than 50 years ago. I've tweaked it over the years, and it's still a family favorite. Warm garlic bread is heavenly on the side.

—Joan Hallford, North Richland Hills, TX

PREP: 15 min. • **COOK:** 6 hours • **MAKES:** 12 servings (3 qt.)

- 1 lb. Italian turkey sausage links
- 1 medium onion, chopped
- 1 medium green pepper, cut into strips
- 1 medium sweet red or yellow pepper, cut into strips
- 1 can (15 oz.) cannellini beans, rinsed and drained
- 1 can (14½ oz.) diced tomatoes, undrained
- 1 jar (14 oz.) pizza sauce
- 2 tsp. Italian seasoning
- 2 garlic cloves, minced
- 2 cans (14½ oz. each) beef broth
- 1 pkg. (5 oz.) Caesar salad croutons
- Shredded part-skim mozzarella cheese

1. Remove casings from sausage. In a large skillet over medium-high heat, cook and crumble sausage until no longer pink. Add onion and peppers; cook until crisp-tender. Drain and transfer to a 6-qt. slow cooker.

2. Add the next 5 ingredients; pour in broth. Cook, covered, on low until vegetables are tender, 6-8 hours. Serve with croutons and cheese.

1 CUP 158 cal., 5g fat (1g sat. fat), 15mg chol., 828mg sod., 19g carb. (4g sugars, 4g fiber), 9g pro.

PAIR IT WITH

Pepperoni Cheese Bread, p. 234

TASTY TWIST ON PIZZA NIGHT

This one tastes like sausage pizza! Stir in your fave pizza toppings. If your pizza preference leans toward pepperoni instead of sausage, you're in luck. Go ahead and use some pepperoni, but microwave it for about 20 seconds before adding it to the soup; you'll remove a lot of the grease that way.

TURKEY SAUSAGE, BUTTERNUT SQUASH & KALE SOUP

Kale and butternut squash are two of my favorite fall veggies. This recipe combines them into a warm and comforting soup. If you love sweet potatoes, sub them for the squash.

—Laura Koch, Lincoln, NE

PREP: 20 min. • **COOK:** 30 min. • **MAKES:** 10 servings (2½ qt.)

- 1 pkg. (19½ oz.) Italian turkey sausage links, casings removed
- 1 medium butternut squash (about 3 lbs.), peeled and cubed
- 2 cartons (32 oz. each) reduced-sodium chicken broth
- 1 bunch kale, trimmed and coarsely chopped (about 16 cups)
- ½ cup shaved Parmesan cheese

1. In a stockpot, cook sausage over medium heat until no longer pink, breaking into crumbles, 8-10 minutes.

2. Add squash and broth; bring to a boil. Gradually stir in kale, allowing it to wilt slightly between additions. Return to a boil. Reduce heat; simmer, uncovered, until vegetables are tender, 15-20 minutes. Top servings with cheese.

1 CUP 163 cal., 5g fat (2g sat. fat), 23mg chol., 838mg sod., 20g carb. (5g sugars, 5g fiber), 13g pro.

BEEFY MUSHROOM SOUP

This is a tasty way to use leftover roast and get supper on the table in about half an hour.

—Ginger Ellsworth, Caldwell, ID

TAKES: 30 min. • **MAKES:** 3 servings

- 1 medium onion, chopped
- ½ cup sliced fresh mushrooms
- 2 Tbsp. butter
- 2 Tbsp. all-purpose flour
- 2 cups reduced-sodium beef broth
- ⅔ cup cubed cooked roast beef
- ½ tsp. garlic powder
- ¼ tsp. paprika
- ¼ tsp. pepper
- ⅛ tsp. salt
- Dash hot pepper sauce
- Shredded part-skim mozzarella cheese, optional

1. In a large saucepan, saute onion and mushrooms in butter until onion is tender; remove with a slotted spoon and set aside. In a small bowl, whisk flour and broth until smooth; gradually add to the pan. Bring to a boil; cook and stir until thickened, 1-2 minutes.

2. Add the roast beef, garlic powder, paprika, pepper, salt, pepper sauce and onion mixture; cook and stir until heated through. Garnish with cheese if desired.

1 CUP 180 cal., 9g fat (5g sat. fat), 52mg chol., 470mg sod., 9g carb. (3g sugars, 1g fiber), 14g pro. **DIABETIC EXCHANGES** 2 lean meat, 2 fat, 1 vegetable.

GRANDMA'S OXTAIL SOUP

This wonderfully rich meal will warm your soul and your taste buds. Oxtail soup is a favorite family heirloom recipe. Don't let the name of this dish turn you off. Oxtail describes the meaty part of the tail of an ox (now commonly cow). The meat is delicious, but requires long and slow cooking.

—Bobbie Keefer, Byers, CO

PREP: 20 min. • **COOK:** 10 hours • **MAKES:** 8 servings (3 qt.)

- 2 lbs. oxtails, trimmed
- 2 Tbsp. olive oil
- 4 medium carrots, sliced (about 2 cups)
- 1 medium onion, chopped
- 2 garlic cloves, minced
- 2 cans (14½ oz. each) diced tomatoes, undrained
- 1 can (15 oz.) beef broth
- 3 bay leaves
- 1 tsp. salt
- 1 tsp. dried oregano
- ½ tsp. dried thyme
- ½ tsp. pepper
- 6 cups chopped cabbage

1. In a large skillet, brown oxtails in oil over medium heat. Remove from pan; place in a 5-qt. slow cooker.

2. Add carrots and onion to drippings; cook and stir until just softened, 3-5 minutes. Add garlic; cook 1 minute longer. Transfer vegetable mixture to slow cooker. Add tomatoes, broth, bay leaves, salt, oregano, thyme and pepper; stir to combine.

3. Cook, covered, on low 8 hours. Add cabbage; cook until cabbage is tender and meat pulls away easily from bones, about 2 hours longer. Remove oxtails; set aside until cool enough to handle. Remove meat from bones; discard bones and shred meat. Return meat to soup. Discard bay leaves.

FREEZE OPTION Freeze cooled stew in freezer containers. To use, partially thaw in refrigerator overnight. Heat through in a saucepan, stirring occasionally; add broth or water if necessary.

1½ CUPS 204 cal., 10g fat (3g sat. fat), 34mg chol., 705mg sod., 14g carb. (8g sugars, 5g fiber), 16g pro.

COOKING WITH OXTAILS

Oxtails can be tough to cut, so it's best to ask the butcher to slice them into pieces (if they aren't already). Trimming the thick pieces of excess fat off the oxtails before cooking will ensure a stew that's flavorful with a velvety mouthfeel.

SPANISH CHICKEN SOUP

A hearty soup that's made from scratch is the perfect antidote for chilly weather. Save leftovers for weekday lunches sent to work in a Thermos or quickly reheated in the microwave.

—*Taste of Home* Test Kitchen

PREP: 15 min. • **COOK:** 50 min. • **MAKES:** 12 servings (3 qt.)

- 1 broiler/fryer chicken (3 to 4 lbs.), cut up
- 2 tsp. adobo seasoning
- 2 Tbsp. olive oil
- 2 celery ribs, chopped
- 1 medium onion, chopped
- 1 medium carrot, chopped
- ¼ cup sofrito tomato cooking base
- 2 qt. water
- 1 bay leaf
- 2 medium Yukon Gold potatoes, peeled and cubed
- 12 oz. fideo noodles or uncooked angel hair pasta, broken into 1-in. pieces
- 1 tsp. salt
- ½ tsp. pepper
- Fresh cilantro leaves, optional

1. Sprinkle chicken with adobo seasoning. In a large stockpot, heat oil over medium heat. Brown chicken on both sides in batches. Remove chicken from pot. Add celery, onion, carrot and sofrito to same pot; cook and stir until onion is tender, 3-4 minutes.

2. Return chicken to pot. Add water and bay leaf; bring to a boil. Reduce heat; cover and simmer 30 minutes. Add potatoes. Simmer, uncovered, until potatoes are almost tender, 8-10 minutes.

3. Remove chicken and bay leaf; discard bay leaf. Let chicken stand until cool enough to handle. Skim fat from broth. Return broth to a simmer; add noodles. Simmer, uncovered, until noodles are tender, 5-7 minutes.

4. Meanwhile, remove chicken from bones; discard bones. Cut chicken into bite-sized pieces; add chicken to broth. Add salt and pepper. Cook and stir until heated through. If desired, garnish with chopped fresh cilantro.

1 CUP 324 cal., 12g fat (3g sat. fat), 52mg chol., 530mg sod., 31g carb. (2g sugars, 2g fiber), 22g pro. **DIABETIC EXCHANGES** 3 lean meat, 2 starch, ½ fat.

PAIR IT WITH

Easy Peasy Biscuits, p. 284

SOUPS

SEAFOOD, MEATLESS & MORE

VEGETARIAN WHITE BEAN SOUP

The culinary experts in our Test Kitchen simmered up this fresh-tasting meatless soup. Hearty with veggies and two kinds of beans, the soup makes a satisfying entree. Round out the meal with warm dinner rolls.

—*Taste of Home* Test Kitchen

TAKES: 30 min. • **MAKES:** 10 servings (2½ qt.)

- 2 small zucchini, quartered lengthwise and sliced
- 1 cup each chopped onion, celery and carrot
- 2 Tbsp. canola oil
- 3 cans (14½ oz. each) vegetable broth
- 1 can (15½ oz.) great northern beans, rinsed and drained
- 1 can (15 oz.) cannellini beans, rinsed and drained
- 1 can (14½ oz.) diced tomatoes, undrained
- ½ tsp. dried thyme
- ½ tsp. dried oregano
- ¼ tsp. pepper
- Minced fresh oregano, optional

In a large saucepan, saute zucchini, onion, celery and carrot in oil over medium heat until crisp-tender, 5-7 minutes. Add the remaining ingredients except fresh oregano. Bring to a boil. Reduce the heat; cover and simmer until vegetables are tender, about 5 minutes. If desired, garnish with fresh oregano.

1 CUP 117 cal., 3g fat (0 sat. fat), 0 chol., 555mg sod., 17g carb. (3g sugars, 5g fiber), 5g pro. **DIABETIC EXCHANGES** 1 starch, ½ fat.

"This soup is absolutely amazing! It quickly made it onto our regular dinner menu lineup. I like to throw in a couple of handfuls of diced potatoes occasionally."

—ANDYS_GIRL1823, TASTEOFHOME.COM

GRILLED WATERMELON GAZPACHO

This is the perfect starter for a summer dinner or lunch. It's cool and tangy with a whole lot of terrific grilled flavor. If you like a little more spice, just add a few more jalapenos.

—George Levinthal, Goleta, CA

PREP: 10 min. + chilling • **GRILL:** 10 min. + cooling • **MAKES:** 4 servings

- 2 Tbsp. olive oil, divided
- ¼ seedless watermelon, cut into three 1½-in.-thick slices
- 1 large beefsteak tomato, halved
- ½ English cucumber, peeled and halved lengthwise
- 1 jalapeno pepper, seeded and halved lengthwise
- ¼ cup plus 2 Tbsp. diced red onion, divided
- 2 Tbsp. sherry vinegar
- 1 Tbsp. lime juice
- ½ tsp. kosher or sea salt
- ¼ tsp. pepper
- 1 small ripe avocado, peeled, pitted and diced

1. Brush 1 Tbsp. olive oil over watermelon slices, tomato, cucumber and jalapeno; grill, covered, on a greased grill rack over medium-high direct heat until seared, 5-6 minutes on each side. Remove from heat, reserving 1 watermelon slice.

2. When cool enough to handle, remove rind from remaining watermelon slices; cut flesh into chunks. Remove skin and seeds from tomato and jalapeno; chop. Coarsely chop cucumber. Combine grilled vegetables; add ¼ cup onion, vinegar, lime juice and seasonings. Process in batches in a blender until smooth, adding remaining olive oil during final minute. If desired, strain through a fine-mesh strainer; adjust seasonings as needed. Refrigerate, covered, until cold.

3. To serve, pour gazpacho into bowls or glasses. Top with diced avocado and remaining onion. Cut reserved watermelon slice into wedges. Garnish bowls or glasses with wedges.

NOTE Wear disposable gloves when cutting hot peppers; the oils can burn skin. Avoid touching your face.

1 CUP 181 cal., 12g fat (2g sat. fat), 0 chol., 248mg sod., 19g carb. (13g sugars, 4g fiber), 2g pro. **DIABETIC EXCHANGES** 2 fat, 1 fruit, 1 vegetable.

PAIR IT WITH

Bread Machine Naan, p. 304

COCONUT CURRY SOUP

I've been a vegetarian since high school, so modifying recipes to fit my meatless requirements is a challenge I enjoy. This rich and creamy soup is packed with nutrients!

—Carissa Sumner, Washington, DC

PREP: 15 min. • **COOK:** 25 min. • **MAKES:** 6 servings

- 1 Tbsp. canola oil
- 2 celery ribs, chopped
- 2 medium carrots, chopped
- 6 garlic cloves, minced
- 1 Tbsp. minced fresh gingerroot
- 2 tsp. curry powder
- ½ tsp. ground turmeric
- 1 can (14½ oz.) vegetable broth
- 1 can (13.66 oz.) light coconut milk
- 1 medium potato (about 8 oz.), peeled and chopped
- ½ tsp. salt
- 1 pkg. (8.8 oz.) ready-to-serve brown rice
- Lime wedges, optional

1. In a large saucepan, heat oil over medium heat. Add celery and carrots; cook and stir for 6-8 minutes or until tender. Add garlic, ginger, curry powder and turmeric; cook 1 minute longer.

2. Add broth, coconut milk, potato and salt; bring to a boil. Reduce the heat; cook, uncovered, 10-15 minutes or until potato is tender. Meanwhile, heat rice according to package directions.

3. Stir rice into soup. If desired, serve with lime wedges.

¾ CUP 186 cal., 8g fat (4g sat. fat), 0 chol., 502mg sod., 22g carb. (3g sugars, 2g fiber), 3g pro. **DIABETIC EXCHANGES** 1½ starch, 1½ fat.

SOPA DE CAMARONES (SHRIMP SOUP)

My daughter and I came up with this soup recipe when she was younger, and it's been a favorite with family and friends ever since. It may even be tastier as leftovers the next day!

—Patti Fair, Valdosta, GA

PREP: 20 min. • **COOK:** 2 hours • **MAKES:** 4 servings

- 3 Tbsp. butter
- 3 celery ribs, sliced
- 1 small onion, chopped
- ⅓ cup lemon juice
- 6 garlic cloves, minced
- 1 to 2 Tbsp. sugar
- 2 cans (14½ oz. each) Mexican petite diced tomatoes, undrained
- 1 lb. peeled and deveined cooked shrimp (61-70 per lb.)
- 1 can (6 oz.) tomato paste
- Hot cooked rice
- Optional: Lime wedges and chopped cilantro

1. In a large skillet, heat butter over medium heat. Add celery and onion; cook and stir until crisp-tender, 3-4 minutes. Add the lemon juice, garlic and sugar; cook for 1 minute longer.

2. Transfer to a 3- or 4-qt. slow cooker. Add undrained tomatoes, shrimp and tomato paste. Cook, covered, on low until heated through, 2-3 hours. Serve with rice and, if desired, lime wedges and chopped cilantro.

1½ CUPS 313 cal., 11g fat (6g sat. fat), 195mg chol., 712mg sod., 26g carb. (16g sugars, 4g fiber), 28g pro.

AMP UP THE FLAVOR

Serve this dish with white rice, such as basmati, to really let the flavors of the Sopa de Camarones shine through and be the highlight.

BEST SEAFOOD CHOWDER

My husband, Chad, is an avid fisherman. When a family party was planned and we had to bring something, we created this recipe using fish from our freezer. The chowder got rave reviews from our relatives.

—Heather Saunders, Belchertown, MA

PREP: 30 min. • **COOK:** 30 min. • **MAKES:** 32 servings (8 qt.)

- ½ lb. sliced bacon, diced
- 2 medium onions, chopped
- 6 cups cubed peeled potatoes
- 4 cups water
- 1 lb. bay or sea scallops, quartered
- 1 lb. lobster meat, cut into 1-in. pieces
- 1 lb. uncooked shrimp (31-40 per lb.), peeled and deveined
- 1 lb. cod, cut into 1-in. pieces
- 1 lb. haddock, cut into 1-in. pieces
- ½ cup butter, melted
- 4 tsp. salt
- 4 tsp. minced fresh parsley
- ½ tsp. curry powder
- 2 qt. whole milk
- 1 can (12 oz.) evaporated milk
- Oyster crackers, optional

1. In a large soup kettle or Dutch oven, cook bacon over medium heat until crisp. Using a slotted spoon, remove to paper towels; set aside drippings. Saute onions in drippings until tender. Add potatoes and water; bring to a boil. Cook for 10 minutes.

2. Add scallops, lobster, shrimp, cod and haddock. Cook 10 minutes or until scallops are opaque, shrimp turn pink and fish flakes easily with a fork. Add butter, salt, parsley and curry powder. Stir in whole milk and evaporated milk; heat through. Garnish with bacon, additional parsley and, if desired, oyster crackers.

1 CUP 193 cal., 9g fat (4g sat. fat), 76mg chol., 625mg sod., 11g carb. (4g sugars, 1g fiber), 17g pro.

"This was outstanding! Even my non-fish-loving husband was in awe, and my son-in-law had three bowls. This recipe is going into my permanent file!"

—COVENANTGALL, TASTEOFHOME.COM

PAIR IT WITH
Ham Biscuits, p. 277

CARROT SOUP

Yukon Gold potatoes—instead of cream—make a smooth carrot soup vegan and add a mild sweetness. If you don't have Yukon Golds on hand, use russet potatoes.

—*Taste of Home* Test Kitchen

TAKES: 30 min. • **MAKES:** 6 servings

- 1 medium onion, chopped
- 2 celery ribs, chopped
- 1 Tbsp. canola oil
- 4 cups vegetable broth
- 1 lb. carrots, sliced
- 2 large Yukon Gold potatoes, peeled and cubed
- 1 tsp. salt
- ¼ tsp. pepper
- Fresh cilantro leaves, optional

1. In a large saucepan, saute onion and celery in oil until tender. Add broth, carrots and potatoes; bring to a boil. Reduce heat; cover and simmer for 15-20 minutes or until vegetables are tender. Remove from heat; cool slightly.

2. Transfer to a blender; cover and process until smooth. Return to pan; stir in salt and pepper. Heat through. If desired, sprinkle with cilantro.

1 CUP 176 cal., 3g fat (0 sat. fat), 0 chol., 710mg sod., 35g carb. (7g sugars, 4g fiber), 4g pro. **DIABETIC EXCHANGES** 2 starch, ½ fat.

FRESH FRUIT SOUP

Entertaining is a big part of a military wife's life—my husband was a career Army man—so my soup got much use! It's a great cool-down after Mexican food, but I've also served it with butter cookies at a baby shower.

—Jenny Sampson, Layton, UT

PREP: 20 min. + chilling • **MAKES:** 10 servings (2½ qt.)

- 1 can (12 oz.) frozen orange juice concentrate, thawed
- 1½ cups sugar
- 1 cinnamon stick (2 in.)
- 6 whole cloves
- ¼ cup cornstarch
- 2 Tbsp. lemon juice
- 2 cups sliced fresh strawberries
- 2 medium bananas, sliced
- 2 cups halved green grapes

1. In a large saucepan, mix orange juice with water according to package directions. Remove ½ cup of juice; set aside. Add sugar, cinnamon stick and cloves to saucepan; bring to a boil. Reduce heat and simmer for 5 minutes.

2. Combine cornstarch and reserved orange juice until smooth; stir into pan. Bring to a boil; cook and stir for 2 minutes or until thickened. Remove from heat and stir in lemon juice.

3. Pour into a large bowl; cover and refrigerate. Just before serving, remove spices and stir in fruit.

1 CUP 238 cal., 0 fat (0 sat. fat), 0 chol., 3mg sod., 60g carb. (53g sugars, 2g fiber), 1g pro.

CABBAGE BARLEY SOUP

My neighbor had an abundance of cabbage, so a group of us had a contest to see who could come up with the best cabbage dish. My vegetarian cabbage soup was a hit and the clear winner.

—Lorraine Caland, Shuniah, ON

PREP: 15 min. • **COOK:** 6¼ hours • **MAKES:** 8 servings (3 qt.)

- 1 cup dried brown lentils, rinsed
- ½ cup medium pearl barley
- 3 medium carrots, chopped
- 2 celery ribs, chopped
- ½ tsp. poultry seasoning
- ¼ tsp. pepper
- 1 bottle (46 oz.) V8 juice
- 4 cups water
- 8 cups shredded cabbage (about 16 oz.)
- ½ lb. sliced fresh mushrooms
- ¾ tsp. salt

1. Place first 8 ingredients in a 5- or 6-qt. slow cooker. Add cabbage. Cook, covered, on low until lentils are tender, 6-8 hours.

2. Stir in mushrooms and salt. Cook, covered, on low until mushrooms are tender, 15-20 minutes.

FREEZE OPTION Freeze cooled soup in freezer containers. To use, partially thaw in refrigerator overnight. Heat through in a saucepan, stirring occasionally; add water if necessary.

1½ CUPS 197 cal., 1g fat (0 sat. fat), 0 chol., 678mg sod., 39g carb. (7g sugars, 9g fiber), 11g pro. **DIABETIC EXCHANGES** 2½ starch, 1 lean meat.

MANHATTAN CLAM CHOWDER

I typically serve this chowder with a tossed salad and hot rolls. It's easy to make and tastes wonderful on a cold winter evening. My family has enjoyed it for more than 30 years.

—Joan Hopewell, Columbus, NJ

PREP: 10 min. • **COOK:** 40 min. • **MAKES:** 8 servings (2 qt.)

- 2 Tbsp. butter
- 1 cup chopped onion
- ⅔ cup chopped celery
- 2 tsp. minced green pepper
- 1 garlic clove, minced
- 2 cups hot water
- 1 cup cubed peeled potatoes
- 1 can (28 oz.) diced tomatoes, undrained
- 2 cans (6½ oz. each) minced clams, undrained
- 1 tsp. salt
- ½ tsp. dried thyme
- ¼ tsp. pepper
- Dash cayenne pepper
- 2 tsp. minced fresh parsley

1. In a large saucepan, heat butter over low heat. Add onion, celery, green pepper and garlic; cook, stirring frequently, 20 minutes. Add water and potatoes; bring to a boil. Reduce heat; simmer, covered, until potatoes are tender, about 15 minutes.

2. Add tomatoes, clams, salt, thyme, pepper and cayenne; heat through. Stir in the parsley. Serve immediately.

1 CUP 91 cal., 3g fat (2g sat. fat), 15mg chol., 652mg sod., 13g carb. (5g sugars, 3g fiber), 5g pro.

CLEANING CLAMS

When buying fresh clams, it's important to clean them thoroughly. For best results, clean your clams as soon as you bring them home from the market. First, check for any clams that are broken, chipped or open, and discard them. Fill a bowl with cold water and submerge the clams for 20-60 minutes to allow them to expel any sand in their systems. Lift each clam individually out of the water and scrub them to rid the shells of any excess grit. Once clean, use them as desired.

PAIR IT WITH
Garlic & Oregano Bread, p. 226

VEGAN SQUASH SOUP

Apple and winter squash are a wonderful match—the perfect pair for this cozy vegan soup. For a slightly different flavor that still features classic fall produce, substitute a ripe pear for the apple.

—*Taste of Home* Test Kitchen

PREP: 50 min. • **COOK:** 45 min. • **MAKES:** 8 servings (3 qt.)

- 1 large butternut squash (4 to 4½ lbs.)
- 1 medium onion, chopped
- 1 medium tart apple, peeled and coarsely chopped
- 1 Tbsp. olive oil
- 6 garlic cloves, minced
- 4 tsp. minced fresh thyme or 2 tsp. dried thyme
- ½ tsp. dried marjoram
- ¼ tsp. salt
- ¼ tsp. pepper
- 8 cups vegetable broth
- Optional: Fresh thyme leaves and coarsely ground black pepper

1. Preheat oven to 400°. Cut squash in half lengthwise; discard seeds. Place squash, cut side down, in a greased 15x10x1-in. baking pan. Bake, uncovered, 45-60 minutes or until tender. Cool slightly. Scoop out flesh; set aside.

2. In a Dutch oven, cook onion and apple in oil until tender. Add garlic; cook 1 minute longer. Stir in seasonings; cook for 10 seconds or until fragrant. Add the broth and squash; bring to a boil. Reduce the heat; simmer, uncovered, 15-20 minutes to allow flavors to blend. Cool slightly. In a blender, cover and process soup in batches until smooth.

3. Return pureed mixture to pan; cook and stir until heated through. If desired, serve with additional thyme and black pepper.

1½ CUPS 148 cal., 2g fat (0 sat. fat), 0 chol., 750mg sod., 33g carb. (10g sugars, 8g fiber), 3g pro.

GARDEN VEGETABLE & HERB SOUP

I submitted this recipe to a local newspaper and won first prize. I make this hearty soup whenever my family needs a good dose of veggies.

—Jody Saulnier, North Woodstock, NH

PREP: 20 min. • **COOK:** 30 min. • **MAKES:** 8 servings (2 qt.)

- 2 Tbsp. olive oil
- 2 medium onions, chopped
- 2 large carrots, sliced
- 1 lb. red potatoes (about 3 medium), cubed
- 2 cups water
- 1 can (14½ oz.) diced tomatoes in sauce
- 1½ cups vegetable broth
- 1½ tsp. garlic powder
- 1 tsp. dried basil
- ½ tsp. salt
- ½ tsp. paprika
- ¼ tsp. dill weed
- ¼ tsp. pepper
- 1 medium yellow summer squash, halved and sliced
- 1 medium zucchini, halved and sliced

1. In a large saucepan, heat oil over medium heat. Add onions and carrots; cook and stir for 4-6 minutes or until onions are tender. Add potatoes and cook for 2 minutes. Stir in water, tomatoes, broth and seasonings. Bring to a boil. Reduce heat; simmer, uncovered, until potatoes and carrots are tender, 8-10 minutes.

2. Add squash and zucchini; cook until vegetables are tender, 8-10 minutes longer. Serve or, if desired, puree mixture in batches, adding additional broth until desired consistency is achieved.

1 CUP 115 cal., 4g fat (1g sat. fat), 0 chol., 525mg sod., 19g carb. (6g sugars, 3g fiber), 2g pro. **DIABETIC EXCHANGES** 1 vegetable, 1 fat, ½ starch.

1

2

3

4

PAIR IT WITH

Copycat Olive Garden Breadsticks, p. 295

ANDOUILLE-SHRIMP CREAM SOUP

This dish is a variation on a creamy southern Louisiana corn stew. The bold flavor of andouille sausage blends beautifully with the shrimp and subtle spices.

—Judy Armstrong, Prairieville, LA

PREP: 20 min. • **COOK:** 30 min. • **MAKES:** 7 servings

- ½ lb. fully cooked andouille sausage links, thinly sliced
- 1 medium onion, chopped
- 2 celery ribs, thinly sliced
- 1 medium sweet red pepper, chopped
- 1 medium green pepper, chopped
- 1 jalapeno pepper, seeded and chopped
- ¼ cup butter, cubed
- 3 garlic cloves, minced
- 2 cups fresh or frozen corn, thawed
- 4 plum tomatoes, chopped
- 1 cup vegetable broth
- 2 Tbsp. minced fresh thyme or 2 tsp. dried thyme
- 1 tsp. chili powder
- ½ tsp. salt
- ½ tsp. pepper
- ¼ to ½ tsp. cayenne pepper
- 1 lb. uncooked shrimp (31-40 per lb.), peeled and deveined
- 1 cup heavy whipping cream

1. In a large skillet, saute first 6 ingredients in butter until vegetables are tender. Add garlic; cook 1 minute longer. Add the corn, tomatoes, broth, thyme, chili powder, salt, pepper and cayenne. Bring to a boil. Reduce heat; simmer, uncovered, for 10 minutes.

2. Stir in shrimp and cream. Bring to a gentle boil. Simmer, uncovered, 8-10 minutes or until shrimp turn pink.

NOTE Wear disposable gloves when cutting hot peppers; the oils can burn skin. Avoid touching your face.

1 CUP 390 cal., 27g fat (15g sat. fat), 185mg chol., 751mg sod., 20g carb. (7g sugars, 4g fiber), 21g pro.

PAIR IT WITH
Herbed Pumpkin Flatbread, p. 292

PRESSURE-COOKER SONORAN CHOWDER

Being from New England originally, I always appreciated a good, rich clam chowder. Living in the Southwest the past 35 years, I have learned to appreciate the Sonoran flavors. This recipe blends a comfort-food memory with my current flavor profiles.

—James Scott, Phoenix, AZ

PREP: 35 min. • **COOK:** 5 min. • **MAKES:** 10 servings (2½ qt.)

- 6 thick-sliced peppered bacon strips, chopped
- 3 Tbsp. butter
- 1 medium onion, chopped
- 1 medium sweet red pepper, chopped
- 2 cans (4 oz. each) chopped green chiles
- 4 garlic cloves, minced
- 3 cans (6½ oz. each) chopped clams, undrained
- 4 cups diced Yukon Gold potatoes (about 1½ lbs.)
- ½ cup chicken stock
- 2 cups half-and-half cream
- 1 envelope taco seasoning
- 2 Tbsp. chopped fresh cilantro, divided

1. Select saute setting on a 6-qt. electric pressure cooker. Adjust for medium heat; add bacon. Cook until crisp, stirring occasionally. Remove with a slotted spoon; drain on paper towels. Discard drippings, reserving 2 Tbsp. in pan. Add butter to drippings in pressure cooker. Add onion, red pepper and chiles; cook and stir for 7-9 minutes or until tender. Add garlic; cook 1 minute longer. Press cancel.

2. Drain clams; pour juice into pressure cooker. Set clams aside. Stir in the potatoes and stock. Lock lid; close pressure-release valve. Adjust to pressure-cook on high for 4 minutes. Allow pressure to release naturally for 4 minutes; quick-release any remaining pressure. Select saute setting and adjust for low heat. Add clams, cream, taco seasoning and 1 Tbsp. cilantro; simmer, uncovered, for 4-5 minutes or until the mixture is heated through, stirring occasionally. Press cancel. Serve with bacon and remaining 1 Tbsp. cilantro.

1 CUP 271 cal., 15g fat (7g sat. fat), 61mg chol., 935mg sod., 23g carb. (4g sugars, 2g fiber), 11g pro.

"Amazing! If you're a fan of clam chowder, then you will not be disappointed."

—WESLEY973, TASTEOFHOME.COM

SEAFOOD SOUP

Salmon, shrimp and loads of veggies make this a flavorful, hearty meal in a bowl.

—Valerie Bradley, Beaverton, OR

PREP: 20 min. • **COOK:** 50 min. • **MAKES:** 6 servings

- 1 Tbsp. olive oil
- 1 small onion, chopped
- 1 small green pepper, chopped
- 2 medium carrots, chopped
- 1 garlic clove, minced
- 1 can (15 oz.) tomato sauce
- 1 can (14½ oz.) diced tomatoes, undrained
- ¾ cup white wine or chicken broth
- 1 bay leaf
- ½ tsp. dried oregano
- ¼ tsp. dried basil
- ¼ tsp. pepper
- ¾ lb. salmon fillets, skinned and cut into ¾-in. cubes
- ½ lb. uncooked shrimp (31-40 per lb.), peeled and deveined
- 3 Tbsp. minced fresh parsley

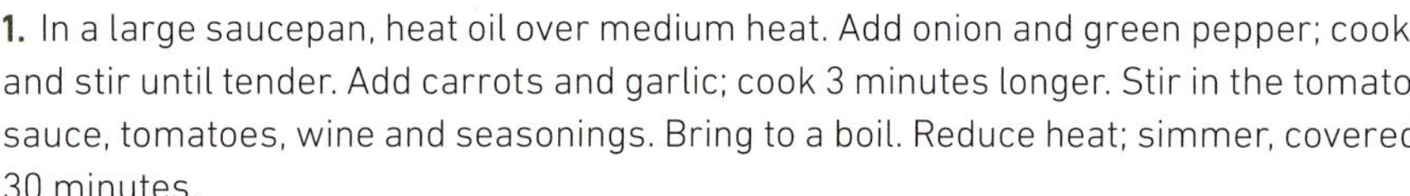

1. In a large saucepan, heat oil over medium heat. Add onion and green pepper; cook and stir until tender. Add carrots and garlic; cook 3 minutes longer. Stir in the tomato sauce, tomatoes, wine and seasonings. Bring to a boil. Reduce heat; simmer, covered, 30 minutes.

2. Stir in salmon, shrimp and parsley. Cook, covered, 7-10 minutes longer or until fish flakes easily with a fork and shrimp turn pink. Discard bay leaf.

1 CUP 213 cal., 9g fat (1g sat. fat), 74mg chol., 525mg sod., 12g carb. (5g sugars, 3g fiber), 18g pro. **DIABETIC EXCHANGES** 2 lean meat, 2 vegetable, ½ fat.

PREPARING SHRIMP FOR SOUP

If you don't know how to clean shrimp, this soup is a great excuse to learn. Use a sharp paring knife to carefully cut a shallow slice in the back of the shrimp, then use the tip of the knife to pull out the black vein running down the back. Not all shrimp will have the vein but most will.

SALMON SWEET POTATO SOUP

I created this recipe as a healthier alternative to whitefish chowder, which is a favorite in the area where I grew up. The salmon and sweet potatoes boost the nutrition, and the slow cooker makes it more convenient. It's especially comforting on a cold fall or winter day!

—Matthew Hass, Ellison Bay, WI

PREP: 20 min. • **COOK:** 5½ hours • **MAKES:** 8 servings (3 qt.)

- 1 Tbsp. olive oil
- 1 medium onion, chopped
- 1 medium carrot, chopped
- 1 celery rib, chopped
- 3 garlic cloves, minced
- 2 medium sweet potatoes, peeled and cut into ½-in. cubes
- 1½ cups frozen corn, thawed
- 6 cups reduced-sodium chicken broth
- 1 tsp. celery salt
- 1 tsp. dill weed
- ½ tsp. salt
- ¾ tsp. pepper
- 1½ lbs. salmon fillets, skin removed and cut into ¾-in. pieces
- 1 can (12 oz.) fat-free evaporated milk
- 2 Tbsp. minced fresh parsley

1. In a large skillet, heat oil over medium heat. Add the onion, carrot and celery; cook and stir until tender, 4-5 minutes. Add garlic; cook 1 minute longer. Transfer to a 5-qt. slow cooker. Add the next 7 ingredients. Cook, covered, on low for 5-6 hours or until sweet potatoes are tender.

2. Stir in salmon, milk and parsley. Cook, covered, 30-40 minutes longer or until fish begins to flake easily with a fork.

1½ CUPS 279 cal., 10g fat (2g sat. fat), 45mg chol., 834mg sod., 26g carb. (13g sugars, 3g fiber), 22g pro. **DIABETIC EXCHANGES** 3 lean meat, 1½ starch, ½ fat.

PAIR IT WITH
No-Knead Harvest
Bread, p. 238

CREAMY VEGAN CAULIFLOWER SOUP

You'll love this cozy, lightened-up version of cauliflower soup. What's our secret ingredient? Coconut milk! Once it is mixed in with the vegetables and the broth, the result is a delicious, silky-smooth soup that's completely dairy free.

—Jenna Urben, McKinney, TX

PREP: 15 min. • **COOK:** 30 min. • **MAKES:** 7 servings

- 1 Tbsp. olive oil
- 1 small onion, chopped
- 1 medium head cauliflower, broken into florets (about 6 cups)
- 1 small potato, peeled and cubed
- 2 cans (14½ oz. each) vegetable broth
- 1 can (13.66 oz.) coconut milk
- ¾ tsp. salt
- ¼ tsp. pepper
- Optional: Nutritional yeast, chopped green onions and fresh herbs

1. In a large saucepan, heat oil over medium heat. Add onion; cook and stir until softened, 2-3 minutes. Stir in cauliflower, potato and broth; bring to a boil. Reduce heat; simmer, covered, about 20 minutes.

2. Remove from heat. Stir in coconut milk, salt and pepper; cool slightly. Puree in batches in a blender or food processor until smooth. If desired, top with nutritional yeast, green onion and herbs.

FREEZE OPTION Before adding toppings, cool soup. Freeze in freezer containers. To use, thaw in refrigerator overnight. Heat through in a saucepan, stirring occasionally. Reblend with blender or immersion blender if coconut milk does not melt fully. Sprinkle with toppings.

1 CUP 158 cal., 11g fat (9g sat. fat), 0 chol., 566mg sod., 12g carb. (4g sugars, 2g fiber), 3g pro.

TASTY TOPPINGS

We like to top our vegan cauliflower soup with nutritional yeast, green onion and herbs, but other delicious options include croutons for crunch, a few thin florets of roasted cauliflower, or even crushed red pepper flakes and hot sauce for a kick.

SHRIMP BISQUE

This bisque combines the perfect blend of seafood and Mexican spices. You'll for sure want seconds!

—Karen Harris, Littleton, CO

TAKES: 30 min. • **MAKES:** 3 cups

- 1 small onion, chopped
- 1 Tbsp. olive oil
- 2 garlic cloves, minced
- 1 Tbsp. all-purpose flour
- 1 cup water
- ½ cup heavy whipping cream
- 1 Tbsp. chili powder
- 2 tsp. sodium-free chicken bouillon granules
- ½ tsp. ground cumin
- ½ tsp. ground coriander
- ½ lb. uncooked shrimp (31-40 per lb.), peeled and deveined
- ½ cup sour cream
- Optional: Fresh cilantro, cubed avocado and additional shrimp

1. In a small saucepan, saute onion in oil until tender. Add garlic; cook 1 minute longer. Stir in flour until blended. Stir in the water, cream, chili powder, bouillon, cumin and coriander; bring to a boil. Reduce heat; cover and simmer for 5 minutes.

2. Cut shrimp into bite-sized pieces; add to soup. Simmer 5 minutes longer or until shrimp turn pink. Gradually stir ½ cup hot soup into sour cream; return all to pan, stirring constantly. Heat through (do not boil). Garnish with cilantro, avocado and additional shrimp if desired.

1 CUP 317 cal., 23g fat (11g sat. fat), 141mg chol., 206mg sod., 11g carb. (4g sugars, 2g fiber), 17g pro.

"Excellent bisque. Easy to make, even if you are a new cook. My husband, who is not a soup fan, asked for seconds. To me, that said it all. This recipe is definitely a keeper."

—PATRICIA K, TASTEOFHOME.COM

PAIR IT WITH
Marina's Golden
Corn Fritters, p. 302

SOUPS

BEANS & LENTILS

TORTELLINI & SPINACH SOUP

I first made this soup in the summer, but when I saw its bright red and green colors, I knew it would make a perfect first course for Christmas dinner.

—Marietta Slater, Justin, TX

TAKES: 25 min. • **MAKES:** 6 servings

- 2 cans (14½ oz. each) vegetable broth
- 1 pkg. (9 oz.) refrigerated cheese tortellini or tortellini of your choice
- 1 can (15 oz.) cannellini beans, rinsed and drained
- 1 can (14½ oz.) Italian diced tomatoes, undrained
- ¼ tsp. salt
- ⅛ tsp. pepper
- 3 cups fresh baby spinach
- 3 Tbsp. minced fresh basil
- ¼ cup shredded Asiago cheese

1. In a large saucepan, bring broth to a boil. Add tortellini; reduce the heat. Simmer, uncovered, 5 minutes. Stir in beans, tomatoes, salt and pepper; return to a simmer. Cook until tortellini are tender, 4-5 minutes longer.

2. Stir in spinach and basil; cook until spinach is wilted. Top servings with cheese.

1 CUP 239 cal., 5g fat (3g sat. fat), 23mg chol., 1135mg sod., 38g carb. (7g sugars, 5g fiber), 11g pro.

"Yummy! Great flavor, hearty and easy to put together. Two thumbs way up!"

—JGA2595176, TASTEOFHOME.COM

PAIR IT WITH
Olive Bread, p. 237

1

2

3

4

5

EASY MULLIGATAWNY SOUP

This soup is a comforting dish that marries both Indian and British ingredients, and it's sure to tantalize your taste buds. It's fragrant, creamy, mildly spicy and simply incredible.

—Anvita Mistry, Erlangen, Germany

TAKES: 35 min. • **MAKES:** 8 servings

- 6 Tbsp. dried split pigeon pea lentils
- 3 Tbsp. uncooked basmati rice
- 2 garlic cloves, minced
- 1 piece fresh gingerroot (1 in.), peeled and minced
- 1 tsp. chili powder
- 1 tsp. ground turmeric
- 1 tsp. ground coriander
- 1 tsp. ground cumin
- 2 Tbsp. ghee
- 1 large onion, chopped
- 1 bay leaf
- 6 medium carrots, chopped
- 2 medium apples, peeled and chopped
- 2 celery ribs, chopped
- 1½ tsp. salt
- ½ tsp. pepper
- 4 cups reduced-sodium vegetable broth
- ¾ cup coconut milk
- 1 tsp. lemon juice
- ½ tsp. garam masala
- ½ tsp. coarsely ground pepper
- ½ cup cooked basmati rice

1. Place uncooked lentils and rice in a small bowl; cover with water. Set aside to soak for 5-10 minutes. Drain and discard water.

2. Use a mortar and pestle to mash garlic, ginger, chili powder, turmeric, coriander and cumin into a curry paste.

3. Heat ghee in a Dutch oven to medium heat; once melted, add onion, curry paste and bay leaf. Cook until fragrant, 1-2 minutes, stirring constantly. Add carrots, apples, celery, salt and pepper; cook until vegetables are crisp-tender, 3-4 minutes, stirring frequently. Stir in broth and soaked lentils and rice. Bring to a low simmer. Cook until lentils are tender, 20-25 minutes. Discard bay leaf.

4. Stir in coconut milk and lemon juice. Serve soup in bowls with rice, topped with garam masala and black pepper.

1 SERVING 184 cal., 7g fat (5g sat. fat), 8mg chol., 571mg sod., 26g carb. (9g sugars, 6g fiber), 5g pro.

POTATO-BEEF BARLEY SOUP

Hash browns add an unexpected twist in this vegetable barley soup. I sometimes throw in some chopped fresh red and yellow peppers for color.

—Kendra McKenzie, Fredericktown, OH

PREP: 10 min. • **COOK:** 30 min. • **MAKES:** 12 servings (4 qt.)

- 1½ lbs. lean ground beef (90% lean)
- 1 large green pepper, chopped
- 7 cups water
- 1 pkg. (32 oz.) frozen cubed hash brown potatoes
- 1 can (28 oz.) crushed tomatoes, undrained
- 2 Tbsp. reduced-sodium soy sauce
- 2½ tsp. garlic powder
- 2½ tsp. dried thyme
- 1½ tsp. salt
- ½ tsp. pepper
- 1 pkg. (16 oz.) frozen cut green beans
- ½ cup quick-cooking barley

1. In a Dutch oven coated with cooking spray, cook beef and green pepper over medium heat until meat is no longer pink; drain.

2. Stir in water, potatoes, tomatoes, soy sauce, garlic powder, thyme, salt and pepper. Bring to a boil. Reduce heat; cover and simmer for 10-15 minutes or until potatoes are tender.

3. Return to a boil. Stir in beans and barley. Reduce heat; cover and simmer until beans and barley are tender, 10-12 minutes. Remove from the heat; let stand for 5 minutes.

1⅓ CUPS 217 cal., 5g fat (2g sat. fat), 35mg chol., 568mg sod., 27g carb. (2g sugars, 5g fiber), 16g pro. **DIABETIC EXCHANGES** 2 lean meat, 1 starch, 1 vegetable.

"I have made this soup several times. It is guest-approved, and I wouldn't hesitate to serve it to company again."

—KAELINHRSE, TASTEOFHOME.COM

FRENCH MARKET SOUP

An old friend gave me this recipe. I think it tastes best the next day, so I recommend preparing it the day before you plan to serve it. Leftovers also freeze well.

—Terri Lowe, Lumberton, TX

PREP: 20 min. + soaking • **COOK:** 4½ hours • **MAKES:** 12 servings (4½ qt.)

- 3 cups assorted dried beans for soup
- 2 smoked ham hocks
- 12 cups water
- 1½ tsp. salt
- ½ tsp. pepper
- 1 can (28 oz.) crushed tomatoes, undrained
- 2 medium onions, chopped
- ¼ to ⅓ cup lemon juice
- 2 garlic cloves, minced
- ½ tsp. chili powder
- 1 lb. smoked kielbasa, chopped
- 1½ cups cubed cooked chicken
- ½ cup dry red wine or chicken broth
- ½ cup minced fresh parsley

1. Sort beans and rinse in cold water. Place beans in a Dutch oven and add water to cover by 2 in. Bring to a boil; boil for 2 minutes. Remove from the heat. Cover and let stand for 1-4 hours or until beans are softened.

2. Drain and rinse beans, discarding liquid; return beans to pan. Add the ham hocks, water, salt and pepper; bring to a boil. Reduce heat. Cover and simmer for 3 hours or until beans are tender.

3. Remove ham hocks; set aside until cool enough to handle. Add tomatoes, onions, lemon juice, garlic and chili powder to beans. Simmer 1 hour longer.

4. Remove ham from bones and cut into cubes; discard bones. Return ham to soup. Stir in kielbasa, chicken, wine and parsley. Simmer for 30-40 minutes or until heated through and as thick as desired.

NOTE This recipe was tested with Bob's Red Mill 13-Bean Soup Mix.

1½ CUPS 291 cal., 14g fat (5g sat. fat), 52mg chol., 840mg sod., 32g carb. (3g sugars, 18g fiber), 23g pro.

OLD-FASHIONED HAM & BEAN SOUP

This old-fashioned version of ham and bean soup starts with dried navy beans, but you could start with great northern beans instead. The first soak of the beans softens them, but they won't get tender until after they are simmered in the second step.

—*Taste of Home* Test Kitchen

PREP: 15 min. + soaking • **COOK:** 1½ hours • **MAKES:** 10 servings (2½ qt.)

- 1 lb. dried navy beans
- 1 Tbsp. canola oil
- 2 medium onions, chopped
- 2 celery ribs, chopped
- 8 cups water
- 1 medium carrot, chopped
- 2 bay leaves
- 1 tsp. dried thyme
- ½ tsp. pepper
- 2 smoked ham hocks
- 2 cups cubed fully cooked ham
- ½ tsp. salt

1. Place beans in a Dutch oven and add water to cover by 2 in. Bring to a boil; boil for 2 minutes. Remove from the heat; cover and let stand for 1-4 hours or until beans are softened. Drain and rinse beans, discarding liquid.

2. In same pan, heat oil over medium heat; add onions and celery. Cook and stir until crisp-tender, 3-5 minutes. Stir in softened beans, 8 cups water, carrot, bay leaves, thyme and pepper. Add ham hocks. Bring to a boil. Reduce heat; cover and simmer for 1¼-1½ hours or until beans are tender.

3. Discard bay leaves. Remove ham hocks and set aside until cool enough to handle. Remove ham from bones and cut into cubes. Discard the bones. Return ham to soup. Stir in cubed ham and salt; heat through.

1 CUP 230 cal., 4g fat (1g sat. fat), 25mg chol., 521mg sod., 31g carb. (3g sugars, 8g fiber), 20g pro. **DIABETIC EXCHANGES** 2 starch, 2 lean meat.

EASY SUBSTITUTION

If you don't have ham hocks, use a ham bone from a ham for this soup. If the ham bone is pretty meaty, feel free to leave out the 2 cups cubed ham. Instead, remove the ham from the bone after cooking, shred or dice it, and return it to the soup.

1

2

3

4

5

PAIR IT WITH
Savory Party Bread,
p. 309

PUMPKIN & BEAN SOUP

I picked up this recipe at my local grocery store during a promotion for creative ways to use pumpkin. Black beans are not usually paired with the hearty fall vegetable, but once I tried the soup, I was a believer! Now it's one of my favorite recipes to make when pumpkin is in season.

—Lori Karavolis, McMurray, PA

PREP: 30 min. • **COOK:** 20 min. • **MAKES:** 10 servings (2½ qt)

- 2 Tbsp. olive oil
- 1 cup chopped sweet onion
- 1 garlic clove, minced
- ½ cup white wine
- 2 cans (15 oz. each) black beans, rinsed and drained
- 1 can (28 oz.) diced tomatoes, undrained
- 2 cups vegetable broth
- 1 can (15 oz.) pumpkin
- 4 tsp. ground coriander
- 3 tsp. ground cumin
- ¾ tsp. salt
- ¼ tsp. cayenne pepper
- ¼ tsp. pepper
- 1 cup heavy whipping cream
- Optional: Chopped fresh cilantro and tortilla chips

1. In a Dutch oven, heat the oil over medium-high heat. Add onion; cook and stir until tender, 4-5 minutes. Add garlic and cook 1 minute longer. Stir in wine. Bring to a boil. Cook until liquid is reduced by half, 3-4 minutes.

2. Add black beans, tomatoes, broth, pumpkin and seasonings. Bring to a boil; reduce heat. Simmer, covered, 20 minutes or until flavors are blended, stirring occasionally. Add cream; heat through. If desired, top soup with chopped cilantro and tortilla chips.

FREEZE OPTION Freeze cooled soup in freezer containers. To use, partially thaw in refrigerator overnight. Heat through, stirring occasionally; add broth if necessary.

1 CUP 221 cal., 12g fat (6g sat. fat), 27mg chol., 608mg sod., 23g carb. (6g sugars, 7g fiber), 6g pro.

SLOW-COOKED BLACK BEAN SOUP

Life can get really crazy with young kids, but I never want to compromise when it comes to cooking. This recipe is healthy and so easy, thanks to the slow cooker!

—Angela Lemoine, Howell, NJ

PREP: 15 min. • **COOK:** 6 hours • **MAKES:** 8 servings

- 2 cans (15 oz. each) black beans, rinsed and drained
- 1 medium onion, finely chopped
- 1 medium sweet red pepper, finely chopped
- 4 garlic cloves, minced
- 2 tsp. ground cumin
- 2 cans (14½ oz. each) vegetable broth
- 1 tsp. olive oil
- 1 cup fresh or frozen corn
- Dash pepper
- Minced fresh cilantro

1. In a 3-qt. slow cooker, combine the first 6 ingredients. Cook, covered, on low for 6-8 hours or until vegetables are softened.

2. Puree soup using an immersion blender. Or cool soup slightly and puree in batches in a blender. Return to slow cooker and heat through.

3. In a small skillet, heat oil over medium heat. Add corn; cook and stir until golden brown, 4-6 minutes. Sprinkle soup with pepper. Garnish with corn and cilantro.

¾ CUP 117 cal., 1g fat (0 sat. fat), 0 chol., 616mg sod., 21g carb. (3g sugars, 5g fiber), 6g pro. **DIABETIC EXCHANGES** 1½ starch.

1

2

3

ITALIAN SAUSAGE BEAN SOUP

During the frigid months, I like to put on a big pot of this soothing soup. It cooks away while I do other things, such as baking bread, crafting or even cleaning.

—Glenna Reimer, Gig Harbor, WA

PREP: 20 min. • **COOK:** 1½ hours • **MAKES:** 8 servings (3 qt.)

- 1 lb. bulk Italian sausage
- 1 medium onion, finely chopped
- 3 garlic cloves, sliced
- 4 cans (14½ oz. each) reduced-sodium chicken broth
- 2 cans (15 oz. each) pinto or cannellini beans, rinsed and drained
- 1 can (14½ oz.) diced tomatoes, undrained
- 1 cup medium pearl barley
- 1 large carrot, sliced
- 1 celery rib, sliced
- 1 tsp. minced fresh sage
- ½ tsp. minced fresh rosemary or ⅛ tsp. dried rosemary, crushed
- 6 cups chopped fresh kale

1. In a Dutch oven, cook and stir sausage and onion over medium heat until meat is no longer pink, 6-7 minutes. Add garlic; cook 1 minute longer. Drain.

2. Stir in broth, beans, tomatoes, barley, carrot, celery, sage and rosemary. Bring to a boil. Reduce heat; cover and simmer for 45 minutes.

3. Stir in kale; return to a boil. Reduce heat; cover and simmer for 25-30 minutes or until vegetables are tender.

1½ CUPS 339 cal., 9g fat (3g sat. fat), 23mg chol., 1100mg sod., 48g carb. (7g sugars, 11g fiber), 19g pro.

BALSAMIC LENTIL SOUP

Balsamic vinegar and honey give this healthy soup a tangy and slightly sweet flavor. Since this soup is slow-cooked, the vegetables and lentils retain their texture and don't turn into mush.

—Colleen Delawder, Herndon, VA

PREP: 15 min. • **COOK:** 5 hours. • **MAKES:** 8 servings (2 qt.)

- 1 carton (32 oz.) reduced-sodium chicken broth
- 3 celery ribs, chopped
- 2 medium carrots, chopped
- 2 medium red potatoes, cut into ½-in. cubes
- 1 cup chopped sweet onion
- 1 cup dried red lentils, rinsed
- 1 Tbsp. honey
- 2 tsp. Italian seasoning
- ½ tsp. salt
- ½ tsp. pepper
- ¼ tsp. crushed red pepper flakes
- ¼ tsp. garlic powder
- ¼ cup balsamic vinegar
- Optional: Shaved Parmesan cheese, fresh parsley, balsamic glaze drizzle

In a 3- or 4-qt. slow cooker, combine first 12 ingredients. Cook, covered, on low until vegetables and lentils are tender, 5-6 hours. Stir in vinegar. Garnish as desired.

1 CUP 145 cal., 0 fat (0 sat. fat), 0 chol., 459mg sod., 28g carb. (7g sugars, 4g fiber), 8g pro. **DIABETIC EXCHANGES** 2 starch.

SECRET INGREDIENT

Balsamic vinegar is one ingredient that always jazzes up soup by adding an unexpected yet fantastic flavor twist. Consider stirring a little balsamic into your favorite soup recipe for a tasty change of pace.

PAIR IT WITH
Rosemary Nut Bread, p. 229

CHICKEN CASSOULET SOUP

After my sister spent a year in France as an au pair, I created this lighter, easier version of traditional French cassoulet for her. It uses chicken instead of the usual duck.

—Bridget Klusman, Otsego, MI

PREP: 35 min. • **COOK:** 6 hours • **MAKES:** 7 servings (about 2¾ qt.)

- ½ lb. bulk pork sausage
- 5 cups water
- ½ lb. cubed cooked chicken
- 1 can (16 oz.) kidney beans, rinsed and drained
- 1 can (15 oz.) black beans, rinsed and drained
- 1 can (15 oz.) garbanzo beans or chickpeas, rinsed and drained
- 2 medium carrots, shredded
- 1 medium onion, chopped
- ¼ cup dry vermouth or chicken broth
- 5 tsp. chicken bouillon granules
- 4 garlic cloves, minced
- 1½ tsp. minced fresh thyme or ½ tsp. dried thyme
- ¼ tsp. fennel seed, crushed
- 1 tsp. dried lavender flowers, optional
- ½ lb. bacon strips, cooked and crumbled
- Additional fresh thyme, optional

1. In a large skillet, cook sausage over medium heat until no longer pink, breaking into crumbles; drain.

2. Transfer to a 4- or 5-qt. slow cooker. Add water, chicken, beans, carrots, onion, vermouth, bouillon, garlic, thyme, fennel and, if desired, lavender. Cover and cook on low for 6-8 hours or until heated through.

3. Divide among serving bowls; sprinkle with bacon. If desired, top with additional fresh thyme.

NOTE Look for dried lavender flowers in spice shops. If using lavender from the garden, make sure it hasn't been treated with chemicals.

1½ CUPS 494 cal., 23g fat (7g sat. fat), 77mg chol., 1821mg sod., 34g carb. (6g sugars, 9g fiber), 34g pro.

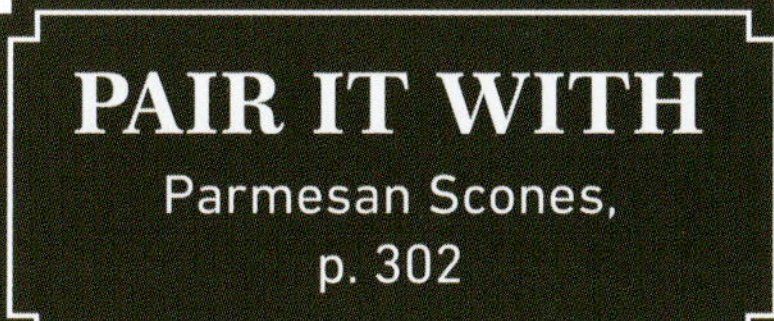

PAIR IT WITH

Parmesan Scones, p. 302

EASY WHITE BEAN SOUP

A Tuscan white bean soup brimming with veggies and spinach delivers a healthy dose of fiber, protein and nutrients in a hearty, comforting bowl. A sprinkling of grated Parmesan adds a rich, nutty note to the finished soup.

—*Taste of Home* Test Kitchen

PREP: 15 min. • **COOK:** 25 min. • **MAKES:** 6 servings

- 1 Tbsp. olive oil
- 1 medium onion, chopped
- 3 garlic cloves, minced
- 1 medium carrot, chopped
- 1 celery rib, chopped
- 2 Tbsp. tomato paste
- 1 tsp. Italian seasoning
- 1 tsp. salt
- ½ tsp. pepper
- ¼ tsp. crushed red pepper flakes
- 1 carton (32 oz.) reduced-sodium vegetable broth
- 4 cups fresh spinach
- 3 cans (15 oz. each) cannellini beans, rinsed and drained
- ¼ cup fresh basil leaves, chopped
- ¼ cup grated Parmesan cheese

1. In a Dutch oven, heat oil over medium heat. Add onion, garlic, carrot and celery; cook and stir until tender, 3-4 minutes. Add tomato paste, Italian seasoning, salt, pepper and pepper flakes. Cook until fragrant, 1-2 minutes. Add broth; bring to a boil. Reduce heat. Simmer, uncovered, about 15 minutes.

2. Stir in spinach, beans and basil; heat through, stirring occasionally. Sprinkle with Parmesan before serving.

1¼ CUPS 236 cal., 4g fat (1g sat. fat), 3mg chol., 871mg sod., 38g carb. (3g sugars, 10g fiber), 11g pro.

RINSE CYCLE?

We call for draining and rinsing the canned white beans in this soup recipe, but it's also fine to pour the cans of beans directly into the pot, if you like. The canning liquid, called aquafaba, will add some viscosity to the cooking liquid for your soup. Note that beans are often canned in salted water, so adding canned bean liquid to any soup can result in a saltier flavor and increase sodium overall.

STAUB

SPINACH & SAUSAGE LENTIL SOUP

During the cooler months of the year, this soup makes regular appearances on our dinner table. It is approved by all, including my picky 6-year-old.

—Kalyn Gensic, Ardmore, OK

PREP: 5 min. • **COOK:** 45 min. • **MAKES:** 6 servings (2 qt.)

- 1 lb. bulk spicy pork sausage
- 1 cup dried brown lentils, rinsed
- 1 can (15 oz.) cannellini beans, rinsed and drained
- 1 carton (32 oz.) reduced-sodium chicken broth
- 1 cup water
- 1 can (14½ oz.) fire-roasted diced tomatoes, undrained
- 6 cups fresh spinach (about 4 oz.)
- Crumbled goat cheese, optional

1. In a Dutch oven, cook and crumble sausage over medium heat until no longer pink, 5-7 minutes; drain.

2. Stir in lentils, beans, broth and water; bring to a boil. Reduce the heat. Simmer, covered, until lentils are tender, about 30 minutes. Stir in tomatoes; heat through.

3. Remove from heat; stir in spinach until wilted. If desired, serve with goat cheese.

FREEZE OPTION Freeze cooled soup in freezer containers. To use, partially thaw in refrigerator overnight. Heat through in a saucepan, stirring occasionally.

1⅓ CUPS 390 cal., 17g fat (5g sat. fat), 41mg chol., 1242mg sod., 37g carb. (3g sugars, 8g fiber), 22g pro.

"Delicious and easy. Next time I make this soup, I will double the recipe so I have some to freeze. Thank you for sharing the recipe. It's a keeper!"

—TERRY, TASTEOFHOME.COM

CHIPOTLE PUMPKIN BUTTERNUT SOUP

This comforting, warm soup will help keep your spirits up in the fall. Using your garden goodies, mix warm spices with some heat from chipotle peppers in adobo sauce. You can use any beans you like and add fresh spinach or kale.

—Teri Schloessmann, Tulsa, OK

PREP: 25 min. • **COOK:** 25 min. • **MAKES:** 10 servings (2½ qt.)

- 2 Tbsp. olive oil
- 1 cup cubed peeled butternut squash
- 1 cup cubed fresh pumpkin
- 1 small onion, chopped
- 12 oz. smoked Polish sausage, sliced
- 1 garlic clove, minced
- 3 cups chicken or vegetable broth
- 1 can (14½ oz.) diced tomatoes, undrained
- 3 oz. cream cheese, cubed
- 1 Tbsp. minced chipotle peppers in adobo sauce
- ½ tsp. ground cumin
- 1 can (15 oz.) black beans, rinsed and drained
- 1 can (11 oz.) Mexicorn, drained
- 2 Tbsp. minced fresh basil

1. In a Dutch oven, heat oil over medium-high heat. Add squash, pumpkin and onion; cook and stir for 6-8 minutes or until crisp-tender. Add sausage and garlic. Cook until sausage is browned, 3-4 minutes.

2. Add broth, tomatoes, cream cheese, chipotle peppers and cumin. Bring to a boil; reduce the heat. Simmer, covered, until squash is tender, about 15 minutes, stirring occasionally. Stir in black beans, Mexicorn and basil; heat through. Garnish with additional basil.

1 CUP 246 cal., 15g fat (5g sat. fat), 34mg chol., 841mg sod., 19g carb. (5g sugars, 3g fiber), 8g pro.

RAMEN & PASTA

CHICKEN RAMEN NOODLE BOWL

This healthier take on ramen uses ingredients I usually have on hand. It is an easy, quick and satisfying lunch. You can also make this with leftover chicken or pork. Fresh lime and/or bean sprouts would be a nice garnish.

—Alicia Rooker, Milwaukee, WI

TAKES: 20 min. • **MAKES:** 2 servings

- 1 pkg. (3 oz.) chicken ramen noodles
- 1 cup frozen stir-fry vegetable blend
- 1 can (5 oz.) chunk white chicken, drained
- 2 medium fresh mushrooms, thinly sliced
- 1 garlic clove, minced
- ½ tsp. Sriracha chili sauce
- 2 soft-boiled large eggs
- 1 green onion, thinly sliced

Cook the noodles and stir-fry blend according to package directions. Stir chicken, mushrooms, garlic, chili sauce and cooked stir-fry blend into noodles; heat through. Divide between 2 bowls. Serve with soft-boiled eggs, green onion and, if desired, additional chili sauce.

1½ CUPS 368 cal., 14g fat (5g sat. fat), 230mg chol., 1199mg sod., 36g carb. (4g sugars, 3g fiber), 24g pro.

FRENCH ONION TORTELLINI SOUP

This soup is delicious and unbelievably fast to make. For a creamy variation, substitute cream of mushroom soup for the French onion soup.

—Marsha Farley, Bangor, ME

TAKES: 30 min. • **MAKES:** 8 servings

- 1 lb. ground beef
- 3½ cups water
- 1 can (28 oz.) diced tomatoes, undrained
- 1 can (10½ oz.) condensed French onion soup, undiluted
- 1 pkg. (9 oz.) frozen cut green beans
- 1 pkg. (9 oz.) refrigerated cheese tortellini
- 1 medium zucchini, chopped
- 1 tsp. dried basil

In a large saucepan, cook the beef over medium heat until no longer pink; drain. Add remaining ingredients; bring to a boil. Cook, uncovered, 7-9 minutes or until tortellini is tender.

1 SERVING 241 cal., 9g fat (4g sat. fat), 43mg chol., 608mg sod., 25g carb. (7g sugars, 4g fiber), 16g pro.

PAIR IT WITH
Almond Flour Bread,
p. 250

PASTA & WHITE BEAN SOUP WITH SUN-DRIED TOMATOES

I have a bean-loving family, so I am always looking for a new bean recipe. This one can be made with chicken broth or vegetable broth to appeal to everyone on your guest list.

—Mary Swartz, Palm Desert, CA

PREP: 20 min. + soaking • **COOK:** 1¼ hours • **MAKES:** 6 servings (2 qt.)

- 1 cup dried great northern beans
- 2 cups finely chopped onions
- 2 medium carrots, chopped
- ½ cup sliced fennel bulb or celery
- ¼ cup olive oil
- 4 garlic cloves, minced
- ¾ tsp. crushed red pepper flakes
- 2 bay leaves
- 4 cans (14½ oz. each) chicken or vegetable broth
- 2 cups uncooked bow tie pasta
- ½ cup oil-packed sun-dried tomatoes, chopped
- ¼ cup minced fresh parsley
- ½ tsp. salt
- Shredded Parmesan cheese, optional

1. Rinse and sort beans; soak according to package directions. Drain and rinse beans; discard liquid and set beans aside.

2. In a Dutch oven, saute onions, carrots and fennel in oil until tender. Add garlic, pepper flakes and bay leaves; cook 1 minute. Add broth and beans.

3. Bring to a boil. Reduce the heat; cover and simmer until beans are almost tender, about 1 hour. Stir in pasta, tomatoes, parsley and salt. Bring to a boil. Reduce heat; cover and simmer for 15 minutes or until beans and pasta are tender. Discard bay leaves. Serve with cheese if desired.

1⅓ CUPS 325 cal., 12g fat (2g sat. fat), 6mg chol., 1433mg sod., 45g carb. (6g sugars, 9g fiber), 12g pro.

DID YOU KNOW?

Sun-dried tomatoes have been dried to remove most of their water content, producing a chewy, intensely flavored tomato product. They are found in the grocery store either packed in oil or dry-packed. The dry-packed sun-dried tomatoes are usually soaked in a liquid to soften them before use.

TOMATO FLORENTINE SOUP

When I get a craving for this comforting soup in summer, I head outside and pick garden-fresh tomatoes and basil. Use whatever kind of pasta you have on hand.

—Engracia Salley, Bristol, RI

PREP: 40 min. • **COOK:** 25 min. • **MAKES:** 9 servings (2¼ qt.)

- 4 garlic cloves, minced
- 3 Tbsp. olive oil
- 8 medium tomatoes, chopped
- 4 cups spicy hot V8 vegetable juice
- ¾ cup uncooked small pasta shells
- ½ tsp. salt
- ⅛ tsp. pepper
- 1 pkg. (10 oz.) fresh baby spinach
- 3 Tbsp. minced fresh basil or 1 Tbsp. dried basil

1. In a large saucepan, saute garlic in oil for 1 minute. Add tomatoes; cook and stir for 5-10 minutes or until tender. Add vegetable juice, pasta, salt and pepper; bring to a boil.

2. Reduce heat; cover and simmer for 20-25 minutes or until pasta is tender. Stir in spinach and basil. Cook 5 minutes longer or until spinach is wilted.

1 CUP 120 cal., 5g fat (1g sat. fat), 0 chol., 376mg sod., 16g carb. (7g sugars, 3g fiber), 4g pro.

GRANDMA'S PRESSURE-COOKER CHICKEN NOODLE SOUP

I have made this soup weekly since I modified my grandma's recipe for the pressure cooker. Chicken soup, especially this one, is quick to make and budget-friendly for any large family.

—Tammy Stanko, Greensburg, PA

PREP: 10 min. • **COOK:** 25 min. + releasing • **MAKES:** 4 servings

- 2 tsp. olive oil
- 4 bone-in chicken thighs
- 2 medium carrots, peeled and sliced into ½-in. pieces
- 1½ celery ribs, sliced into ½-in. pieces
- 6 cups reduced-sodium chicken broth
- ½ tsp. salt
- ⅛ tsp. pepper
- ½ pkg. (8 oz.) fine egg noodles, cooked
- Chopped fresh parsley, optional

1. Select saute setting on a 3- or 6-qt. electric pressure cooker and adjust for medium heat; add oil. Brown chicken thighs. Press cancel. Add carrots, celery and broth to pressure cooker. Lock lid; close pressure-release valve. Adjust to pressure-cook on high for 10 minutes. Allow pressure to release naturally for 10 minutes, then quick-release any remaining pressure.

2. Stir in salt and pepper. Evenly divide noodles among 4 serving bowls; top each bowl with 1 chicken thigh and broth. If desired, sprinkle with parsley.

2 CUPS SOUP WITH 1 CHICKEN THIGH 389 cal., 29g fat (5g sat. fat), 112mg chol., 1262mg sod., 25g carb. (4g sugars, 2g fiber), 31g pro.

SINGAPORE NOODLE SOUP

This hearty noodle soup is a beloved favorite in Southeast Asia, especially Singapore, where it is called laksa. *It is perfect for busy dinners because it has protein, starch and vegetables cooked together in one pot. Every home has its own recipe. You can serve it with lime juice or chili garlic paste.*

—Loanne Chiu, Fort Worth, TX

PREP: 15 min. • **COOK:** 25 min. • **MAKES:** 6 servings (2¼ qt.)

- 1 carton (32 oz.) seafood stock
- 1 can (13.66 oz.) coconut milk
- 2 Tbsp. grated fresh gingerroot
- 2 Tbsp. massaman curry paste or red curry paste
- 1 Tbsp. fish sauce or soy sauce
- 3 tsp. grated lime zest
- 2 tsp. brown sugar
- 2 cups frozen stir-fry vegetable blend
- 1 small sweet red pepper, chopped
- 1½ lbs. uncooked shrimp (26-30 per lb.), peeled and deveined
- 8 oz. refrigerated angel hair pasta
- 2 Tbsp. lime juice
- 2 Tbsp. chopped fresh basil

1. In a large saucepan, combine first 7 ingredients. Bring to a boil. Reduce heat; simmer, uncovered, 15 minutes.

2. Stir in vegetables and red pepper. Return to a boil. Add shrimp and pasta. Cook until shrimp turn pink and pasta is tender, 4-5 minutes. Stir in lime juice and basil. If desired, garnish with additional basil.

1½ CUPS 359 cal., 13g fat (11g sat. fat), 157mg chol., 952mg sod., 33g carb. (6g sugars, 2g fiber), 27g pro.

"This soup is absolutely delicious, quick, healthy and a hit in our household! My husband loves it so much that he asks me to make it every week. Trust me, this soup won't disappoint!"

—MICHELE945, TASTEOFHOME.COM

PAIR IT WITH
Icebox Potato Rolls, p. 283

CHINESE BEEF NOODLE SOUP

This peppercorn-infused beef soup is brimming with comfort, spice and classic Chinese ingredients: gingerroot, star anise, chili bean paste and Szechuan chiles. Serve this piping hot with noodles and a scattering of freshly chopped green onion and cilantro.

—Tria Wen, San Francisco, CA

PREP: 15 min. • **COOK:** 1½ hours • **MAKES:** 6 servings

- 1 Tbsp. canola oil
- 1 Tbsp. Szechuan peppercorns
- 1½ lbs. boneless beef chuck roast, cut into 2-in. cubes
- 3 pieces fresh gingerroot (¼ in.), sliced
- 4 cups water
- ½ cup reduced-sodium soy sauce
- 2 Tbsp. Shaoxing cooking wine
- 1 Tbsp. rock sugar or honey
- 2 tsp. chili bean paste
- 5 whole star anise
- 2 bay leaves
- 2 green onions, thinly sliced
- 2 dried Szechuan chiles
- ½ tsp. salt
- 2 medium carrots, chopped
- 2 medium daikon radishes, chopped
- 14 oz. uncooked Chinese noodles
- Optional: Fresh cilantro leaves, sesame oil

1. In a Dutch oven or large saucepot, heat oil over medium heat. Add peppercorns; cook until fragrant, 1-2 minutes, stirring constantly. Using a slotted spoon, remove peppercorns; discard.

2. In same pan, over medium-high heat, add beef and ginger. Cook, stirring often, until beef is browned, 8-10 minutes. Add water, soy sauce, wine, sugar, chili bean paste, star anise, bay leaves, green onion, dried chiles and salt; bring to a boil. Reduce heat; cover and simmer for 30 minutes.

3. Stir in carrots and radishes. Continue to simmer for 55-60 minutes longer or until vegetables are tender. Remove and discard star anise, bay leaves and dried chiles.

4. Meanwhile, cook noodles according to package directions; drain. Add noodles to the soup.

5. Serve in bowls with additional green onion, additional chili bean paste, cilantro leaves and sesame oil as desired.

1 SERVING 512 cal., 15g fat (5g sat. fat), 74mg chol., 1963mg sod., 57g carb. (9g sugars, 5g fiber), 35g pro.

USE YOUR NOODLE

Dried noodles are convenient and economical, making them an obvious choice for Asian-inspired soups. If you live near an Asian grocery store, however, and have access to fresh noodles, it will definitely make for a treat. No matter which noodles you use, be sure not to overcook them, as they'll continue to soften in the hot soup.

COPYCAT OLIVE GARDEN CHICKEN GNOCCHI SOUP

My family loves making soup because it's a great way to use up vegetables, and we have leftovers for days. I made this soup once, and the recipe made it into my soup Rolodex!

—Risa Lichtman, Portland, OR

PREP: 15 min. • **COOK:** 25 min. • **MAKES:** 8 servings (2 qt.)

- ¼ cup butter, cubed
- 1 cup finely chopped celery
- 1 cup shredded carrots
- 1 small onion, finely chopped
- 4 garlic cloves, minced
- ½ cup all-purpose flour
- 5 cups chicken broth
- 1 pkg. (16 oz.) potato gnocchi
- 1½ cups cubed cooked chicken breast
- 1 cup fresh baby spinach
- 1 cup heavy whipping cream
- 1 tsp. minced fresh thyme
- ½ tsp. salt
- ¼ tsp. pepper
- Sliced chives

1. In a Dutch oven, melt butter over medium heat. Add celery, carrots, onion and garlic; cook and stir for 4-6 minutes or until crisp-tender. Stir in flour until blended. Gradually whisk in broth. Bring to a boil. Reduce heat; simmer, uncovered, until slightly thickened, 4-5 minutes, stirring occasionally.

2. Stir in gnocchi and chicken. Cook for 4-6 minutes or until gnocchi is heated through and tender. Reduce the heat to medium-low. Stir in spinach, cream, thyme, salt and pepper; heat through. Garnish with chives.

1 CUP 362 cal., 19g fat (11g sat. fat), 78mg chol., 1058mg sod., 35g carb. (3g sugars, 3g fiber), 14g pro.

GETTING TO KNOW GNOCCHI

You don't have to cook gnocchi before adding it to most soups. The simmering soup is the perfect temperature for cooking gnocchi, so just drop them straight in! If you are using frozen gnocchi, add a few extra minutes to the cooking time to ensure that they cook through.

1

2

3

4

5

STAUB
STAUB

CHORIZO & CHICKPEA SOUP

CHORIZO & CHICKPEA SOUP

The chorizo sausage adds its own spice to the broth, creating delicious flavor with no need for additional seasonings. And while it's cooking, the whole house smells amazing.

—Jaclyn McKewan, Lancaster, NY

PREP: 15 min. • **COOK:** 8¼ hours • **MAKES:** 6 servings

- 3 cups water
- 2 celery ribs, chopped
- 2 fully cooked Spanish chorizo links (3 oz. each), cut into ½-in. pieces
- ½ cup dried chickpeas or garbanzo beans
- 1 can (14½ oz.) petite diced tomatoes, undrained
- ½ cup ditalini or other small pasta
- ½ tsp. salt

Place water, celery, chorizo and chickpeas in a 4- or 5-qt. slow cooker. Cook, covered, on low until chickpeas are tender, 8-10 hours. Stir in tomatoes, pasta and salt; cook, covered, on high until pasta is tender, 15-20 minutes longer.

FREEZE OPTION Freeze cooled soup in freezer containers. To use, partially thaw in refrigerator overnight. Heat through in a saucepan, stirring occasionally; add broth or water if necessary.

1 CUP 180 cal., 8g fat (3g sat. fat), 18mg chol., 569mg sod., 23g carb. (3g sugars, 6g fiber), 9g pro. **DIABETIC EXCHANGES** 1½ starch, 1 high-fat meat.

OODLES OF NOODLES SOUP

When my godchild, Alex, was young, I often gave her children's cookbooks for her birthday or other special occasions. We'd plan an entire menu from the books, prepare the meal together and serve it to her family. This soup recipe was a favorite.

—Lorri Reinhardt, Big Bend, WI

PREP: 15 min. • **COOK:** 30 min. • **MAKES:** 6 servings

- ¾ lb. boneless skinless chicken breasts, cubed
- 2 medium carrots, sliced
- 1 small onion, chopped
- 2 celery ribs, sliced
- 1 garlic clove, minced
- 5 cups water
- ¼ tsp. pepper
- 2 pkg. (3 oz. each) chicken ramen noodles

1. In a large saucepan coated with cooking spray, saute the chicken, carrots, onion, celery and garlic until chicken is no longer pink. Add water, pepper and contents of seasoning packets from noodles. Bring to a boil. Reduce heat; cover and simmer for 15-20 minutes or until carrots are tender.

2. Break noodles into pieces and add to soup; cover and cook for 3 minutes or until noodles are tender.

1 CUP 137 cal., 4g fat (2g sat. fat), 31mg chol., 309mg sod., 13g carb. (3g sugars, 1g fiber), 13g pro.

PORK EDAMAME SOUP

My husband grew up in a traditional Asian household and says this soup delivers the authentic taste. I think the Asian hot chili sauce is what makes the dish, but any type of hot sauce would give it a delicious kick!

—Kari Sue, Bend, OR

PREP: 25 min. • **COOK:** 4 hours 10 min. • **MAKES:** 6 servings (2¼ qt.)

- 4 tsp. canola oil
- 2 lbs. boneless country-style pork ribs, trimmed, cut into 1-in. cubes
- 2 medium carrots, cut into 1-in. pieces
- 1 medium sweet red pepper, cut into 1-in. pieces
- 1 can (8 oz.) sliced water chestnuts, drained
- 6 garlic cloves, minced
- 2 Tbsp. soy sauce
- 1 Tbsp. hoisin sauce
- 1 Tbsp. minced fresh gingerroot
- 2 tsp. Sriracha chili sauce
- 2 cans (14½ oz. each) chicken broth
- 1 pkg. (10 oz.) frozen shelled edamame, thawed
- 1 pkg. (3 oz.) ramen noodles
- Thinly sliced green onions, optional

1. In a large skillet, heat oil over medium-high heat. Brown pork in batches. Remove to a 5-qt. slow cooker. Stir in next 9 ingredients.

2. Cook, covered, on low for 4-5 hours or until meat and vegetables are tender. Stir in edamame. Break up noodles slightly; stir into soup, discarding or saving seasoning packet for another use. Cook, covered, on low for 10-15 minutes or until noodles are al dente. Serve immediately. If desired, top with green onion.

1½ CUPS 455 cal., 23g fat (7g sat. fat), 90mg chol., 1134mg sod., 25g carb. (6g sugars, 4g fiber), 36g pro.

PAIR IT WITH

Copycat Texas Roadhouse Rolls, p. 274

EASY POT STICKER SOUP

My husband and I have soup often, so I'm always coming up with something new. I saw pot stickers in the freezer and decided to feature them in an Asian soup, and the result was delicious. Rice vinegar adds just the right tang, and green onion and carrots make a fresh garnish. Stir in chopped cabbage or bok choy, if you'd like. A little sesame oil goes a long way, but you can always add a bit more.

—Darlene Brenden, Salem, OR

PREP: 15 min. • **COOK:** 5¼ hours • **MAKES:** 6 servings (2 qt.)

- ½ lb. Chinese or napa cabbage, thinly sliced
- 2 celery ribs, thinly sliced
- 2 medium carrots, cut into matchsticks
- ⅓ cup thinly sliced green onions
- 2 to 3 Tbsp. soy sauce
- 2 Tbsp. rice vinegar
- 3 garlic cloves, minced
- 2 tsp. minced fresh gingerroot or ½ tsp. ground ginger
- ½ tsp. sesame oil
- 6 cups reduced-sodium chicken broth
- 1 pkg. (16 oz.) frozen chicken pot stickers
- Crispy chow mein noodles, optional

In a 4-qt. slow cooker, combine first 9 ingredients. Stir in broth. Cook, covered, on low until vegetables are tender, 5-6 hours. Add pot stickers; cook, covered, on high 15-20 minutes or until heated through. If desired, sprinkle with chow mein noodles before serving.

1⅓ CUPS 198 cal., 6g fat (2g sat. fat), 28mg chol., 1302mg sod., 23g carb. (5g sugars, 2g fiber), 13g pro.

"This is very clever, very easy and very delicious! I loved it!"

—GUEST2233, TASTEOFHOME.COM

EASY SHRIMP & SCALLOPS RAMEN SOUP

This recipe is delicious and so easy to make at home on a weeknight. You can add any vegetables, seafood or meat that you have on hand.

—Aleni Salcedo, East Elmhurst, NY

TAKES: 30 min. • **MAKES:** 6 servings (2¼ qt.)

- ½ lb. sea scallops
- ½ lb. uncooked shrimp (16-20 per lb.), peeled and deveined
- 2 pkg. (3 oz. each) shrimp ramen noodles
- 2 tsp. sesame oil
- 2 garlic cloves, minced
- 2 cartons (32 oz. each) chicken broth
- 2 Tbsp. lime juice
- 3 cups fresh bean sprouts
- Optional toppings: Fresh cilantro leaves, black and white sesame seeds and lime wedges

1. Sprinkle scallops and shrimp with contents of 1 seasoning packet from noodles (discard second packet or save for another use). In a Dutch oven, heat sesame oil over medium heat. In batches, cook scallops and shrimp until scallops are firm and opaque and shrimp turn pink. Remove and keep warm. In the same pan, add garlic; cook 1 minute longer.

2. Add broth and lime juice. Bring to a boil; reduce the heat. Add noodles. Cook for 3 minutes. Add bean sprouts. Return scallops and shrimp to pan; heat through. Serve with optional toppings as desired.

1½ CUPS 231 cal., 8g fat (3g sat. fat), 59mg chol., 1603mg sod., 24g carb. (4g sugars, 1g fiber), 17g pro.

"What a great way to dress up ramen soup! Because we have four teens in the house, I doubled the shrimp, and yet the kids were still fighting over seconds and thirds. Next time I'll have to double the recipe! This is a super easy and fun weeknight meal."

—PUNKYJOE81, TASTEOFHOME.COM

LEMONY MUSHROOM-ORZO SOUP FOR TWO

LEMONY MUSHROOM-ORZO SOUP FOR TWO

This is a versatile soup that works as a first course or as a side for a sandwich lunch. It's loaded with mushrooms and orzo pasta—and lemon livens up its flavor.

—Edrie O'Brien, Denver, CO

TAKES: 30 min. • **MAKES:** 2 servings

- 2½ cups sliced fresh mushrooms
- 2 green onions, chopped
- 1 Tbsp. olive oil
- 1 garlic clove, minced
- 1½ cups reduced-sodium chicken broth
- 1½ tsp. minced fresh parsley
- ¼ tsp. dried thyme
- ⅛ tsp. pepper
- ¼ cup uncooked orzo pasta
- 1½ tsp. lemon juice
- ⅛ tsp. grated lemon zest

1. In a small saucepan, saute mushrooms and green onion in oil until tender. Add garlic; cook 1 minute longer. Stir in broth, parsley, thyme and pepper.

2. Bring to a boil. Stir in orzo, and lemon juice and zest. Cook 5-6 minutes or until pasta is tender.

1 CUP 191 cal., 8g fat (1g sat. fat), 0 chol., 437mg sod., 24g carb. (4g sugars, 2g fiber), 9g pro. **DIABETIC EXCHANGES** 1½ fat, 1 starch, 1 vegetable.

BEEF & NOODLE SOUP

I take advantage of convenience items to prepare this hearty soup when I'm short on time. Bowls of the chunky mixture are chock-full of ground beef, noodles and vegetables.

—Arlene Lynn, Lincoln, NE

TAKES: 30 min. • **MAKES:** 8 servings (2 qt.)

- 1 lb. ground beef
- 1 can (46 oz.) V8 juice
- 1 envelope onion soup mix
- 1 pkg. (3 oz.) beef ramen noodles
- 1 pkg. (16 oz.) frozen mixed vegetables

1. In a large saucepan, cook beef over medium heat until no longer pink; drain. Stir in V8 juice, soup mix, contents of noodle seasoning packet and mixed vegetables.

2. Bring to a boil. Reduce heat; simmer, uncovered, for 6 minutes or until vegetables are tender. Return to a boil; stir in noodles. Cook for 3 minutes or until the noodles are tender.

1 CUP 230 cal., 9g fat (3g sat. fat), 35mg chol., 984mg sod., 23g carb. (6g sugars, 4g fiber), 14g pro.

RAVIOLI SOUP

We adore everything pasta, so I used it as the inspiration for this unique soup. The meaty tomato base pairs perfectly with the cheesy ravioli pillows. My family can't get enough of this soup!

—Shelley Way, Cheyenne, WY

PREP: 20 min. • **COOK:** 45 min. • **MAKES:** 10 servings (2½ qt.)

- 1 lb. ground beef
- 2 cups water
- 2 cans (one 28 oz., one 14½ oz.) crushed tomatoes
- 1 can (6 oz.) tomato paste
- 1½ cups chopped onions
- ¼ cup minced fresh parsley
- 2 garlic cloves, minced
- ¾ tsp. dried basil
- ½ tsp. sugar
- ½ tsp. dried oregano
- ½ tsp. onion salt
- ½ tsp. salt
- ¼ tsp. pepper
- ¼ tsp. dried thyme
- 1 pkg. (9 oz.) refrigerated cheese ravioli
- ¼ cup grated Parmesan cheese
- Optional: Additional minced fresh parsley or fresh oregano leaves

1. In a Dutch oven, cook beef over medium heat until no longer pink, 5-7 minutes, breaking it into crumbles; drain. Add water, tomatoes, tomato paste, onions, parsley, garlic, basil, sugar, oregano, onion salt, salt, pepper and thyme; bring to a boil. Reduce heat; cover and simmer for 30 minutes.

2. Cook ravioli according to package directions; drain. Add to soup and heat through. Stir in Parmesan cheese. If desired, sprinkle with additional parsley or oregano leaves.

1 CUP 235 cal., 8g fat (4g sat. fat), 42mg chol., 542mg sod., 25g carb. (5g sugars, 4g fiber), 17g pro.

FRESH, FROZEN OR REFRIGERATED?

Feel free to use fresh homemade ravioli or frozen ravioli in this soup instead of the refrigerated variety. You can even mix things up with tortellini. Just be sure to cook the pasta first, and remember to drain the pasta well before adding it to soup.

PAIR IT WITH
Pull-Apart
Garlic Bread, p. 261

COPYCAT OLIVE GARDEN MINESTRONE SOUP

This Olive Garden-style minestrone soup is brimming with bright vegetables, creamy beans and pasta in a rich, tomatoey broth. It's colorful and hearty—what more could you ask for? (Besides some warm, buttery breadsticks!)

—Lauren Habermehl, Pewaukee, WI

TAKES: 40 min. • **MAKES:** 12 servings

- 2 Tbsp. olive oil
- 1 cup chopped onion
- ½ cup chopped celery
- ½ cup chopped carrot
- 4 garlic cloves, minced
- 2 tsp. Italian seasoning
- 2 tsp. salt
- ½ tsp. pepper
- ⅓ cup tomato paste
- 1 can (14½ oz.) diced tomatoes
- 4 cups reduced-sodium chicken broth
- 1 can (15½ oz.) white kidney or cannellini beans, rinsed and drained
- 1 can (15½ oz.) kidney beans, rinsed and drained
- ¾ cup uncooked small pasta shells
- 1 small zucchini, chopped
- ½ cup fresh or frozen cut green beans
- 2 cups fresh spinach, chopped
- 1 Tbsp. minced fresh parsley
- 1 Tbsp. minced fresh basil
- ¼ cup grated Parmesan cheese

1. Heat oil in a stockpot to medium heat. Add onion, celery and carrot; cook until slightly soft, 4-5 minutes. Add garlic, Italian seasoning, salt and pepper; cook for 1-2 minutes or until fragrant. Stir in tomato paste; cook until bubbly, 1-2 minutes.

2. Add tomatoes and broth; bring to a simmer. Stir in beans and pasta shells. Bring to a simmer; cook until pasta is almost cooked, 6-7 minutes. Stir in zucchini, green beans and spinach. Cook 2-3 minutes longer or until vegetables are crisp-tender and pasta is al dente. Stir in parsley and basil. Garnish with Parmesan and, if desired, additional minced fresh basil.

1 SERVING 212 cal., 5g fat (1g sat. fat), 2mg chol., 1145mg sod., 32g carb. (6g sugars, 7g fiber), 11g pro.

DIY RAMEN SOUP

This go-to soup, prepared and served in a canning jar, is a healthier alternative to most commercial varieties. Feel free to customize the veggies to suit your taste.

—Michelle Clair, Seattle, WA

TAKES: 25 min. • **MAKES:** 2 servings

- 1 pkg. (3 oz.) ramen noodles
- 1 Tbsp. reduced-sodium chicken base
- 1 to 2 tsp. Sriracha chili sauce
- 1 tsp. minced fresh gingerroot
- ½ cup shredded carrots
- ½ cup shredded cabbage
- 2 radishes, halved and sliced
- ½ cup sliced fresh shiitake mushrooms
- 1 cup shredded cooked chicken breast
- ¼ cup fresh cilantro leaves
- 2 lime wedges
- 1 hard-boiled large egg, halved
- 4 cups boiling water

1. Cook ramen noodles according to package directions (do not use seasoning packet); cool.

2. In each of two 1-qt. wide-mouth canning jars, layer half the noodles, chicken base, chili sauce, ginger, carrots, cabbage, radishes, mushrooms, chicken and cilantro in the order listed. Place lime wedges and egg halves in two 4-oz. glass jars or other airtight containers. Cover all 4 containers and refrigerate until ready to serve.

TO SERVE Pour 2 cups boiling water into each 1-qt. jar; let stand until warmed through or until the chicken base has dissolved. Stir to combine seasonings. Squeeze lime juice over soup; place an egg half on top.

1 SERVING 380 cal., 6g fat (1g sat. fat), 147mg chol., 1386mg sod., 47g carb. (4g sugars, 3g fiber), 32g pro.

"This is one of my favorite food-prep recipes. It's a tasty, quick lunch or an easy dinner. I usually double the recipe and sometimes add other things such as more veggies."

—KARELIRAY, TASTEOFHOME.COM

MEATBALL SOUP

MEATBALL SOUP

This soup is just like a meal in a bowl and great for chilly days. To satisfy heartier appetites, serve it with a sandwich.

—Sue Miller, Walworth, WI

PREP: 15 min. • **COOK:** 35 min. • **MAKES:** 5 servings

- 1 large egg, lightly beaten
- ¼ cup dry bread crumbs
- ¼ cup minced fresh parsley
- 2 Tbsp. grated Parmesan cheese
- ¼ tsp. garlic salt, optional
- ⅛ tsp. pepper
- ½ lb. lean ground beef (90% lean)
- 4 cups reduced-sodium beef broth
- 1 can (16 oz.) kidney beans, rinsed and drained
- 1 can (14½ oz.) stewed tomatoes
- 1 medium carrot, thinly sliced
- 1 tsp. Italian seasoning
- ¼ cup uncooked tiny shell pasta
- Minced fresh parsley, optional

1. In a small bowl, combine first 6 ingredients. Crumble beef over mixture and mix lightly but thoroughly. Shape into 1-in. balls. Brown meatballs in a large saucepan; drain. Add the broth, beans, tomatoes, carrot and Italian seasoning. Bring to a boil. Reduce heat; cover and simmer for 10 minutes.

2. Add pasta; simmer until meat is no longer pink and pasta is tender, 10 minutes longer. If desired, top with minced fresh parsley and additional grated Parmesan cheese.

FREEZE OPTION Divide cooled soup in individual portions; freeze up to 3 months.

1½ CUPS 248 cal., 5g fat (2g sat. fat), 70mg chol., 778mg sod., 30g carb. (8g sugars, 6g fiber), 20g pro.

RAMEN BROCCOLI SOUP

Cheese and garlic powder are the secret to this tasty and heartwarming soup. Loaded with noodles, it hits the spot on cool winter days.

—Luella Dirks, Emelle, AL

TAKES: 20 min. • **MAKES:** 7 servings

- 5 cups water
- 1 pkg. (16 oz.) frozen broccoli cuts
- 2 pkg. (3 oz. each) chicken ramen noodles
- ¼ tsp. garlic powder
- 3 slices American cheese, cut into strips

1. In a large saucepan, bring water to a boil. Add broccoli; return to a boil. Reduce heat; cover and simmer for 3 minutes. Return to a boil. Break noodles into small pieces; add to water. Cook for 3 minutes longer, stirring occasionally.

2. Remove from heat. Add garlic powder, cheese and contents of seasoning packets from the noodles; stir until cheese is melted. Serve immediately.

1 CUP 150 cal., 6g fat (4g sat. fat), 6mg chol., 573mg sod., 20g carb. (2g sugars, 2g fiber), 5g pro. **DIABETIC EXCHANGES** 1 starch, 1 vegetable, 1 fat.

OLD-FASHIONED TURKEY NOODLE SOUP

Make the most of leftover turkey with a delicious homemade soup. Roasting the turkey bones, garlic and vegetables adds a rich flavor without added fat.

—*Taste of Home* Test Kitchen

PREP: 5 hours + chilling • **COOK:** 30 min. • **MAKES:** 10 servings (3¾ qt.)

BROTH

- 1 leftover turkey carcass (from a 12- to 14-lb. turkey)
- 2 cooked turkey wings, meat removed
- 2 cooked turkey drumsticks, meat removed
- 1 turkey neck bone
- 1 medium unpeeled onion, cut into wedges
- 2 small unpeeled carrots, cut into chunks
- 6 to 8 garlic cloves, peeled
- 4 qt. plus 1 cup cold water, divided

SOUP

- 3 qt. water
- 5 cups uncooked egg noodles
- 2 cups diced carrots
- 2 cups diced celery
- 3 cups cubed cooked turkey
- ¼ cup minced fresh parsley
- 2½ tsp. salt
- 2 tsp. dried thyme
- 1 tsp. pepper

1. Place turkey carcass, bones from wings and drumsticks, neck bone, onion, carrots and garlic in a 15x10x1-in. baking pan coated with cooking spray. Bake, uncovered, at 400° for 1 hour, turning once.

2. Transfer carcass, bones and vegetables to an 8-qt. stockpot. Add 4 qts. cold water; set aside. Pour 1 cup cold water into baking pan, stirring to loosen browned bits. Add to pot. Bring to a boil. Reduce heat; cover and simmer for 3-4 hours.

3. Cool slightly. Strain broth; discard bones and vegetables. Set stockpot in an ice-water bath until broth cools, stirring occasionally. Cover and refrigerate overnight.

4. Skim fat from broth. Cover and bring to a boil. Reduce the heat to a simmer. Meanwhile, in a Dutch oven, bring 3 qts. water to a boil. Add noodles and carrots; cook for 4 minutes. Add celery; cook for 5-7 minutes longer or until noodles and vegetables are tender. Drain; add to simmering broth. Add turkey; heat through. Stir in parsley, salt, thyme and pepper.

1½ CUPS 188 cal., 4g fat (1g sat. fat), 66mg chol., 670mg sod., 17g carb. (2g sugars, 2g fiber), 20g pro. **DIABETIC EXCHANGES** 2 lean meat, 1 starch.

NIFTY NOODLES

Egg noodles are a fantastic choice for turkey soup because of their chewy texture and comforting flavor. You can use any small pasta shape that fits on a spoon too, such as orzo, macaroni or farfalle (bow tie pasta).

SOUPS

CREAMY & CHEESY

SOPA AJOBLANCO

This white gazpacho was a staple when I was young; I remember slurping it directly from the bowl. It's made from stale bread and on-hand seasonings, and topped with grapes for a traditional touch.

—Francine Lizotte, Langley, BC

PREP: 20 min. + standing • **COOK:** 5 min. • **MAKES:** 4 servings

- 1 cup blanched almonds
- 1½ cups cubed white bread, crusts removed
- ⅓ cup heavy whipping cream or unsweetened almond milk
- 2½ cups reduced-sodium chicken broth
- 3 Tbsp. sherry vinegar
- 2 garlic cloves, minced
- ½ tsp. fine sea salt
- ¼ tsp. white pepper
- ½ cup plus 1 Tbsp. olive oil, divided
- ⅛ tsp. hot Hungarian paprika
- ¼ cup halved green grapes
- ¼ cup chopped blanched almonds

1. Rinse almonds in cold water; drain. Place in a large bowl and add enough water to cover by 3 in. Cover and let stand overnight. Spread bread cubes onto a baking sheet; let stand overnight.

2. Place 1 cup bread cubes in a small bowl. Pour the cream over bread; let stand for 15 minutes. Drain almonds, discarding soaking liquid. Transfer almonds to a blender. Add bread mixture, broth, vinegar, garlic, salt and pepper; process until blended. While processing, gradually add ½ cup oil in a steady stream. Transfer to a large bowl. Refrigerate, covered, at least 6 hours.

3. In a large skillet, heat remaining 1 Tbsp. oil over medium heat; stir in paprika. Add remaining ½ cup bread cubes; cook and stir until golden brown, 3-4 minutes.

4. Remove soup from refrigerator. Stir to redistribute settled out oil. Divide soup among 4 bowls; top with croutons, grapes, chopped almonds and additional oil.

1 CUP WITH 2 TBSP. TOPPING 660 cal., 62g fat (11g sat. fat), 23mg chol., 677mg sod., 19g carb. (6g sugars, 5g fiber), 14g pro.

BEST CREAM OF TOMATO SOUP

Creamy, rich and bursting with brightness, this soup is the ultimate sidekick to a grilled cheese sandwich.

—Josh Rink, Milwaukee, WI

PREP: 20 min. • **COOK:** 30 min. • **MAKES:** 16 servings (4 qt.)

- 3 Tbsp. olive oil
- 3 Tbsp. butter
- ¼ to ½ tsp. crushed red pepper flakes
- 3 large carrots, peeled and chopped
- 1 large onion, chopped
- 2 garlic cloves, minced
- 2 tsp. dried basil
- 3 cans (28 oz. each) whole peeled tomatoes, undrained
- 1 container (32 oz.) chicken stock
- 2 Tbsp. tomato paste
- 3 tsp. sugar
- 1 tsp. salt
- ½ tsp. pepper
- 1 cup heavy whipping cream, optional
- Optional toppings: Thinly sliced fresh basil leaves and grated Parmesan cheese

1. In a 6-qt. stockpot or Dutch oven, heat oil, butter and pepper flakes over medium heat until the butter is melted. Add carrots and onion; cook, uncovered, over medium heat, stirring frequently, until vegetables are softened, 8-10 minutes. Add garlic and basil; cook and stir 1 minute longer. Stir in tomatoes, stock, tomato paste, sugar, salt and pepper; mix well. Bring to a boil. Reduce heat; simmer, uncovered, to let flavors blend, 20-25 minutes.

2. Remove pan from heat. Using a blender, puree the soup in batches until smooth. If desired, slowly stir in heavy cream, stirring continuously to incorporate. Return pan to stove to heat through. If desired, top servings with fresh basil and Parmesan cheese.

1 CUP 104 cal., 5g fat (2g sat. fat), 6mg chol., 572mg sod., 15g carb. (10g sugars, 2g fiber), 3g pro. **DIABETIC EXCHANGES** 1 starch, 1 fat.

TASTY TOPPINGS

We topped this comforting soup with fresh basil and cheese, but if you're looking to get creative, try topping it with bacon crumbles, croutons, sliced black olives, broken tortilla chips, sliced pepperoni or even crushed potato chips.

AVGOLEMONO SOUP

While avgolemono *may be tricky to pronounce if you didn't grow up eating traditional Greek food, the recipe couldn't be simpler. This quintessential soup uses pantry staples and results in a meal that's pure comfort food.*

—Lauren Habermehl, Pewaukee, WI

PREP: 20 min. • **COOK:** 2½ hours • **MAKES:** 4 servings

- 2 lbs. bone-in chicken thighs or chicken leg quarters
- 4 cups water
- 1 medium onion, quartered
- 2 large carrots, cut into chunks
- 2 celery ribs, cut into chunks
- 1 to 2 bay leaves
- ¼ cup uncooked long grain rice, rinsed
- 1 large egg white, room temperature
- 3 large egg yolks, room temperature
- 1 Tbsp. grated lemon zest
- ¼ cup lemon juice
- 1 tsp. salt
- ½ tsp. pepper
- Optional: Fresh parsley, dill and oregano

1. Place first 6 ingredients in a Dutch oven. Slowly bring to a boil; reduce heat until mixture is just at a simmer. Simmer, covered, for 2 hours.

2. Remove the chicken; let stand until cool enough to handle. Strain broth, discarding vegetables and bay leaves. Reserve 1 cup broth. Return remaining broth to a simmer. Add rice; simmer, covered, 10-15 minutes or until tender.

3. Meanwhile, beat egg whites until soft peaks form. Add egg yolks and beat until frothy, 1-2 minutes. Slowly add lemon zest and juice; stir to combine. Gradually add reserved broth into egg mixture. Beat until well blended, 1-2 minutes.

4. Slowly pour the egg mixture into rice mixture; stir to combine. Return soup to a simmer. Add salt and pepper; cook and stir, continuously, 8-10 minutes or until soup thickens.

5. Meanwhile, remove meat from bones; discard bones. Shred chicken. Serve soup with shredded chicken and, if desired, fresh parsley, dill, oregano and additional lemon zest.

1 CUP 392 cal., 22g fat (7g sat. fat), 245mg chol., 701mg sod., 12g carb. (1g sugars, 0 fiber), 34g pro.

1

2

3

4

5

6

PAIR IT WITH
Herb-Cheese Rolls, p. 266

PUMPKIN WITH SMOKED GOUDA SOUP

I love the smell of this rich, cheesy soup as it bubbles on the stove. The Gouda adds a delightful smokiness that just says autumn to me. Unlike most cream soups, this freezes well!

—Kerry Dingwall, Wilmington, NC

PREP: 20 min. • **COOK:** 35 min. • **MAKES:** 9 servings (2¼ qt.)

- 4 bacon strips, chopped
- 1 medium onion, chopped
- 3 garlic cloves, minced
- 6 cups chicken broth
- 1 can (29 oz.) solid-pack pumpkin
- ½ tsp. salt
- ¼ tsp. ground nutmeg
- ⅛ tsp. pepper
- 1 cup heavy whipping cream
- 1 cup shredded Gouda cheese
- 2 Tbsp. minced fresh parsley
- Additional shredded Gouda cheese, optional

1. In a Dutch oven, cook bacon over medium heat until crisp. Remove with a slotted spoon; drain on paper towels. Discard drippings, reserving 1 Tbsp. in pan. Saute the onion in drippings until tender. Add garlic; cook 1 minute longer.

2. Stir in the broth, pumpkin, salt, nutmeg and pepper. Bring to a boil. Reduce heat; simmer, uncovered, for 10 minutes. Cool slightly.

3. In a blender, process soup in batches until smooth. Return all to pan. Stir in cream; heat through. Add cheese; stir until melted. Sprinkle each serving with fresh parsley, bacon and, if desired, additional cheese.

FREEZE OPTION Freeze cooled soup in freezer containers. To use, partially thaw soup in refrigerator overnight. Transfer to a saucepan; heat through, stirring frequently. Do not boil.

1 CUP 214 cal., 17g fat (9g sat. fat), 58mg chol., 970mg sod., 11g carb. (5g sugars, 4g fiber), 7g pro.

PAIR IT WITH

Sweet Potato & Pesto Slow-Cooker Bread, p. 231

CREAM OF CELERY SOUP

This creamy soup is easy to make and full of flavor. It uses celery ribs and seed, sweet yellow onion, a touch of dry sherry, and heavy whipping cream for richness. Add a perfectly toasted grilled cheese sandwich for an irresistibly comforting meal.

—Colleen Delawder, Herndon, VA

PREP: 10 min. • **COOK:** 25 min. • **MAKES:** 6 servings

- 3 Tbsp. butter
- 1 lb. celery ribs, chopped (about 3 cups)
- 1 medium onion, chopped
- 2 garlic cloves, minced
- 1¼ tsp. salt
- 1 tsp. celery seed, crushed
- ½ tsp. pepper
- 5 Tbsp. all-purpose flour
- 4 cups reduced-sodium chicken broth
- ½ cup heavy whipping cream
- 1 Tbsp. sherry, optional

In a Dutch oven, melt butter over medium heat. Add celery and onion; cook until the celery is soft and slightly caramelized on the edges, 8-10 minutes. Stir in garlic, salt, celery seed and pepper; cook 1 minute longer. Stir in flour; cook for 1-2 minutes or until browned, stirring constantly. Slowly whisk in chicken broth; bring to a simmer until thickened, 4-5 minutes, whisking frequently. Add cream and, if desired, sherry; simmer until thickened, 4-5 minutes longer.

1 CUP 179 cal., 13g fat (8g sat. fat), 38mg chol., 1001mg sod., 11g carb. (3g sugars, 2g fiber), 4g pro.

AMP UP THE FLAVOR

Celery leaves are a delicious addition to cream of celery soup. Chop them finely and stir them in at the end of cooking to add extra flavor and a pop of freshness, or use them as a garnish for added color and texture.

CAJUN POTATO SOUP

This soup is the perfect mash-up between southern comfort and your grandma's beloved potato soup recipe. Made with traditional ingredients like chunks of potatoes, cheese and cream, the soup gets a fiery kick from spicy andouille sausage and Cajun seasoning for a well-rounded blend of flavors.

—Lauren Habermehl, Pewaukee, WI

PREP: 20 min. • **COOK:** 40 min. • **MAKES:** 12 servings (3 qt.)

- 13½ oz. fully cooked andouille sausage links, cut into ¼-in. slices
- 2 Tbsp. butter
- 2 Tbsp. olive oil
- 3 garlic cloves, minced
- ½ tsp. crushed red pepper flakes
- 1 medium onion, chopped
- 1 medium sweet red pepper, chopped
- 1 celery rib, chopped
- 1 carton (32 oz.) chicken broth
- 3 tsp. Cajun seasoning
- ½ tsp. smoked paprika
- ¼ tsp. kosher salt
- 4 large russet potatoes, peeled and cut into 1-in. cubes
- 1 cup heavy whipping cream
- ¾ cup shredded cheddar cheese
- ¼ cup grated Parmesan cheese
- ¼ cup chopped fresh parsley

1. In a Dutch oven over medium heat, cook and stir sausage until edges are lightly browned, 3-5 minutes. Remove sausage to a bowl.

2. In the same pan, melt butter and heat oil over medium heat. Add garlic and pepper flakes; cook and stir for 1 minute. Add onion, red pepper and celery. Cook and stir until vegetables are softened, 5-7 minutes.

3. Stir in the broth, Cajun seasoning, paprika and salt. Bring to a boil. Add potatoes. Reduce heat; simmer, uncovered, 15-18 minutes or until potatoes are tender.

4. Reduce heat to low. Stir in cream, cheddar cheese and Parmesan cheese until cheese is melted. Add sausage and parsley. Heat through. If desired, serve with additional parsley.

1 CUP 305 cal., 21g fat (10g sat. fat), 77mg chol., 812mg sod., 21g carb. (3g sugars, 2g fiber), 11g pro.

PAIR IT WITH
Tender Whole Wheat
Rolls, p. 281

CORN CHOWDER WITH TURKEY & BACON

This recipe uses Thanksgiving leftovers to create a rich and creamy turkey chowder. My grandmother would even add chopped hard-boiled eggs to this dish, which gave it a nice richness.

—Susan Bickta, Kutztown, PA

PREP: 25 min. • **COOK:** 50 min. • **MAKES:** 16 servings (4 qt.)

- 1 lb. thick-sliced bacon strips, chopped
- 3 celery ribs, sliced
- 1 medium onion, chopped
- 1 medium carrot, chopped
- ½ cup chopped red onion
- 1 bay leaf
- ¼ cup all-purpose flour
- 1 carton (32 oz.) chicken stock
- 1 can (10½ oz.) condensed cream of chicken soup, undiluted
- 1 pkg. (8 oz.) cream cheese, softened
- ¾ cup 2% milk
- ¾ cup heavy whipping cream
- 3½ cups frozen corn (about 17.5 oz.)
- 2½ cups cubed cooked turkey
- 2 cups refrigerated shredded hash brown potatoes (about 10 oz.)
- ¾ cup turkey gravy
- 1 Tbsp. dried parsley flakes
- Thinly sliced green onions, optional

1. In a Dutch oven, cook bacon over medium heat until crisp, stirring occasionally. Remove with a slotted spoon; drain on paper towels. Discard drippings, reserving ¼ cup in pan. Add celery, onion, carrot, red onion and bay leaf to pan; cook and stir over medium-high heat until vegetables are tender, 8-10 minutes.

2. Stir in flour until blended; gradually whisk in chicken stock. Bring to a boil, stirring constantly; cook and stir for 2 minutes. Add the soup, cream cheese, milk and cream; mix well. Stir in corn, turkey, hash browns, gravy, parsley and ¾ cup cooked bacon; reduce heat. Cook, covered, for 20 minutes, stirring occasionally.

3. Discard bay leaf. Serve with remaining bacon and, if desired, green onion.

1 CUP 289 cal., 19g fat (9g sat. fat), 63mg chol., 603mg sod., 17g carb. (4g sugars, 2g fiber), 14g pro.

"This soup is absolutely phenomenal! Hubby and I couldn't stop raving about how creamy and flavorful it was. I can't say enough about how delicious it is. I highly recommend it!"

—CYNANDTOM, TASTEOFHOME.COM

CREAM OF POTATO SOUP

This soup is comfort food, especially when the temperatures take a plunge. I serve this often—it's a simple supper that can be prepared in no time.

—Ruth Ann Stelfox, Raymond, AB

TAKES: 30 min. • **MAKES:** 2 servings

- 2 medium potatoes, peeled and diced
- 1 cup water
- 2 Tbsp. chopped onion
- 2 Tbsp. butter
- 2 Tbsp. all-purpose flour
- 3 cups whole milk
- ½ tsp. salt
- ⅛ tsp. celery salt
- Dash pepper
- Paprika and minced fresh parsley

1. Place the potatoes and water in a saucepan; bring to a boil over medium-high heat. Cover and cook until tender; drain and set aside.

2. In same pan, saute onion in butter until tender. Stir in flour until blended. Gradually stir in milk. Bring to a boil; cook and stir for 2 minutes or until thickened. Reduce heat; add the potatoes, salt, celery salt and pepper. Cook until heated through, 2-3 minutes. Sprinkle with paprika and parsley and, if desired, additional pepper.

1 SERVING 482 cal., 24g fat (15g sat. fat), 80mg chol., 982mg sod., 53g carb. (20g sugars, 2g fiber), 16g pro.

"I tried to make potato soup many times in my life, and every time it was a disaster. I tried this recipe and the soup was awesome! I can't believe I made really good potato soup for the first time. Hooray!"

—ROXANNE48, TASTEOFHOME.COM

1

2

3

4

SMOKY & SPICY VEGETABLE BISQUE

On an ordinary night, I make my bisque a complete meal by serving it with a side of bruschetta or a Caprese salad. For a special-occasion feast, it makes a terrific first course, setting off the richer dishes beautifully with a bit of heat and smoke.

—Juliana Inhofer, Rocklin, CA

PREP: 1 hour • **COOK:** 30 min. • **MAKES:** 6 servings

- 2 large onions, cut into 8 wedges
- 4 large tomatoes, cut into 8 wedges
- 1 large sweet red pepper, cut into 8 wedges
- 4 garlic cloves, halved
- ¼ cup olive oil
- 2 cans (14½ oz. each) reduced-sodium chicken broth
- ½ cup fat-free half-and-half
- ½ cup coarsely chopped fresh basil
- 1 small chipotle pepper in adobo sauce, seeded
- ½ tsp. pepper
- ¼ tsp. salt
- Fresh basil leaves, optional

1. Line a 15x10x1-in. baking pan with foil and coat the foil with cooking spray. Place the onions, tomatoes, red pepper and garlic in pan. Drizzle with oil and toss to coat.

2. Bake, uncovered, at 425° until tender and browned, 40-45 minutes, stirring occasionally.

3. In a large saucepan, combine broth, half-and-half, basil, chipotle pepper, pepper, salt and roasted vegetables. Bring to a boil. Reduce heat; simmer, uncovered, for 20-25 minutes. Cool slightly.

4. In a blender, process soup in batches until smooth. Return all to pan; heat through. Garnish with basil leaves if desired.

NOTE Wear disposable gloves when cutting hot peppers; the oils can burn skin. Avoid touching your face.

1 CUP 157 cal., 9g fat (1g sat. fat), 0 chol., 528mg sod., 15g carb. (9g sugars, 3g fiber), 5g pro.

PAIR IT WITH
Rosemary Nut Bread,
p. 229

CREAMY TUSCAN CHICKEN SOUP

Tuscan chicken soup, also known as Marry Me Chicken Soup, proves that to get to the heart, you have to go through the stomach. This creamy, cheesy soup is complemented with heavy Italian seasoning, bright sun-dried tomatoes and protein-rich rotisserie chicken, leaving everyone with a happy and full belly.

—Nancy Mock, Southbridge, MA

PREP: 20 min. • **COOK:** 30 min. • **MAKES:** 10 servings (2½ qt.)

- 1 Tbsp. oil from jar of julienned oil-packed sun-dried tomatoes
- 1 Tbsp. olive oil
- 1 medium onion, finely chopped
- ½ cup julienned oil-packed sun-dried tomatoes
- 2 Tbsp. tomato paste
- 2 garlic cloves, minced
- 6 cups chicken broth
- 1 tsp. Italian seasoning
- ½ tsp. salt
- ½ tsp. pepper
- ½ tsp. garlic powder
- 2 cups uncooked elbow macaroni or small pasta shells
- 2 cups shredded rotisserie chicken
- 2 cups chopped fresh spinach
- 2 cups whole milk
- ½ cup grated Parmesan cheese

1. In a Dutch oven, heat oil from sun-dried tomatoes and olive oil over medium heat. Add onion; cook and stir until softened, 4-6 minutes. Add sun-dried tomatoes, tomato paste and garlic. Cook 2 minutes longer.

2. Stir in broth, Italian seasoning, salt, pepper and garlic powder. Bring to a boil. Stir in pasta. Reduce heat; simmer, uncovered, until pasta is al dente, about 10 minutes. Stir in chicken and spinach. Cook and stir until heated through and spinach is wilted.

3. In a small saucepan, warm milk over medium heat. Ladle a small amount of soup into milk, then slowly stir warm milk mixture into the Dutch oven. Stir in Parmesan cheese. If desired, serve with additional Parmesan cheese.

1 CUP 205 cal., 9g fat (3g sat. fat), 33mg chol., 774mg sod., 18g carb. (4g sugars, 1g fiber), 14g pro.

CHICKEN CHOICES

You can make this soup with cooked chicken breasts instead of rotisserie chicken. Cut the chicken into bite-sized pieces and simmer it in the broth for about 30 minutes before adding the pasta. Alternatively, you can use shredded leftover chicken breasts, or bake chicken breasts and shred them once they're cool enough to handle.

CHEESEBURGER SOUP

A local restaurant serves a similar soup but wouldn't share its recipe with me. I developed my own, modifying a recipe I already had for potato soup. I was really pleased with the way this all-American dish turned out.

—Joanie Shawhan, Madison, WI

PREP: 30 min. • **COOK:** 25 min. • **MAKES:** 8 servings (2 qt.)

- ½ lb. ground beef
- 4 Tbsp. butter, divided
- ¾ cup chopped onion
- ¾ cup shredded carrots
- ¾ cup diced celery
- 1 tsp. dried basil
- 1 tsp. dried parsley flakes
- 1¾ lbs. (about 4 cups) cubed peeled potatoes
- 3 cups chicken broth
- ¼ cup all-purpose flour
- 8 to 16 oz. Velveeta, cubed
- 1½ cups whole milk
- ¾ tsp. salt
- ¼ to ½ tsp. pepper
- ¼ cup sour cream
- Optional: Onion rings and thinly sliced green onions

1. In a large saucepan over medium heat, cook and crumble beef until no longer pink, 6-8 minutes; drain and remove from pan. In same saucepan, melt 1 Tbsp. butter over medium heat. Saute onion, carrots, celery, basil and parsley until the vegetables are tender, about 10 minutes. Add potatoes, broth and beef; bring to a boil. Reduce heat; simmer, covered, 10-12 minutes or until potatoes are tender.

2. Meanwhile, in a small skillet, melt remaining 3 Tbsp. butter. Add flour; cook and stir until bubbly, 3-5 minutes. Add to soup; bring to a boil. Cook and stir for 2 minutes. Reduce heat to low. Stir in cheese, milk, salt and pepper; cook until cheese melts. Remove from heat; blend in sour cream. If desired, serve with onion rings and green onion.

1 CUP 354 cal., 20g fat (11g sat. fat), 70mg chol., 1012mg sod., 31g carb. (7g sugars, 3g fiber), 14g pro.

"This is absolutely delicious, loaded with flavor and so comforting to eat. It's like a hug in a bowl."

—SHERRY640, TASTEOFHOME.COM

1

2

3

4

5
6
7
8

GREEN CHILE BUTTERNUT SQUASH SOUP

This delicious, easy Mexican-inspired soup can be made in a slow cooker. I like to cook it overnight, blend it in the morning and store it in the refrigerator. That way, all I have to do when I get home is heat it up and savor it.

—Colleen Delawder, Herndon, VA

PREP: 15 min. • **COOK:** 6 hours • **MAKES:** 8 servings (2 qt.)

- 6 cups cubed peeled butternut squash
- 3 cups reduced-sodium chicken broth
- 1 can (10 oz.) green enchilada sauce
- 1 Tbsp. chili powder
- 1½ tsp. ground cumin
- ½ tsp. sea salt
- ½ tsp. pepper
- ½ tsp. onion powder
- ½ tsp. garlic powder
- ½ tsp. dried oregano
- ¼ tsp. crushed red pepper flakes
- 1 cup heavy whipping cream
- Optional: Crispy tortilla strips, sliced jalapeno pepper and fresh cilantro leaves

1. Combine the first 11 ingredients in a 6-qt. slow cooker. Cook, covered, on low until vegetables are soft, 6-7 hours.

2. Puree soup using an immersion blender. Or cool slightly and puree soup in batches in a blender; return to slow cooker. Stir in heavy cream; heat through. If desired, top with crispy tortilla strips, jalapeno and cilantro leaves, and sprinkle with additional chili powder.

FREEZE OPTION Freeze cooled soup in freezer containers. To use, partially thaw in refrigerator overnight. Heat through in a saucepan, stirring occasionally; add broth if necessary.

1 CUP 185 cal., 12g fat (7g sat. fat), 34mg chol., 539mg sod., 19g carb. (5g sugars, 3g fiber), 4g pro.

ROASTED GARLIC SOUP

Creamy soup is comforting on a cold day, but one made with mellow, rich roasted garlic somehow hits the spot in a way that many other soups don't. A tablespoon of dry sherry is optional but definitely upgrades the flavor. Avoid cooking sherry because those are packed with unneeded salt.

—Megan Taylor, Greenfield, WI

PREP: 10 min. • **COOK:** 25 min. • **MAKES:** 4 servings

- 3 whole garlic bulbs
- 1 Tbsp. olive oil
- 2 Tbsp. butter
- 1 medium onion, chopped
- 1¼ tsp. salt
- 1 tsp. minced fresh thyme
- 1 tsp. minced fresh sage
- ½ tsp. pepper
- 5 Tbsp. all-purpose flour
- 4 cups reduced-sodium chicken broth
- 1 bay leaf
- ½ cup heavy whipping cream
- 1 Tbsp. sherry, optional
- Optional: Grated Parmesan cheese, fresh coarsely ground black pepper

1. Preheat oven to 425°. Remove papery outer skin from garlic bulb, but do not peel or separate cloves. Cut tops off of garlic bulbs, exposing individual cloves; brush with oil. Wrap in heavy-duty foil. Bake until cloves are softened, 30-35 minutes. Unwrap and cool for 10 minutes. Squeeze garlic cloves into a bowl; mash with a fork until smooth.

2. In a Dutch oven, melt butter over medium heat. Add onion; cook for 8-10 minutes or until slightly caramelized on edges. Stir in garlic, salt, thyme, sage and pepper; cook 1 minute longer. Stir in the flour; cook until browned, 1-2 minutes, stirring constantly. Slowly whisk in broth; add bay leaf. Bring to a simmer. Cook for 8-10 minutes or until thickened, whisking frequently. Add cream and, if desired, sherry.

3. Remove soup from heat; cool slightly. Discard bay leaf. Process soup in batches in a blender until smooth, return to pan. If desired, top with Parmesan and pepper.

1 CUP 286 cal., 20g fat (11g sat. fat), 49mg chol., 1367mg sod., 21g carb. (3g sugars, 1g fiber), 7g pro.

PAIR IT WITH
Soft Beer Pretzel
Nuggets, p. 306

POTATO BEER CHEESE SOUP

This satisfying potato soup has a velvety texture that's not too thick or too thin. The subtle flavors of beer and cheese balance each other nicely, creating a soup that's sure to warm you head to toe.

—Patti Lavell, Islamorada, FL

PREP: 25 min. • **COOK:** 30 min. • **MAKES:** 8 servings (2 qt.)

- 2 lbs. potatoes (about 6 medium), peeled and cubed
- 1 small onion, chopped
- 2 cups water
- 1½ cups 2% milk
- 1 cup beer or chicken broth
- 2 Tbsp. Worcestershire sauce
- 2 chicken bouillon cubes
- ¾ tsp. salt
- ½ tsp. ground mustard
- ½ tsp. white pepper
- 2 cups shredded cheddar cheese
- Optional: Salad croutons, crumbled cooked bacon, minced chives and coarsely ground pepper

1. Place potatoes, onion and water in a large saucepan. Bring to a boil. Reduce heat; cover and cook for 15-20 minutes or until tender. Remove from heat; cool slightly (do not drain). In a blender, cover and process mixture in batches until smooth. Return all to the pan and heat through.

2. Stir in milk, beer, Worcestershire sauce, bouillon, salt, mustard and white pepper; heat through. Stir in cheese just until melted. If desired, top with croutons, bacon, chives and/or pepper.

1 CUP 225 cal., 11g fat (6g sat. fat), 32mg chol., 711mg sod., 21g carb. (5g sugars, 1g fiber), 10g pro.

"Very good soup for a cool evening. I used jalapeno cheddar cheese for extra flavor. I will certainly make it again."

—LORRAINT200, TASTEOFHOME.COM

CHEESE CHICKEN SOUP

Kids won't think twice about eating vegetables once they're incorporated into this creamy and cheesy soup.

—LaVonne Lundgren, Sioux City, IA

TAKES: 30 min. • **MAKES:** 8 servings (2⅔ qt.)

- 4 cups shredded cooked chicken breast
- 3½ cups water
- 2 cans (10¾ oz. each) condensed cream of chicken soup, undiluted
- 1 pkg. (16 oz.) frozen mixed vegetables, thawed
- 1 can (14½ oz.) diced potatoes, drained
- 1 lb. Velveeta, cubed
- Minced chives, optional

In a Dutch oven, combine the first 5 ingredients. Bring to a boil. Reduce heat; cover and simmer until vegetables are tender, 8-10 minutes. Stir in cheese just until melted (do not boil). If desired, top with minced fresh chives.

1⅓ CUPS 429 cal., 22g fat (11g sat. fat), 116mg chol., 1464mg sod., 23g carb. (6g sugars, 4g fiber), 33g pro.

CREAMY CORN CRAB SOUP

This creamy soup is fast, easy and very tasty. Corn really stars in this delectable recipe, and crabmeat makes it a little more special. It's sure to impress both busy cooks and lovers of flavorful homemade food.

—Carol Ropchan, Willingdon, AB

TAKES: 30 min. • **MAKES:** 6 servings

- 1 medium onion, chopped
- 2 Tbsp. butter
- 3 cups chicken broth
- 3 cups frozen corn
- 3 medium potatoes, peeled and diced
- 1 can (6 oz.) crabmeat, drained, flaked and cartilage removed
- 1 cup whole milk
- ¼ tsp. pepper, plus more for optional topping
- Optional: Minced chives and crushed red pepper flakes

1. In a large saucepan, saute onion in butter until tender. Add the broth, corn and potatoes; bring to a boil. Reduce heat; cover and simmer for 15 minutes. Remove from heat; cool slightly.

2. In a blender, puree half the corn mixture. Return to pan. Stir in the crab, milk and pepper; cook over low heat until heated through (do not boil). If desired, top with fresh cracked pepper, chives and crushed red pepper flakes.

1¼ CUPS 219 cal., 6g fat (3g sat. fat), 44mg chol., 702mg sod., 33g carb. (6g sugars, 3g fiber), 10g pro. **DIABETIC EXCHANGES** 2 starch, 1 lean meat, 1 fat.

CHEESE CHICKEN SOUP

SOUPS

STEWS & CHILI

PRESSURE-COOKER BEEF & FARRO STEW

This pressure-cooked stew is loaded with tender beef and lots of veggies. It's comforting and filling, so it's sure to become a family favorite.

—Kaylen Friederich, Reno, NV

PREP: 40 min. • **COOK:** 30 min. + releasing • **MAKES:** 12 servings (4 qt.)

- 1 boneless beef chuck roast (about 2 lbs.), cut into 1-in. pieces
- 1½ tsp. salt
- ½ tsp. pepper
- 2 Tbsp. olive oil, divided
- 6 large carrots, cut into ½-in. pieces
- 3 celery ribs, chopped
- 1 large onion, chopped
- 6 garlic cloves, minced
- ¼ cup tomato paste
- 1 cup dry red wine
- 6 cups beef stock
- 4 large Yukon Gold potatoes, peeled and cut into 1-in. pieces
- ½ lb. fresh mushrooms, sliced
- ¾ cup farro, rinsed
- 3 bay leaves
- 1 tsp. garlic powder
- 1 tsp. dried thyme

1. Sprinkle beef with salt and pepper. Select saute or browning setting on a 6-qt. electric pressure cooker. Adjust for medium heat; add 1 Tbsp. oil. When oil is hot, brown beef in batches. Set aside.

2. Add remaining 1 Tbsp. oil, carrots, celery and onion to pressure cooker; cook and stir until vegetables are crisp-tender, 5-7 minutes.

3. Add garlic; cook 1 minute longer. Add tomato paste. Cook and stir until fragrant, about 1 minute. Add wine, stirring to loosen browned bits.

4. Return beef to pressure cooker. Stir in stock, potatoes, mushrooms, farro, bay leaves, garlic powder and thyme. Press cancel.

5. Lock lid; close the pressure-release valve. Adjust to pressure-cook on high for 30 minutes. Let pressure release naturally for 15 minutes; quick-release any remaining pressure. If desired, skim fat from stew. Discard bay leaves.

FREEZE OPTION Freeze cooled stew in freezer containers. To use, partially thaw in refrigerator overnight. Heat through in a saucepan, stirring occasionally; add broth or water if necessary.

1⅓ CUPS 360 cal., 10g fat (3g sat. fat), 49mg chol., 619mg sod., 43g carb. (6g sugars, 5g fiber), 22g pro. **DIABETIC EXCHANGES** 3 starch, 3 lean meat, ½ fat.

"Made this last night. The meat came out so tender and tasted amazing! Since I cook for just myself, I am happily freezing the rest."

—ADELE942, TASTEOFHOME.COM

PAIR IT WITH
Sage & Gruyere
Sourdough Bread, p. 215

GREEN CHILE CHICKEN CHILI

This easy chili is loaded with chicken and beans. The spicy heat can be tamed a bit with cool sour cream.

—Fred Lockwood, Plano, TX

PREP: 25 min. • **COOK:** 5 hours • **MAKES:** 10 servings (3½ qt.)

- 4 bone-in chicken breast halves (14 oz. each)
- 2 medium onions, chopped
- 2 medium green peppers, chopped
- 1 cup pickled jalapeno slices
- 1 can (4 oz.) chopped green chiles
- 2 jars (16 oz. each) salsa verde
- 2 cans (15½ oz. each) navy beans, rinsed and drained
- 1 cup sour cream
- ½ cup minced fresh cilantro
- Optional toppings: Shredded Colby-Monterey Jack cheese, sour cream and crushed tortilla chips

1. Place chicken, onions, peppers, jalapenos and chiles in a 5- or 6-qt. slow cooker. Pour salsa over top. Cover and cook on low for 5-6 hours or until chicken is tender.

2. Remove chicken; cool slightly. Shred chicken with 2 forks, discarding skin and bones; return meat to slow cooker. Stir in beans, sour cream and cilantro; heat through. Serve with toppings as desired.

FREEZE OPTION Before adding sour cream, cilantro and toppings, cool chili. Freeze in freezer containers. To use, partially thaw in refrigerator overnight. Heat through in a saucepan, stirring occasionally and adding water if necessary. Stir in sour cream and cilantro. Serve with toppings as desired.

NOTE Wear disposable gloves when cutting hot peppers; the oils can burn skin. Avoid touching your face.

1⅓ CUPS 320 cal., 7g fat (4g sat. fat), 79mg chol., 1187mg sod., 30g carb. (5g sugars, 7g fiber), 32g pro.

"I make this at least once a month, and it lasts a couple of days (barely). It's easy, budget friendly and so yummy!"

—KOENIGSFM, TASTEOFHOME.COM

WEST AFRICAN CHICKEN STEW

I really love authentic African flavors, but they can be hard to come by in the U.S. This recipe features a delicious combination of ingredients such as peanut butter, sweet potatoes and black-eyed peas, all of which are readily available.

—Michael Cohen, Los Angeles, CA

PREP: 20 min. • **COOK:** 30 min. • **MAKES:** 8 servings (2½ qt.)

- 1 lb. boneless skinless chicken breasts, cut into 1-in. cubes
- ½ tsp. salt
- ¼ tsp. pepper
- 3 tsp. canola oil, divided
- 1 medium onion, thinly sliced
- 6 garlic cloves, minced
- 2 Tbsp. minced fresh gingerroot
- 2 cans (15½ oz. each) black-eyed peas, rinsed and drained
- 1 can (28 oz.) crushed tomatoes
- 1 large sweet potato, peeled and cut into 1-in. cubes
- 1 cup reduced-sodium chicken broth
- ¼ cup creamy peanut butter
- 1½ tsp. minced fresh thyme or ½ tsp. dried thyme, divided
- ¼ tsp. cayenne pepper
- Hot cooked brown rice, optional

1. Sprinkle chicken with salt and pepper. In a Dutch oven, cook chicken over medium heat in 2 tsp. oil for 4-6 minutes or until no longer pink; remove and set aside.

2. In same pan, saute onion in remaining oil until tender. Add garlic and ginger; cook 1 minute longer.

3. Stir in the peas, tomatoes, sweet potato, broth, peanut butter, 1¼ tsp. thyme and cayenne. Bring to a boil. Reduce heat; cover and simmer for 15-20 minutes or until potato is tender. Add chicken; heat through.

4. Serve with rice if desired. Sprinkle with remaining thyme.

1¼ CUPS 275 cal., 7g fat (1g sat. fat), 31mg chol., 636mg sod., 32g carb. (5g sugars, 6g fiber), 22g pro. **DIABETIC EXCHANGES** 3 lean meat, 2 vegetable, 1 starch, 1 fat.

PAIR IT WITH

Sea Salt Sticks, p. 314

COMFORTING BARLEY & PUMPKIN BEEF STEW

There's nothing more comforting than a bowl of beef stew unless, of course, it's steaming hot and loaded with barley. Now that's comfort food at its best!

—Colleen Delawder, Herndon, VA

PREP: 30 min. • **COOK:** 6 hours • **MAKES:** 9 servings (about 3½ qt.)

- ¼ cup all-purpose flour
- 3 Tbsp. cornstarch
- 1½ tsp. salt, divided
- 1½ tsp. pepper, divided
- 1½ lbs. beef stew meat
- 3 Tbsp. olive oil
- 1 large sweet onion, finely chopped
- 2 cartons (32 oz. each) beef broth
- 1 can (15 oz.) pumpkin
- 1 cup medium pearl barley
- 1 tsp. dried thyme
- ¼ tsp. garlic powder
- ¼ tsp. crushed red pepper flakes
- Optional: Minced fresh parsley and additional red pepper flakes

1. In a shallow dish, mix flour, cornstarch, 1 tsp. salt and 1 tsp. pepper. Add beef, a few pieces at a time, and toss to coat. In a large skillet, heat oil over medium-high heat; brown meat in batches.

2. Transfer meat to a 5- or 6-qt. slow cooker; leave drippings in pan. In same skillet, cook and stir onion in drippings until tender, 6-8 minutes; add to slow cooker. Stir in broth, pumpkin, barley, thyme, garlic powder, red pepper flakes and remaining ½ tsp. salt and ½ tsp. pepper. Cook, covered, on low until meat is tender, 6-8 hours. Serve with parsley and additional pepper flakes if desired.

1½ CUPS 211 cal., 8g fat (2g sat. fat), 35mg chol., 819mg sod., 20g carb. (3g sugars, 4g fiber), 15g pro. **DIABETIC EXCHANGES** 2 lean meat, 1 starch, 1 fat.

MEXICAN PORK & HOMINY STEW

This aromatic pork stew, also known as pozole, is a southwestern delicacy. I make it in the slow cooker so it can simmer away on its own. The rich, brothy soup is delicious, much like a tamale in a bowl.

—Joan Hallford, North Richland Hills, TX

PREP: 30 min. • **COOK:** 6 hours • **MAKES:** 8 servings (about 2¾ qt.)

- 2 cups water
- 1 large poblano pepper, seeded and chopped
- 1 jalapeno pepper, seeded and chopped
- 1 can (14½ oz.) fire-roasted diced tomatoes, undrained
- 1 medium onion, chopped
- 4 garlic cloves, minced
- 2 tsp. ground cumin
- ½ tsp. dried oregano
- 2 lbs. boneless country-style pork ribs, cubed
- 1 can (29 oz.) hominy, rinsed and drained
- 2 cups reduced-sodium chicken broth
- 1 Tbsp. lime juice
- 1 tsp. kosher salt
- ¼ tsp. pepper

Optional: Fried tortilla strips, cubed avocado, sliced radishes, lime wedges and cilantro leaves

1. In a saucepan, combine water, poblano and jalapeno. Bring to a boil. Reduce heat; simmer until tender, about 10 minutes. Remove from heat; cool slightly. Place mixture in a blender. Add tomatoes, onion, garlic, cumin and oregano; cover and process until smooth.

2. Transfer to a 5- or 6-qt. slow cooker. Stir in pork, hominy, broth, lime juice, salt and pepper. Cook, covered, on low for 6-8 hours or until pork is tender. If desired, serve with optional ingredients.

FREEZE OPTION Freeze cooled stew in freezer containers. To use, partially thaw in refrigerator overnight. Heat through in a saucepan, stirring occasionally; add broth if necessary.

1⅓ CUPS 257 cal., 10g fat (4g sat. fat), 65mg chol., 1005mg sod., 16g carb. (3g sugars, 4g fiber), 22g pro.

PAIR IT WITH
Ham Biscuits, p. 277

SEAFOOD GUMBO

Gumbo is one of the dishes that makes Louisiana cuisine so famous. We live across the border in Texas and can't get enough of this traditional Cajun dish featuring okra, shrimp, spicy seasonings and what is called the holy trinity—onions, green peppers and celery. This recipe calls for seafood, but you could also use chicken, duck or sausage.

—Ruth Aubey, San Antonio, TX

PREP: 20 min. • **COOK:** 30 min. • **MAKES:** 24 servings (6 qt.)

- 1 cup all-purpose flour
- 1 cup canola oil
- 4 cups chopped onion
- 2 cups chopped celery
- 2 cups chopped green pepper
- 1 cup sliced green onions
- 4 cups chicken broth
- 8 cups water
- 4 cups sliced okra
- 2 Tbsp. paprika
- 1 Tbsp. salt
- 2 tsp. oregano
- 1 tsp. ground black pepper
- 6 cups small shrimp, rinsed and drained or seafood of your choice
- 1 cup minced fresh parsley
- 2 Tbsp. Cajun seasoning

1. In a heavy Dutch oven, combine flour and oil until smooth. Cook over medium-high heat for 5 minutes, stirring constantly. Reduce heat to medium. Cook and stir about 10 minutes longer or until mixture is reddish brown.

2. Add onion, celery, green pepper and green onion; cook and stir for 5 minutes. Add chicken broth, water, okra, paprika, salt, oregano and pepper. Bring to a boil; reduce heat and simmer, covered, for 10 minutes.

3. Add shrimp and parsley. Simmer, uncovered, about 5 minutes longer or until the shrimp or other seafood is done. Remove from heat; stir in Cajun seasoning.

1 CUP 166 cal., 10g fat (1g sat. fat), 96mg chol., 900mg sod., 10g carb. (2g sugars, 2g fiber), 10g pro.

MAKE-AHEAD ROUX

Making a roux with flour is common when preparing homemade gravy, but a roux works for gumbo too. To make it ahead, cook the roux until it reaches the desired color, and let it cool slightly in the pan. Then store it in an airtight container in the refrigerator. It lasts in the fridge for up to 6 months and in the freezer for up to 1 year. When you're ready to use it, add the roux to the Dutch oven. Once hot, add the vegetables and cook as directed.

TURKEY CABBAGE STEW

Chock-full of ground turkey, cabbage, carrots and tomatoes, this stew delivers down-home comfort food fast!

—Susan Lasken, Woodland Hills, CA

TAKES: 30 min. • **MAKES:** 6 servings

- 1 lb. lean ground turkey
- 1 medium onion, chopped
- 3 garlic cloves, minced
- 4 cups chopped cabbage
- 2 medium carrots, sliced
- 1 can (28 oz.) diced tomatoes, undrained
- ¾ cup water
- 1 Tbsp. brown sugar
- 1 Tbsp. white vinegar
- 1 tsp. salt
- 1 tsp. dried oregano
- ¼ tsp. dried thyme
- ¼ tsp. pepper

1. Cook turkey, onion and garlic in a large saucepan over medium heat until meat is no longer pink, 5-7 minutes, breaking turkey into crumbles; drain.

2. Add the remaining ingredients. Bring to a boil; cover and simmer for 12-15 minutes or until vegetables are tender.

FREEZE OPTION Freeze cooled stew in freezer containers. To use, partially thaw in refrigerator overnight. Heat through in a saucepan, stirring occasionally; add water if necessary.

1 CUP 180 cal., 6g fat (2g sat. fat), 52mg chol., 674mg sod., 16g carb. (10g sugars, 5g fiber), 17g pro. **DIABETIC EXCHANGES** 2 vegetable, 2 lean meat.

"This is a big winner in my book—healthy but still comfort food. I enjoy the touch of sweet and the blend of herbs. Together they give this stew some welcome complex flavors."

—KATISHA, TASTEOFHOME.COM

PRESSURE-COOKER SPRING-THYME CHICKEN STEW

During a long winter (and spring), we were in need of something warm, comforting and bright. This stew always reminds me of the days Mom would make her chicken soup for me.

—Amy Chase, Vanderhoof, BC

PREP: 25 min. • **COOK:** 10 min. • **MAKES:** 4 servings

- 1 lb. small red potatoes, halved
- 1 large onion, finely chopped
- ¾ cup shredded carrots
- 6 garlic cloves, minced
- 2 tsp. grated lemon zest
- 2 tsp. dried thyme
- ½ tsp. salt
- ¼ tsp. pepper
- 1½ lbs. boneless skinless chicken thighs, cut into 1-in. pieces
- 2 cups reduced-sodium chicken broth, divided
- 2 bay leaves
- 3 Tbsp. all-purpose flour
- 2 Tbsp. minced fresh parsley

1. Place potatoes, onion and carrots in a 6-qt. electric pressure cooker. Top with garlic, lemon zest, thyme, salt and pepper. Place chicken over top. Add 1¾ cups chicken broth and bay leaves.

2. Lock lid; close pressure-release valve. Adjust to pressure-cook on high for 5 minutes. Quick-release pressure. A thermometer inserted in chicken should read at least 170°.

3. Remove chicken; keep warm. Discard bay leaves. In a small bowl, mix flour and remaining ¼ cup broth until smooth; stir into pressure cooker. Select saute setting and adjust for low heat. Simmer, stirring constantly, for 1-2 minutes or until slightly thickened. Return chicken to pressure cooker; heat through. Sprinkle servings with parsley.

1 SERVING 389 cal., 13g fat (3g sat. fat), 113mg chol., 699mg sod., 31g carb. (4g sugars, 4g fiber), 37g pro. **DIABETIC EXCHANGES** 5 lean meat, 2 vegetable, 1½ starch.

HOT SURFACE
Hamilton Beach
KEEP WARM
OFF
LOW
HIGH

SLOW-COOKED PORK STEW

Try this comforting stew that's easy to put together, and it tastes like you've been working hard in the kitchen all day. It's even better served over polenta, egg noodles or mashed potatoes.

—Nancy Elliott, Houston, TX

PREP: 15 min. • **COOK:** 5 hours • **MAKES:** 8 servings (2 qt.)

- 2 pork tenderloins (1 lb. each), cut into 2-in. pieces
- 1 tsp. salt
- ½ tsp. pepper
- 2 large carrots, cut into ½-in. slices
- 2 celery ribs, coarsely chopped
- 1 medium onion, coarsely chopped
- 3 cups beef broth
- 2 Tbsp. tomato paste
- ⅓ cup pitted dried plums (prunes), chopped
- 4 garlic cloves, minced
- 2 bay leaves
- 1 fresh rosemary sprig
- 1 fresh thyme sprig
- ⅓ cup Greek olives, optional
- Optional: Chopped fresh parsley and hot cooked mashed potatoes

1. Sprinkle pork with salt and pepper; transfer to a 4-qt. slow cooker. Add carrots, celery and onion. In a small bowl, whisk together broth and tomato paste; pour over vegetables. Add plums, garlic, bay leaves, rosemary, thyme and, if desired, olives. Cook, covered, on low until meat and vegetables are tender, 5-6 hours.

2. Discard bay leaves, rosemary and thyme. If desired, sprinkle stew with parsley and serve with potatoes.

1 CUP 177 cal., 4g fat (1g sat. fat), 64mg chol., 698mg sod., 9g carb. (4g sugars, 1g fiber), 24g pro. **DIABETIC EXCHANGES** 3 lean meat, ½ starch.

TENDERIZING TIPS

You can take an extra step to guarantee that the pork in this stew melts in your mouth. To do so, before you cook the pork, tenderize it by lightly pounding it with a mallet evenly across the surface, being careful not to overwork the meat. You can also try marinating the pork in acidic ingredients like lemon juice or vinegar before cooking, which helps break down tough proteins.

VEGETARIAN SKILLET CHILI

This chili is comfort food to me—it makes me feel warm and fuzzy. I make it for both vegetarians and non-vegetarians, and it is loved by all.

—Casey Hill, London, UK

PREP: 15 min. • **COOK:** 55 min. • **MAKES:** 8 servings

1 Tbsp. olive oil
1 small red onion, chopped
3 garlic cloves, minced
1 medium sweet red pepper, chopped
1 medium zucchini, chopped
1 small carrot, chopped
2 cans (14 oz. each) crushed tomatoes
1 can (14 oz.) black beans, rinsed and drained
1 can (14 oz.) kidney beans, rinsed and drained
1 cup water
1 Tbsp. paprika
1 Tbsp. ground cumin
1 Tbsp. chili powder
1 Tbsp. ground cinnamon
1 tsp. cayenne pepper
Optional: lime wedges and chopped fresh cilantro

In a large skillet, heat olive oil over medium heat. Add onion and garlic; cook and stir for 3-5 minutes. Add red pepper, zucchini and carrot. Cook and stir until vegetables are tender, about 10 minutes. Add tomatoes, beans, water and seasonings. Reduce heat and simmer, uncovered, about 40 minutes, adding more water as needed. Serve with lime and cilantro if desired.

1 CUP 140 cal., 2g fat (0 sat. fat), 0 chol., 304mg sod., 24g carb. (5g sugars, 8g fiber), 7g pro. **DIABETIC EXCHANGES** 1½ starch, 1 lean meat, ½ fat.

TASTY TOPPINGS FOR BIG FLAVOR

You can add a little more zip to your vegetarian chili by adding extra cayenne and chili powder. We also recommend topping this chili with shredded cheese and crushed tortilla chips.

PAIR IT WITH
Homemade Fry Bread, p. 296

TURKEY STEW WITH DUMPLINGS

My husband and I love dumplings, and this mild-tasting, homey dish has flavorful ones floating on a tasty turkey and vegetable stew. It hits the spot on chilly fall and winter days.

—Rita Taylor, St. Cloud, MN

PREP: 30 min. • **COOK:** 45 min. • **MAKES:** 12 servings

- 8 medium carrots, cut into 1-in. chunks
- 4 celery ribs, cut into 1-in. chunks
- 1 cup chopped onion
- ½ cup butter, cubed
- 2 cans (10½ oz. each) condensed beef consomme, undiluted
- 4⅔ cups water, divided
- 2 tsp. salt
- ¼ tsp. pepper
- 3 cups cubed cooked turkey
- 2 cups frozen cut green beans
- ½ cup all-purpose flour
- 2 tsp. Worcestershire sauce

DUMPLINGS

- 1½ cups all-purpose flour
- 2 tsp. baking powder
- 1 tsp. salt
- 2 Tbsp. minced parsley
- ⅛ tsp. poultry seasoning
- ¾ cup 2% milk
- 1 large egg

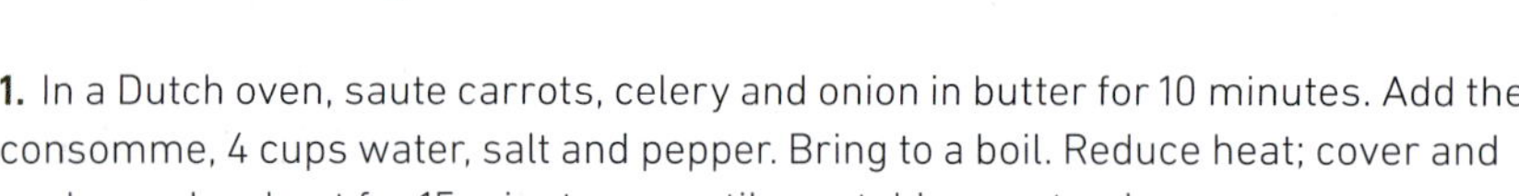

1. In a Dutch oven, saute carrots, celery and onion in butter for 10 minutes. Add the consomme, 4 cups water, salt and pepper. Bring to a boil. Reduce heat; cover and cook over low heat for 15 minutes or until vegetables are tender.

2. Add turkey and beans; cook for 5 minutes. Combine flour, Worcestershire sauce and remaining water until smooth; stir into turkey mixture. Bring to a boil. Reduce heat; cover and simmer for 5 minutes or until thickened.

3. For dumplings, combine the flour, baking powder and salt in a large bowl. Stir in parsley and poultry seasoning. Combine milk and egg; stir into flour mixture just until moistened. Drop mixture by tablespoonfuls onto simmering stew. Cover and simmer for 20 minutes or until a toothpick inserted in a dumpling comes out clean (do not lift the cover while simmering).

1 SERVING 255 cal., 11g fat (6g sat. fat), 68mg chol., 995mg sod., 24g carb. (6g sugars, 3g fiber), 15g pro.

BUFFALO CHICKEN CHILI

This chili is rich in the best way. The cream cheese, blue cheese and tangy hot sauce join forces for a dinner recipe everyone will love.

—Peggy Woodward, Shullsburg, WI

PREP: 10 min. • **COOK:** 5½ hours • **MAKES:** 6 servings

- 1 can (15½ oz.) navy beans, rinsed and drained
- 1 can (14½ oz.) chicken broth
- 1 can (14½ oz.) fire-roasted diced tomatoes
- 1 can (8 oz.) tomato sauce
- ½ cup Buffalo wing sauce
- ½ tsp. onion powder
- ½ tsp. garlic powder
- 1 lb. boneless skinless chicken breast halves
- 1 pkg. (8 oz.) cream cheese, cubed and softened
- Optional toppings: Crumbled blue cheese, chopped celery and chopped green onions

1. In a 4- or 5-qt. slow cooker, combine first 7 ingredients. Add chicken. Cover and cook on low for 5-6 hours or until chicken is tender.

2. Remove chicken; shred with 2 forks. Return to slow cooker. Stir in cream cheese. Cover and cook on low until cheese is melted, about 30 minutes. Stir until blended. Serve with toppings as desired.

NOTE Leftovers won't freeze well due to the cream cheese, which can curdle when frozen.

1¼ CUPS 337 cal., 16g fat (8g sat. fat), 80mg chol., 1586mg sod., 25g carb. (5g sugars, 5g fiber), 25g pro.

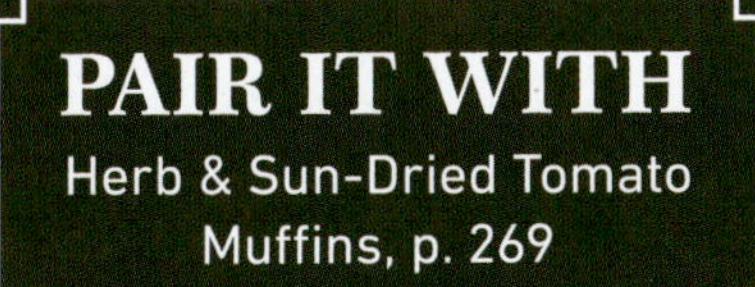

PAIR IT WITH

Herb & Sun-Dried Tomato Muffins, p. 269

"Absolutely to die for! I made this for guests, and they were licking their bowls clean. Thank you so much for such a quick, easy and delicious recipe. Our guests begged for the recipe."

—LADYJACK, TASTEOFHOME.COM

THE BEST BEEF STEW

Our beef stew recipe has tons of flavor, thanks to its blend of herbs and the addition of red wine and balsamic vinegar. Learn how to make this comforting classic and take it to the next level.

—James Schend, Pleasant Prairie, WI

PREP: 30 min. • **COOK:** 2 hours • **MAKES:** 6 servings (2¼ qt.)

- 1½ lbs. beef stew meat, cut into 1-in. cubes
- ½ tsp. salt, divided
- 6 Tbsp. all-purpose flour, divided
- ½ tsp. smoked paprika
- 1 Tbsp. canola oil
- 3 Tbsp. tomato paste
- 2 tsp. herbes de Provence
- 2 garlic cloves, minced
- 2 cups dry red wine
- 2 cups beef broth
- 1½ tsp. minced fresh rosemary, divided
- 2 bay leaves
- 3 cups cubed peeled potatoes
- 3 cups coarsely chopped onions (about 2 large)
- 2 cups sliced carrots
- 2 Tbsp. cold water
- 2 Tbsp. balsamic or red wine vinegar
- 1 cup fresh or frozen peas
- Additional fresh rosemary, optional

1. In a small bowl, toss beef and ¼ tsp. salt. In a large bowl, combine 4 Tbsp. flour and paprika. Add beef, a few pieces at a time, and toss to coat.

2. In a Dutch oven, brown beef in oil over medium heat. Stir in tomato paste, herbes de Provence and garlic; cook until fragrant and color starts to darken slightly. Add wine; cook until mixture just comes to a boil. Simmer for 5 minutes or until reduced by half. Stir in broth, 1 tsp. rosemary and bay leaves. Bring to a boil. Reduce the heat; cover and simmer until meat is almost tender, about 1½ hours.

3. Add potatoes, onions and carrots. Cover; simmer until meat and vegetables are tender, about 30 minutes longer.

4. Discard the bay leaves. In a small bowl, combine remaining ½ tsp. rosemary, remaining ¼ tsp. salt and remaining 2 Tbsp. flour. Add cold water and vinegar; stir until smooth. Stir into stew. Bring to a boil; add peas. Cook, stirring, until thickened, about 2 minutes. If desired, top with additional fresh rosemary.

1½ CUPS 366 cal., 11g fat (3g sat. fat), 71mg chol., 605mg sod., 40g carb. (9g sugars, 6g fiber), 28g pro. **DIABETIC EXCHANGES** 3 lean meat, 2½ starch, ½ fat.

COPYCAT WENDY'S CHILI

I don't eat a lot of fast food, but when I do I try to pick things that are fairly healthy. I found that Wendy's chili is one of the healthiest items on its menu. So when I needed to bring chili to a potluck, I tried to re-create Wendy's recipe—and I think I got it pretty close.

—Margo Zoerner, Pleasant Prairie, WI

PREP: 20 min. • **COOK:** 1 hour • **MAKES:** 20 servings (5 qt.)

2½ lbs. ground beef
2 cups chopped onion
1 cup chopped celery
3 Tbsp. chili powder
1 Tbsp. ground cumin
1 tsp. pepper
1 can (4 oz.) chopped green chiles
1 garlic clove, minced
1 can (46 oz.) tomato juice
4 cups V8 juice
1 can (28 oz.) diced tomatoes, undrained
2 cans (16 oz. each) kidney beans, rinsed and drained
2 cans (16 oz. each) pink beans or pinto beans, rinsed and drained
Optional: Sour cream, cubed avocado, shredded cheddar cheese and sliced jalapeno pepper

1. In a large Dutch oven, cook beef over medium heat until meat is no longer pink; drain. Continue to cook until beef is browned, 4-5 minutes longer. Add onion and celery; cook until tender. Stir in chili powder, cumin and pepper; cook for 1 minute. Add green chiles and garlic; cook 1 minute longer.

2. Stir in juices and tomatoes. Bring to a boil. Reduce heat; simmer, uncovered, for 20 minutes. Add beans and simmer 20 minutes longer or until thickened to desired consistency. If desired, serve with sour cream, avocado, cheese and jalapenos.

FREEZE OPTION Freeze the cooled chili in freezer containers. To use, partially thaw in refrigerator overnight. Heat through in a saucepan, stirring occasionally; add water if necessary.

NOTE This recipe was tested with Goya Pink Beans (Habichuelas Rosadas).

1 CUP 225 cal., 7g fat (3g sat. fat), 35mg chol., 595mg sod., 23g carb. (7g sugars, 6g fiber), 17g pro.

"Wow! This is delicious. The V8 juice is a creative addition, and it has the perfect amount of spice."

—JENNIFER3031, TASTEOFHOME.COM

PAIR IT WITH
Herb-Cheese Rolls, p. 266

BREADS

Bread Basics 200

Yeast & Rising 208

Quick & Easy 240

Rolls, Biscuits & More 264

Special & Savory 290

BREAD BASICS

Don't let bread baking intimidate you! From coast to coast, home bakers relish the satisfaction of baking buttery breads, biscuits, rolls and more for family and friends. It's easy when you know the basics.

BREAD TYPES

Breads can largely be divided into two categories.

YEAST BREADS

These breads depend on a living organism for their height and texture. Yeast breads fall into two main varieties: kneaded and batter.

Kneaded breads are traditionally worked by hand to develop the gluten in the dough. Modern gadgets—a bread machine or a stand mixer fitted with a dough hook—take the work out of kneading, but the dough itself is still kneaded.

Batter breads are beaten with a mixer to develop the gluten. They use less flour, so their dough is stickier than kneaded yeast breads. The finished breads have a coarser texture and a rugged crust.

QUICK BREADS

These loaves get a lift from leaveners such as baking soda or baking powder. The beauty of quick breads is right in the name—they're ready to pop in the oven and start baking right away.

INGREDIENTS FOR YEAST BREAD

Ingredients and their particular qualities affect bread's texture, density and crust. Understanding the job of each ingredient will help you comprehend the science of yeast breads.

FLOURS

Wheat flour contains an elastic protein called gluten, which is developed during kneading and gives bread its structure. Flours with high gluten content (hard flours), such as bread flour or all-purpose flour, yield the best results. Whole wheat and rye flours (soft flours) have less gluten; used alone, they make an extremely dense loaf. These flours are often used in combination with bread flour or all-purpose flour to achieve lighter, airier results.

YEAST

This microorganism consumes sugars in sweeteners and flours and produces carbon dioxide gas that stretches gluten strands to give breads a light, airy texture. Store yeast in the refrigerator or freezer.

SWEETENERS

The food for yeast; sweeteners also tenderize, add flavor, promote browning and lengthen shelf life. White or brown sugar, molasses, honey and maple syrup are common sweeteners used in yeast breads.

SALT

Controls the yeast's growth. Always use the quantity of salt given in the recipe—too much salt will prevent the yeast from growing, but not enough will let the yeast grow too fast too soon, and then collapse.

LIQUIDS

Water and milk are the primary liquids used in bread. Water gives a crunchy crust; milk gives a softer crust and a more tender crumb. Always warm the liquid to the temperature stated in the recipe. Too cold, and the yeast will be slow to activate; too hot, and it will kill the yeast.

FATS (AND EGGS)

Tenderize, add moisture, carry flavor and give richness to breads.

TYPES OF YEAST

Always use the type of yeast called for in a recipe. Learning the differences in yeast, however, can help take your bread baking to new heights!

WET YEAST

Wet yeast, or fresh yeast, can be tricky to come by so it isn't usually called for in at-home baking recipes. Wet yeast must be refrigerated as it has a shelf life of only two weeks. That said, wet yeast activates much quicker than dry yeast because of its moisture content. To use wet yeast, you should first break up the compressed block into smaller crumbles. Then it can be measured and added straight to the dough.

DRY YEAST

Dry yeasts are the types of yeast you're most likely to find in your grocery store's baking aisle. They have a longer shelf life—typically up to two years from the packaging date. But not all varieties of dry yeast are created equal. Depending on your recipe, you may find that active dry yeast or instant yeast is preferred.

ACTIVE DRY YEAST

This is the most commonly used type of yeast. It must be proofed before adding to dough (see "Proofing Yeast" at right) in order to activate the dormant organism. A standard packet of yeast contains approximately 2½ tsp. To use active dry yeast in recipes that call for instant yeast, increase the yeast amount by 25%.

INSTANT AND RAPID-RISE YEASTS

These yeasts are finely granulated and can cut the rising time for dough by up to half. They can be added directly to the dry ingredients and do not need proofing. Instant and rapid-rise yeast can be used interchangeably; rapid-rise yeast may contain dough conditioners, like ascorbic acid, to promote the quick rise. To use instant yeast in recipes that call for active dry yeast, use 25% less than the recipe specifies.

BREAD MACHINE YEAST

Turn to this yeast when using a bread machine. The fine, small granules can be mixed easily into the dough. Like rapid-rise yeast, this type of yeast may contain dough conditioners.

CAKE YEAST *(aka Fresh Yeast or Compressed Yeast)*

Cake yeast is proofed at a lower temperature (80°-90°), and is most suitable for breads with a long, cool rise time. Due to its short shelf life, it may be difficult to find—check the dairy case.

OSMOTOLERANT YEAST

Designed for sugar-heavy doughs, this yeast is not as common as dry yeasts but is becoming more readily available. Look for it at specialty food stores.

PROOFING YEAST

When we talk yeast breads, the term "proof" pops up in two ways: proofing yeast and proofing dough. Proofing the dough comes after kneading (see p. 202).

Proofing yeast ensures that it is alive and ready to create carbon dioxide.

Dissolve one ¼-oz. packet of active dry yeast in a dish with 1 tsp. sugar and ½ cup warm water (between 105°-115°).

Leave the yeast mixture alone for 5-10 minutes to let the yeast do its work; when it starts to bubble and foam, you know it's alive and ready for bread.

1

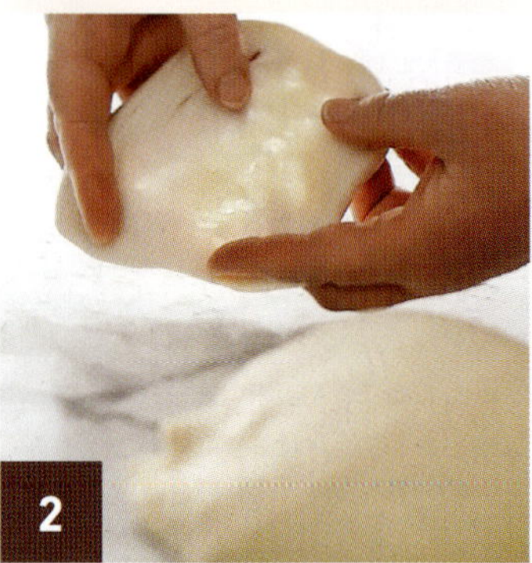
2

KNEADING

Kneading helps develop gluten, giving yeast bread its structure.

Fold the top of dough toward you. With your palms, push dough with a rolling motion away from you. Turn dough a quarter turn; repeat folding, kneading and turning until dough is smooth and elastic. Add a little flour to the surface as needed to avoid sticking.

Next, test the dough's elasticity (see right) before moving on to the "Windowpane Test." Tear off a piece of dough and stretch it between your fingers. If you can stretch it until you can see light through it when you hold it up, it's ready; if it tears, it needs more work.

PROOFING DOUGH

For the proofing (rising) stage, place dough in a greased bowl and cover it, then set the bowl in a warm (75° or above), humid and stable environment. Here are three tried-and-true ways to proof bread in cold and warm kitchens alike.

PROOF AT ROOM TEMPERATURE

The traditional way to proof bread is in a glass bowl at room temperature. Cover the bowl with a damp paper towel or cloth. If your bowl is deep enough, use plastic wrap. If working with a particularly sticky dough, rub a tiny amount of oil onto some plastic wrap to help prevent the dough from sticking. (A spritz of cooking spray works too.)

PROOF BREAD IN THE OVEN

This technique works best with heavier doughs and is not recommended for sourdough breads. Place a glass baking dish on your oven's bottom rack and fill it with boiling water; place your bowl of dough on the middle or top rack. Refresh the water every 30-45 minutes or until dough has doubled in size.

Some oven lights radiate enough heat for proofing even without turning on the heat. Turn on the light, then after about 30 minutes, use an oven thermometer to check the temperature; if the oven is 75° or above, set your bowl of dough in the oven and shut the door, leaving the light on.

PROOF BREAD WITH A SLOW COOKER

Fill your slow cooker halfway with water and set it to the low setting. Put the lid on upside down, cover it with a dish towel, then set your bowl of dough on top.

TESTING ELASTICITY

How do you know when your bread is done proofing? Depending on temperature, humidity, the freshness of your yeast and the type of dough, proofing can take from 1-3 hours. When ready, your dough should have expanded to roughly twice its original size and have a full, puffed appearance. To test the dough's elasticity, let it rest about 1 minute and then press it with your finger. If the indentation springs back slightly, it's ready. If the indentation stays, it's **underproofed** and won't rise properly during baking. If the dough looks stretched across the top and springs back instantly when pressed, it's **overproofed** and may crack and collapse when baked.

What should you do if your dough is underproofed? If your dough isn't rising, the yeast might be past its prime or your water may have been the wrong temperature (too hot and the yeast will die; too cold and the yeast won't grow). Always use fresh yeast and invest in a thermometer to help your yeast get the job done. You'll be on your way to a perfect loaf of homemade bread in no time.

How do you fix overproofed dough? You can fix overproofed dough by kneading and pushing the air out of the dough. Then reshape and place your bread back into your desired proofing container. Allow it to proof as normal, and then bake.

REASONS YOUR BREAD ISN'T RISING

The little organisms that help your bread rise require extra care—warm temperatures, food and just-right conditions. If any of these variables are off, the dough may not rise the way it should. Here are some of the most common reasons your bread isn't getting the right lift.

1 YEAST IS TOO OLD

To make sure your yeast is ready to go, be sure to proof it before adding it to your dough.

2 LIQUID IS THE WRONG TEMPERATURE

Too hot and the yeast will die; too cool and the yeast won't grow. Be sure that the liquid you are using is between 105°-115°.

3 TOO MUCH SALT

Salt controls the yeast so that it doesn't ferment too quickly—but too much salt can keep the yeast from doing its job. Measure carefully and never pour yeast and salt directly on top of one another in your mixing bowl.

4 TOO MUCH SUGAR

Sweet doughs take longer to rise because sugar absorbs the liquid in the dough so the yeast isn't as efficient. (Sweet doughs often proof overnight in the refrigerator.) Measure carefully, don't add extra sugar, and allow cinnamon rolls and other sweet doughs plenty of time to rise.

5 TOO MUCH FLOUR

Be mindful of your measurements and how much flour your dough picks up during kneading—too much can make the dough stiff and dry instead of slightly sticky and elastic. Use a bench scraper to scrape the dough off your work surface rather than being tempted to keep adding flour.

6 USING WHOLE GRAINS

White flour creates gluten strands that give bread an airy texture, while whole wheat and other alternative flours don't develop gluten as easily or at all. Use a recipe specially formulated for those flours. If you want to add wheat flour to a recipe you already love, keep some all-purpose flour in the equation to help the bread rise.

7 CRUST IS TOO DRY

The dough should be nice and moist; if a crust develops on top of the dough during proofing, it can be difficult for the bread to rise in the oven later. Cover your dough with a damp tea towel while proofing. Or spritz the dough with water and cover with a towel.

BAKING AT HIGH ALTITUDES

At elevations above 3,000 feet, the lower air pressure makes the yeast rise more quickly (in as little as half the time). Keep an eye on your dough, and use about one-third less yeast than called for in the recipe. Watch your flour content too. Add the flour slowly, and don't add any more than absolutely necessary to make the dough manageable. It will also bake more quickly, so be sure to check for doneness a few minutes before the minimum baking time.

PUNCH THE BREAD DOWN!

After proofing, you'll need to "punch down" the dough. The action isn't an actual fast punch—just press down firmly with your knuckles to remove some of the air.

STORING YOUR FINISHED LOAF

Because it doesn't contain preservatives, it can be a race to finish a loaf before it goes stale.

Homemade bread lasts 3-4 days when stored in a bread box on the counter. For long-term storage, however, you can freeze it. Wrapped tightly, bread lasts for up to 6 months in the freezer.

HOW TO MAKE

QUICK & EASY BREAD BOWLS

Impress your friends by serving cream soups in bread bowls. These bowls come together with just a few ingredients.

—Rachel Preus, Marshall, MI

PREP: 35 min. + rising • **BAKE:** 20 min. + cooling • **MAKES:** 6 servings

- 2 Tbsp. active dry yeast
- 3 cups warm water (110°-115°)
- 2 Tbsp. sugar
- 2 tsp. salt
- 6½ to 7½ cups bread flour
- Optional: Cornmeal and sesame seeds

1. In a small bowl, dissolve yeast in warm water. In a large bowl, combine sugar, salt, yeast mixture and 3 cups flour; beat on medium speed for 3 minutes. Stir in enough remaining flour to form a soft dough (dough will be sticky).

2. Turn onto a floured surface; knead until smooth and elastic, 6-8 minutes. Place in a greased bowl, turning once to grease the top. Cover with a kitchen towel and let rise in a warm place until doubled, about 30 minutes.

3. Preheat the oven to 500°. Punch down the dough. Divide and shape into 6 balls. Place 3 in. apart on 2 baking sheets that have been greased or, if desired, generously sprinkled with cornmeal. Cover with a kitchen towel; let rise in a warm place until doubled, about 15 minutes. Spray loaves with water; if desired, generously sprinkle with sesame seeds. Using a sharp knife, score tops with shallow cuts in an "X" pattern. Bake for 2 minutes. Reduce oven setting to 425°. Bake for 16-18 minutes or until golden brown and internal temperature reaches 190°-200°. Remove from pans to wire racks to cool completely.

4. Cut a thin slice off the top of each loaf. Hollow out the bottom portion of each loaf, leaving a ½-in. shell. Discard the removed bread or save for another use, such as croutons.

1 BREAD BOWL 283 cal., 1g fat (0 sat. fat), 0 chol., 396mg sod., 57g carb. (2g sugars, 2g fiber), 10g pro.

1

2

USE IT WITH

Potato Beer Cheese Soup, p. 171

HOW TO MAKE

BISCUIT BAKING MIX

You need just four common pantry staples to put together this versatile mix. I use it in recipes that call for a store-bought baking mix.

—Tami Christman, Soda Springs, ID

TAKES: 5 min. • **MAKES:** 12 cups

- 9 cups all-purpose flour
- ¼ cup baking powder
- 1 Tbsp. salt
- 2 cups shortening

1. In a large bowl, mix flour, baking powder and salt; cut in shortening until mixture resembles coarse crumbs.

2. Once mixture is well combined, place biscuit mix in an airtight container. Label it with a "use by" date (obtained from shortening package). Store it in a cool, dry place or freeze up to 8 months.

¼ CUP MIX 159 cal., 8g fat (2g sat. fat), 0 chol., 248mg sod., 18g carb. (0 sugars, 1g fiber), 2g pro.

USE IT WITH

Flaky Italian Biscuits, p. 270

CUTTING IN SHORTENING

"Cutting in" refers to the step of baking recipes where shortening, lard or butter is added to dry flour. The process coats the flour proteins with fat, allowing a flaky texture to develop when the pastry bakes. If you're working with a large amount of pastry dough, you may want to use a pastry blender or food processor, but you can also use your fingertips when working with small recipes like this one.

HOW TO MAKE

SOURDOUGH STARTER

Some 25 years ago, I received this recipe and some starter from a good friend, who is now a neighbor. I use it to make many loaves of the sourdough French bread.
—Delila George, Junction City, OR

PREP: 10 min. + standing • **MAKES:** about 3 cups

- 2 cups all-purpose flour
- 1 pkg. (¼ oz.) active dry yeast
- 2 cups warm water (110°-115°)

1. In a covered 4-qt. ceramic or glass bowl or container, mix flour and yeast. Gradually stir in warm water until smooth. Cover loosely with a kitchen towel; let stand in a warm place for 2-4 days or until mixture is bubbly and sour smelling and a clear liquid has formed on top. (Starter may darken, but if starter turns another color or develops an offensive odor or mold, discard it and start over.)

2. Transfer starter to a jar with a lid. Refrigerate starter until ready to use. Use and replenish starter, or nourish it, once every 1-2 weeks.

TO USE AND REPLENISH STARTER Stir to blend in any liquid on top. Remove the amount of starter needed; bring to room temperature before using. For each ½ cup starter removed, add ½ cup flour and ½ cup warm water to the remaining starter and stir until smooth. Cover loosely and let stand in a warm place 1-2 days or until light and bubbly. Stir; cover tightly and refrigerate.

TO NOURISH STARTER Remove half the starter. Stir in equal parts of flour and warm water. Cover loosely and let stand in a warm place 1-2 days or until light and bubbly. Stir; cover tightly and refrigerate.

1 TBSP. 19 cal., 0 fat (0 sat. fat), 0 chol., 0 sod., 4g carb. (0 sugars, 0 fiber), 1g pro.

1

2

3

SOURDOUGH STARTER FAQS

What is the best flour for a sourdough starter? Bread flour is best for sourdough starters, but all-purpose flour can also be used.

What happens if you don't nourish or feed your sourdough starter? Forgetting to nourish your sourdough starter for long periods will kill the yeast and organisms you've worked hard to cultivate. If you've only missed one feeding, you may be able to bring it back with some nourishing and careful watching.

WHAT IS SOURDOUGH BREAD?

Here's what separates this fermented loaf from other types of yeast breads.

WHAT'S THE HISTORY?

Sourdough has been around longer than most other breads—although the term "sourdough" is a new one. Sourdough got its start before commercial yeasts and mass production were introduced in the 19th century.

WHY IS IT DIFFERENT?

Unlike other yeast bread recipes that use baker's yeast as the leavening agent, traditional sourdough recipes use a starter made of water and flour. The starter ferments over time, producing natural yeast and the slightly acidic flavor that sets sourdough apart. Sourdough bread is also known for its crusty yet airy texture. Although sourdough bread can be relatively easy to make, it can be intimidating for new bakers because it's more time consuming than other types of homemade bread. It's often made by hand (rather than in a bread machine), which gives it a rustic quality.

WHAT MAKES IT SOUR?

The sourness of the bread comes from the acids produced in the starter. The ingredients, plus a warm environment, create a perfect storm for the starter to ferment and take on that signature sour flavor. If you'd like to make a more sour loaf, find a cool spot for the dough to rise. Or when mixing the starter, use a higher ratio of flour to water.

USE IT WITH

Country Crust Sourdough Bread *(shown here)*, p. 221
Sage & Gruyere Sourdough Bread, p. 215

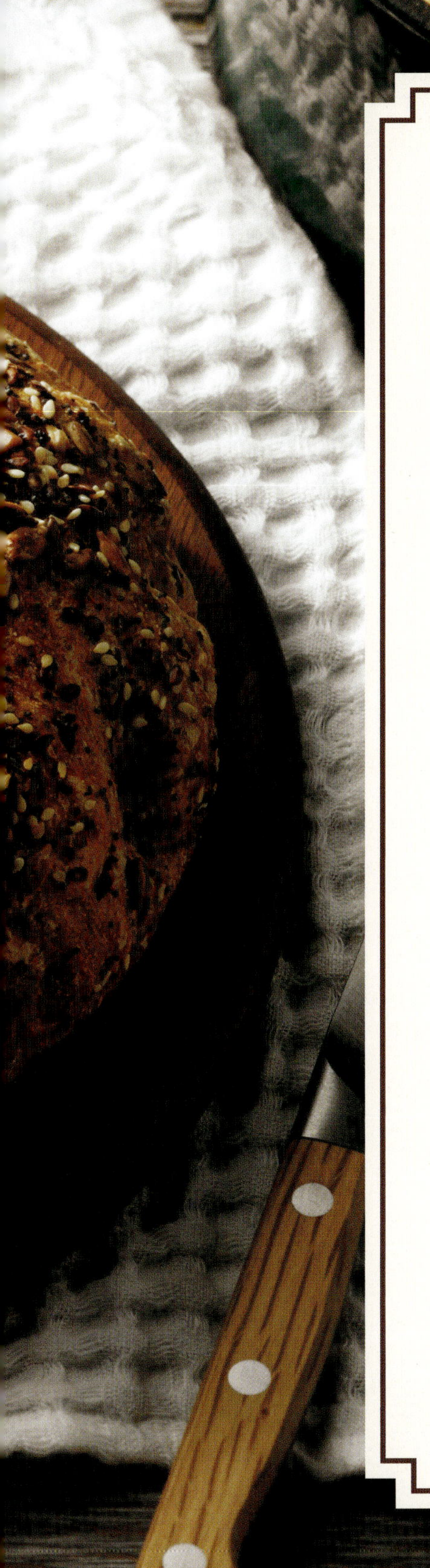

BREADS

YEAST & RISING

SAVORY STUFFING BREAD

Poultry seasoning and celery salt make this hearty loaf taste just like stuffing. It's the perfect bread to serve with turkey during the holidays, and it's nice for making sandwiches with the leftovers.

—Elizabeth King, Duluth, MN

PREP: 30 min. + rising • **BAKE:** 20 min. + cooling • **MAKES:** 2 loaves (16 pieces each)

- 2 Tbsp. sugar
- 2 pkg. (¼ oz. each) active dry yeast
- 1½ tsp. poultry seasoning
- ½ tsp. salt
- ½ tsp. celery salt
- ½ tsp. pepper
- 5½ to 6 cups all-purpose flour
- ¼ cup butter, cubed
- 1 small onion, finely chopped
- 1 can (14½ oz.) chicken broth
- 2 large eggs, room temperature

1. In a large bowl, mix sugar, yeast, seasonings and 2 cups flour. In a small saucepan, heat butter over medium-high heat. Add onion; cook and stir for 2-3 minutes or until tender. Stir in broth; heat to 120°-130°. Add to dry ingredients; beat on medium speed for 2 minutes. Add eggs; beat on high for 2 minutes. Stir in enough remaining flour to form a soft dough (dough will be sticky).

2. Turn dough onto a well-floured surface; knead for 6-8 minutes or until smooth and elastic. Place in a greased bowl, turning once to grease the top. Cover and let rise in a warm place until doubled, about 1 hour.

3. Punch down dough. Turn onto a lightly floured surface; divide in half. Shape into 2 loaves. Place in 2 greased 9x5-in. loaf pans, seam side down.

4. Cover with kitchen towels; let rise in a warm place until doubled, about 30 minutes.

5. Preheat oven to 375°. Bake for 18-22 minutes or until golden brown. Remove from pans to wire racks to cool completely.

1 PIECE 102 cal., 2g fat (1g sat. fat), 16mg chol., 127mg sod., 18g carb. (1g sugars, 1g fiber), 3g pro.

"This recipe is awesome! Thank you! I made loaves for Thanksgiving to give as gifts."

—GUEST95782978, TASTEOFHOME.COM

1
2
3
4
5

PASKA EASTER BREAD

Paska is a traditional Easter bread prepared with lots of eggs, making it much richer than ordinary sweet breads. The beautiful braided top will earn you many compliments.

—Millie Cherniwchan, Smoky Lake, AB

PREP: 40 min. + rising • **BAKE:** 50 min. • **MAKES:** 2 loaves (12 pieces each)

- 2 pkg. (¼ oz. each) active dry yeast
- 1 tsp. plus ⅓ cup sugar, divided
- 4 cups warm water (110° to 115°), divided
- 1 cup nonfat dry milk powder
- 13½ to 14½ cups all-purpose flour, divided
- 6 large eggs, room temperature, beaten
- ½ cup butter, melted
- 1 Tbsp. salt

EGG GLAZE

- 1 large egg
- 2 Tbsp. water

1. In a large bowl, dissolve yeast and 1 tsp. sugar in 1 cup warm water. Let stand for 5 minutes. Add remaining 3 cups water. Beat in milk powder and 5 cups flour until smooth. Cover and let rise in a warm place until bubbly, about 20 minutes. Add eggs, butter, salt and remaining ⅓ cup sugar; mix well. Stir in enough remaining flour to form a soft dough.

2. Turn out onto a floured surface; knead until smooth and elastic, 8-10 minutes. Place in a greased bowl, turning once to grease top. Cover and let rise in a warm place until doubled, about 1 hour.

3. Punch down dough. Turn out onto a lightly floured surface; divide dough in half and set 1 portion aside. Divide remaining portion in half; press each portion into a well-greased 10-in. springform pan. Divide reserved dough into 6 balls. Shape each ball into a 30-in. rope; make 2 braids of 3 ropes each. Place a braid around the edge of each pan, forming a circle. Trim ends of braids, reserving dough scraps. Pinch ends of braids to seal.

4. Shape the scraps into 2 long thin ropes; form into rosettes or crosses. Place 1 decoration on center of each loaf. Cover and let rise until doubled, about 1 hour.

5. For glaze, in a small bowl, beat egg and water; brush over dough. Bake at 350° for 50-60 minutes or until golden brown. Remove from pans to wire racks to cool.

1 PIECE 342 cal., 6g fat (3g sat. fat), 73mg chol., 380mg sod., 60g carb. (7g sugars, 2g fiber), 11g pro.

OLD-FASHIONED BROWN BREAD

This chewy bread boasts a slightly sweet flavor that will take you back to the old days.
—Patricia Donnelly, Kings Landing, NB

PREP: 20 min. + rising • **BAKE:** 35 min. • **MAKES:** 2 loaves (16 pieces each)

- 2⅓ cups boiling water
- 1 cup old-fashioned oats
- ½ cup butter, cubed
- ⅓ cup molasses
- 5½ to 6½ cups all-purpose flour
- 5 tsp. active dry yeast
- 2 tsp. salt

1. In a large bowl, pour boiling water over oats. Stir in butter and molasses. Let stand until mixture cools down to 110°-115°, stirring occasionally.

2. In a second bowl, combine 3½ cups flour, yeast and salt. Beat in oat mixture until blended. Stir in enough remaining flour to form a soft dough.

3. Turn dough onto a floured surface; knead until smooth and elastic, 6-8 minutes. Place in a greased bowl, turning once to grease top. Cover and let rise in a warm place until doubled, about 1 hour.

4. Punch down dough. Turn onto a lightly floured surface; divide in half. Shape into loaves. Place in 2 greased 9x5-in. loaf pans. Cover and let rise until doubled, about 30 minutes. Preheat oven to 375°.

5. Bake until golden brown, 35-40 minutes. Remove from pans to wire racks to cool.

1 PIECE 124 cal., 3g fat (2g sat. fat), 8mg chol., 170mg sod., 21g carb. (2g sugars, 1g fiber), 3g pro.

"One of my favorite breads. The molasses adds just the right amount of sweetness plus a beautiful color."

—EBRAMKAMP, TASTEOFHOME.COM

PAIR IT WITH

French Market Soup, p. 105

SAGE & GRUYERE SOURDOUGH BREAD

A Sourdough Starter gives loaves extra flavor and helps the rising process. This bread with sage and Gruyere cheese comes out so well that I'm thrilled to share it.

—Debra Kramer, Boca Raton, FL

PREP: 35 min. + rising • **BAKE:** 25 min. • **MAKES:** 1 loaf (16 pieces)

- ½ cup Sourdough Starter (p.206)
- 1⅛ tsp. active dry yeast
- ⅓ cup warm water (110° to 115°)
- ½ cup canned pumpkin
- ½ cup shredded Gruyere cheese, divided
- 4 tsp. butter, softened
- 1 Tbsp. sugar
- 1 Tbsp. minced fresh sage
- 1 tsp. salt
- 2¼ to 2¾ cups all-purpose flour
- 1 large egg, lightly beaten

1. Let Sourdough Starter come to room temperature before using.

2. In a small bowl, dissolve yeast in warm water. In a large bowl, combine Sourdough Starter, pumpkin, ¼ cup cheese, butter, sugar, sage, salt, yeast mixture and 1 cup of flour; beat on medium speed until smooth. Stir in enough remaining flour to form a stiff dough (dough will be slightly sticky).

3. Turn dough onto a floured surface; knead until smooth and elastic, 6-8 minutes. Place in a greased bowl, turning once to grease top. Cover and let rise in a warm place until doubled, about 1 hour.

4. Punch down dough. Turn onto a lightly floured surface; shape dough into a round loaf. Place on a greased baking sheet. Cover with a kitchen towel; let rise in a warm place until doubled, about 30 minutes. Preheat oven to 375°.

5. Brush egg over loaf; sprinkle with remaining ¼ cup cheese. Bake until golden brown, 25-30 minutes. Remove from pan to a wire rack to cool.

1 PIECE 98 cal., 3g fat (1g sat. fat), 18mg chol., 186mg sod., 15g carb. (1g sugars, 1g fiber), 3g pro.

HOMEMADE PUMPERNICKEL BREAD

This bread is our favorite. It uses molasses rather than sugar, and rye and whole wheat flour instead of white. Unsweetened chocolate is the secret ingredient!

—Julie Wesson, Wilton, WI

PREP: 30 min. + rising • **BAKE:** 15 min. + cooling • **MAKES:** 1 mini loaf (4 pieces)

- 1 tsp. active dry yeast
- ⅓ cup warm water (110° to 115°)
- 1 Tbsp. molasses
- 1 Tbsp. reduced-fat stick margarine, softened
- ½ oz. unsweetened chocolate, melted
- ¾ tsp. white vinegar
- ¼ tsp. salt
- ¾ cup rye flour
- ¼ to ½ cup whole wheat flour

1. In a bowl, dissolve yeast in warm water. Add molasses, margarine, chocolate, vinegar, salt, rye flour and 3 Tbsp. whole wheat flour. Beat until smooth. Stir in enough remaining flour to form a soft dough.

2. Turn onto a floured surface; knead until smooth and elastic, 6-8 minutes. Place in a bowl coated with cooking spray, turning once to coat top. Cover and let rise in a warm place until doubled, about 1 hour.

3. Punch down dough. Shape into a round loaf. Place on a baking sheet coated with cooking spray. With a sharp knife, make 3 shallow slashes across top of loaf. Cover and let rise until doubled, about 30 minutes.

4. Bake at 375° for 15-20 minutes or until bread sounds hollow when tapped. Remove to a wire rack to cool.

1 PIECE 145 cal., 4g fat (1g sat. fat), 0 chol., 170mg sod., 25g carb. (4g sugars, 4g fiber), 4g pro.

PUMPERNICKEL POINTERS

What can you use if you don't have any rye flour? In pumpernickel bread, there's honestly no substitute for the flavor of rye flour. However, if you're out of rye flour or do not prefer it, you can use whole wheat flour or even buckwheat flour instead.

What can you do if the Homemade Pumpernickel Bread dough is too sticky? Kneading bread dough, especially a sticky one, can be tricky! So avoid the temptation to add lots of extra flour to the dough, which risks the bread becoming tough. It can be helpful to lightly dust the work surface and your hands with a thin coating of flour before kneading. You can also use butter or cooking spray to grease your hands.

PAIR IT WITH
Cream of Celery Soup,
p. 157

PAIR IT WITH
Meatball Soup, p. 145

CRUSTY HOMEMADE BREAD

Crackling homemade bread makes an average day extraordinary. Enjoy this beautiful loaf as is, or stir in a few favorites such as cheese, garlic, herbs and dried fruit.

—Megumi Garcia, Milwaukee, WI

PREP: 20 min. + chilling • **BAKE:** 50 min. • **MAKES:** 1 loaf (16 pieces)

- 1½ tsp. active dry yeast
- 1¾ cups warm water (110° to 115°)
- 3½ cups plus 1 Tbsp. all-purpose flour, divided
- 2 tsp. salt
- 1 Tbsp. cornmeal or additional flour

1. In a large bowl, dissolve the yeast in warm water. Using a rubber spatula, stir in 3½ cups flour and salt to form a soft, sticky dough. Do not knead. Cover and let rise at room temperature for 1 hour.

2. Stir down dough (dough will be sticky). Turn onto a floured surface; with floured hands pat into a 9-in. square. Fold square into thirds, forming a 9x3-in. rectangle. Fold rectangle into thirds, forming a 3-in. square. Place in a large greased bowl, turning once to grease the top. Cover and let rise at room temperature until almost doubled, about 1 hour.

3. Punch down dough and repeat folding process. Return dough to bowl; refrigerate, covered, overnight.

4. Grease the bottom of a disposable foil roasting pan with sides at least 4 in. high; dust pan with cornmeal. Turn dough onto a floured surface. Knead gently 6-8 times; shape into a 6-in. round loaf. Place into prepared pan; dust top with remaining 1 Tbsp. flour. Cover pan and let rise at room temperature until dough expands to 7½ in. long, about 1¼ hours.

5. Preheat oven to 500°. Using a sharp knife, make a ¼-in.-deep slash across top of dough. Cover pan tightly with foil. Bake on lowest oven rack for 25 minutes.

6. Reduce oven setting to 450°. Remove foil; bake bread until deep golden brown, 25-30 minutes. Remove loaf to a wire rack to cool.

1 PIECE 105 cal., 0 fat (0 sat. fat), 0 chol., 296mg sod., 22g carb. (0 sugars, 1g fiber), 3g pro.

QUICK & EASY DONENESS TESTS

If you see that your bread is getting very brown on top before it's finished baking, drape a piece of foil over the top to protect it. The bread is done once it sounds hollow when tapped on the bottom with your knuckles (though you'll likely only be able to test this once the bread has cooled). Another way to check is with a digital thermometer—when the temperature at the center of the loaf reaches 190°, the bread is done.

SWEDISH LIMPA BREAD

I've entered my bread in several fairs, and it has won every single time! Orange and anise give it a subtle but wonderful flavor.

—Beryl Parrott, Franklin, MB

PREP: 30 min. + rising • **BAKE:** 30 min. • **MAKES:** 2 loaves (12 pieces each)

- ½ cup packed light brown sugar
- ¼ cup dark molasses
- ¼ cup butter, cubed
- 2 Tbsp. grated orange zest
- 1½ tsp. salt
- 1 tsp. aniseed, lightly crushed
- 1 cup boiling water
- 1 cup cold water
- 2 pkg. (¼ oz. each) active dry yeast
- ½ cup warm water (110° to 115°)
- 4½ cups all-purpose flour
- 3 to 4 cups rye flour
- 2 Tbsp. cornmeal
- 2 Tbsp. butter, melted

1. In a large bowl, combine brown sugar, molasses, butter, orange zest, salt, aniseed and boiling water; stir until brown sugar is dissolved and butter is melted. Stir in cold water; let stand until mixture cools to 110°-115°.

2. Meanwhile, in a large bowl, dissolve yeast in warm water. Stir in molasses mixture; mix well.

3. Add all-purpose flour and 1 cup rye flour. Beat on medium speed for 3 minutes. Stir in enough remaining rye flour to form a stiff dough.

4. Turn onto a floured surface; knead until smooth and elastic, 6-8 minutes. Place in a greased bowl, turning once to grease top. Cover and let rise in a warm place until doubled, about 1 hour.

5. Punch down dough. Turn onto a lightly floured surface; divide in half. Shape dough into 2 oval loaves. Grease 2 baking sheets and sprinkle them lightly with cornmeal. Place loaves on prepared pans. Cover and let rise until doubled, about 30 minutes.

6. Preheat oven to 350°. With a sharp knife, make 4 shallow slashes across top of each loaf. Bake until golden brown, 30-35 minutes. Remove to wire racks; brush with butter.

1 PIECE 186 cal., 3g fat (2g sat. fat), 8mg chol., 172mg sod., 35g carb. (7g sugars, 3g fiber), 4g pro.

COUNTRY CRUST SOURDOUGH BREAD

Use your Sourdough Starter (p. 206) to make this easy-peasy bread! For many years, I've been making 45 loaves of this bread for an annual Christmas bazaar, where we feed bread and soup to over 300 folks.

—Beverley Whaley, Camano Island, WA

PREP: 20 min. + rising • **BAKE:** 30 min. • **MAKES:** 2 loaves (16 pieces each)

- 2 pkg. (¼ oz. each) active dry yeast
- 1¼ cups warm water (110° to 115°)
- 1 cup Sourdough Starter (p. 206)
- 2 large eggs, room temperature
- ¼ cup sugar
- ¼ cup vegetable oil
- 1 tsp. salt
- 6 to 6½ cups all-purpose flour
- Melted butter

1. In a large bowl, dissolve yeast in warm water. Add Sourdough Starter, eggs, sugar, oil, salt and 3 cups flour. Beat until smooth. Stir in enough remaining flour to form a soft dough.

2. Turn onto a floured surface; knead until smooth and elastic, 6-8 minutes. Place in a greased bowl, turning once to grease top. Cover and let rise in a warm place until doubled, about 1 hour.

3. Punch down dough. Turn onto a lightly floured surface; divide in half. Shape into loaves. Place in 2 greased 8x4-in. loaf pans. Cover and let rise until doubled, about 45 minutes.

4. Bake at 375° until golden brown, 30-35 minutes. Remove from pans to wire racks to cool. Brush with butter.

1 PIECE 113 cal., 2g fat (0 sat. fat), 12mg chol., 79mg sod., 20g carb. (2g sugars, 1g fiber), 3g pro.

"This recipe, made with Taste of Home's Sourdough Starter recipe, knocked it out of the park on the first try. It's an excellent recipe that will be my go-to bread from now on."

—BRIANSCHMIDT, TASTEOFHOME.COM

DUTCH OVEN RAISIN WALNUT BREAD

On a cold day, nothing is better than a warm, crusty bread filled with raisins and walnuts.

—Catherine Ward, Mequon, WI

PREP: 15 min. + rising • **BAKE:** 50 min. + cooling • **MAKES:** 1 loaf (32 pieces)

- 6 to 7 cups (125 grams per cup) all-purpose flour
- ¼ cup sugar
- 2 tsp. active dry yeast
- 2 tsp. ground cinnamon
- 2 tsp. salt
- 1 cup raisins
- 1 cup chopped walnuts
- 3 cups cool water (70° to 75°)

1. In a large bowl, whisk 6 cups flour, sugar, yeast, cinnamon and salt. Stir in raisins and walnuts; add water and enough remaining flour to form a moist, shaggy dough. Do not knead. Cover and let rise in a cool place until doubled, 7-8 hours.

2. Preheat oven to 450°; place a Dutch oven with lid on the center rack and heat for at least 30 minutes. Once the Dutch oven is heated, turn dough onto a generously floured surface. Using a metal scraper or spatula, quickly shape into a round loaf. Gently place on top of a piece of parchment.

3. Using a sharp knife, make a ¼-in.-deep slash across top of loaf. Using parchment, immediately lower loaf into heated Dutch oven. Cover; bake for 30 minutes. Uncover and bake until loaf is deep golden brown and sounds hollow when tapped on bottom, 20-30 minutes longer, partially covering if the bread is browning too much. Remove loaf from Dutch oven and cool completely on wire rack.

1 PIECE 130 cal., 3g fat (0 sat. fat), 0 chol., 149mg sod., 24g carb. (4g sugars, 1g fiber), 3g pro.

DUTCH OVEN YEAST BREAD Use 3-3½ cups flour instead of 6-7 cups, and reduce the yeast to 1 tsp. and salt to 1 tsp. Omit the sugar, cinnamon, raisins and walnuts. Decrease water to 1½ cups and bake 5-10 minutes less if needed. Follow the recipe as directed.

NO DUTCH OVEN?

The glory of this bread is that it bakes up so beautifully in a Dutch oven. If you don't have a Dutch oven, however, you can bake it in a traditional cast-iron skillet on a baking sheet instead.

1

2

3

4

5

COPYCAT CHEESECAKE FACTORY BROWN BREAD

If you've ever eaten at The Cheesecake Factory, you know about their addictive, subtly sweet brown bread. This copycat version brings four loaves to your kitchen so you'll never have to go without.

—Lauren Habermehl, Pewaukee, WI

PREP: 40 min. + rising • **BAKE:** 25 min. • **MAKES:** 4 loaves

- 2¼ tsp. instant or active dry yeast
- 1¼ cups water, warmed to 105°-115°
- 1 Tbsp. sugar
- 2½ cups bread flour
- 1½ cups whole wheat flour
- 1½ Tbsp. cocoa powder
- 1 tsp. salt
- ¼ cup honey
- 2 Tbsp. molasses
- 1 tsp. instant espresso powder
- ¼ cup yellow cornmeal, for dusting the bottoms of the loaves
- ¼ cup old-fashioned oats
- Softened butter, optional

1. In bowl of a stand mixer fitted with a dough hook, combine yeast, warm water and sugar. Let sit for 5 minutes or until foamy. Meanwhile, in a separate bowl, sift together bread flour, whole wheat flour, cocoa powder and salt; set aside.

2. To mixing bowl, add honey, molasses and espresso powder; stir to combine. Add sifted ingredients; blend on low speed for 2-3 minutes. Increase speed to medium-low; knead until dough is smooth and elastic and begins to pull away from sides of bowl, 6-8 minutes.

3. Transfer dough to a clean, lightly oiled bowl; cover. Let rise in a warm place until doubled in size, about 1½ hours.

4. Place the cornmeal in a shallow dish or tray; set aside. Turn dough onto a lightly floured surface and divide it into 4 equal-sized portions. Roll each into a smooth log about 8-in. long; press each loaf into cornmeal to lightly coat the bottom. Transfer loaves to a parchment-lined baking sheet about 4-in. apart. Gently brush the loaves with water; sprinkle lightly with rolled oats. Cover loosely with a clean towel; let rise in a warm place until doubled, about 1 hour. Meanwhile, preheat the oven to 350°.

5. Uncover loaves; bake for 25-35 minutes. Remove; let cool slightly. Serve warm with butter if desired.

1 PIECE 158 cal., 1g fat (0 sat. fat), 0 chol., 285mg sod., 34g carb. (7g sugars, 2g fiber), 5g pro.

GARLIC & OREGANO BREAD

Homemade bread can be easy! Literally, just stir up the dough. No kneading. No sweating. Use a rubber spatula for easy cleanup.

—Megumi Garcia, Milwaukee, WI

PREP: 30 min. + chilling • **BAKE:** 50 min. • **MAKES:** 1 loaf (16 pieces)

- 1½ tsp. active dry yeast
- 1¾ cups water (70° to 75°)
- 3½ cups plus 1 Tbsp. all-purpose flour, divided
- 2 tsp. salt
- 1 Tbsp. cornmeal or additional flour
- ½ cup garlic cloves, peeled and quartered
- ¼ cup 2% milk
- 2 Tbsp. minced fresh oregano

1. In a small bowl, dissolve yeast in water. In a large bowl, mix 3½ cups flour and salt. Using a rubber spatula, stir in the yeast mixture to form a soft, sticky dough. Do not knead. Cover and let rise at room temperature for 1 hour.

2. Punch down dough. Turn onto a lightly floured surface. Pat into a 9-in. square. Fold dough into thirds, forming a 9x3-in. rectangle. Fold the rectangle into thirds, forming a 3-in. square. Turn dough over; place in a greased bowl. Cover and let rise at room temperature until almost doubled, about 1 hour.

3. Punch down dough and repeat folding process. Return dough to bowl; refrigerate, covered, overnight.

4. Dust bottom of a disposable foil roasting pan with cornmeal. In a small microwave-safe bowl, combine garlic and milk; microwave on high for 45 seconds. Drain garlic, discarding milk. Turn dough onto a floured surface; knead in garlic and oregano. Shape dough into a 6-in. round loaf.

5. Transfer loaf to prepared pan; dust top with remaining 1 Tbsp. flour. Cover pan; let rise at room temperature until dough expands to a 7½-in. loaf, about 1¼ hours.

6. Preheat oven to 500°. Using a sharp knife, make a ¼-in.-deep slash across top of loaf. Cover pan tightly with foil. Bake on lowest oven rack for 25 minutes.

7. Reduce oven setting to 450°. Remove foil; bake 25-30 minutes longer or until deep golden brown. Remove loaf to a wire rack to cool.

1 PIECE 112 cal., 0 fat (0 sat. fat), 0 chol., 297mg sod., 23g carb. (0 sugars, 1g fiber), 3g pro. **DIABETIC EXCHANGES** 1½ starch.

CARAWAY BREAD

A rustic round loaf of this bread is delicious when eaten warm, as a base for sandwiches, alongside soup or as toast. If you want to experiment, add sliced chives or sunflower seeds, or substitute other herbs, such as dried rosemary or thyme, for the caraway.

—Frances Conklin, Cottonwood, ID

PREP: 20 min. + rising • **BAKE:** 20 min. • **MAKES:** 1 loaf (8 wedges)

- 1 pkg. (¼ oz.) active dry yeast
- 1⅓ cups warm water (110° to 115°)
- 2 to 3 tsp. caraway seeds
- 1 tsp. salt
- 1 tsp. honey
- ¾ cup whole wheat flour
- 2½ to 3 cups all-purpose flour
- 2 tsp. cornmeal

1. In a small bowl, dissolve yeast in warm water. In a large bowl, combine caraway seeds, salt, honey, yeast mixture, whole wheat flour and 1½ cups all-purpose flour; beat on medium speed until smooth. Stir in enough remaining flour to form a stiff dough (dough will be sticky).

2. Turn dough onto a floured surface; knead until smooth and elastic, 6-8 minutes. Place in a greased bowl, turning once to grease top. Cover and let rise in a warm place until doubled, about 1 hour.

3. Grease a 15x10x1-in. baking pan; sprinkle with cornmeal. Punch down dough. Turn onto a lightly floured surface. Shape into a round loaf; place on prepared pan. Cover with greased plastic wrap and let rise in a warm place until almost doubled, about 30 minutes. Preheat oven to 425°.

4. Using a sharp knife, cut a large X in top of loaf. Bake on a lower oven rack until golden brown, 20-25 minutes. Remove from pan to a wire rack to cool.

1 WEDGE 191 cal., 1g fat (0 sat. fat), 0 chol., 297mg sod., 40g carb. (1g sugars, 3g fiber), 6g pro.

ROSEMARY NUT BREAD

I received this recipe from a friend who was moving into a new apartment. To celebrate, she made this bread to share, and now it is served at many of my family functions.

—Robin Haas, Cranston, RI

PREP: 25 min. + rising • **BAKE:** 20 min. • **MAKES:** 1 loaf (9 pieces)

- 1¼ tsp. active dry yeast
- ½ cup warm water (110°-115°)
- ¼ cup whole wheat flour
- 1½ to 1¾ cups all-purpose flour
- 2 Tbsp. honey
- 1 Tbsp. olive oil
- 1½ tsp. dried rosemary, crushed
- ½ tsp. salt
- ⅓ cup finely chopped walnuts

1. In a small bowl, dissolve yeast in warm water. In a large bowl, mix whole wheat flour and ¼ cup all-purpose flour; stir in yeast mixture. Cover and let stand, about 15 minutes. Add honey, olive oil, rosemary, salt and ¾ cup all-purpose flour; beat on medium speed until smooth. Stir in walnuts and enough remaining all-purpose flour to form a soft dough.

2. Turn dough onto a floured surface; knead until smooth and elastic, 6-8 minutes. Place in a greased bowl, turning once to grease top. Cover and let rise in a warm place until doubled, about 45 minutes.

3. Punch down dough. Turn onto a lightly floured surface; divide into thirds. Roll each into a 12-in. rope. Place ropes on a greased baking sheet and braid. Pinch ends to seal; tuck under. Cover with a kitchen towel; let rise in a warm place until almost doubled, about 30 minutes.

4. Preheat oven to 375°. Bake until golden brown, 20-25 minutes. Remove from pan to a wire rack to cool.

1 PIECE 145 cal., 4g fat (0 sat. fat), 0 chol., 132mg sod., 23g carb. (4g sugars, 1g fiber), 4g pro.

"I made this bread for Thanksgiving and everyone really enjoyed it. I'd suggest adding an egg wash if you want it to have a shine, but other than that it was really pretty!"

—KIMBERLY869, TASTEOFHOME.COM

SWEET POTATO & PESTO SLOW-COOKER BREAD

I like to bake fresh bread at home both as a way to offer my family a delicious accompaniment to their dinners and simply because I enjoy the process. Baking bread in the slow cooker allows you to achieve a tender, perfectly baked loaf without turning on the oven. It's especially helpful in the summer when the house gets too warm. Baking bread this way eliminates the need for a second rise, which is a nice timesaver. This beautiful slow-cooked braided loaf is one of my favorite recipes.

—Shauna Havey, Roy, UT

PREP: 45 min. + rising • **COOK:** 3 hours + cooling • **MAKES:** 1 loaf (12 pieces)

- 1 pkg. (¼ oz.) active dry yeast
- ⅔ cup warm half-and-half cream (110° to 115°)
- 1 large egg, room temperature
- 1 cup canned sweet potato puree or canned pumpkin
- 1 tsp. sugar
- 1 tsp. kosher salt
- ¼ tsp. ground nutmeg
- 3½ to 4 cups bread flour
- 1 container (7 oz.) refrigerated prepared pesto
- ½ cup plus 2 Tbsp. grated Parmesan cheese, divided

1. Dissolve yeast in warm cream. In a large bowl, combine egg, sweet potato puree, sugar, salt, nutmeg, yeast mixture and 2 cups flour; beat on medium speed until smooth. Stir in enough remaining flour to form a soft dough (dough will be sticky).

2. Turn onto a lightly floured surface; knead until smooth and elastic, 6-8 minutes. Place in a greased bowl, turning once to grease top. Cover and let rise in a warm place until doubled, about 1 hour.

3. Punch down dough. Turn onto a lightly floured surface; roll dough into a 18x9-in. rectangle. Spread pesto to within 1 in. of edges; sprinkle with ½ cup Parmesan. Roll up jelly-roll style, starting with a long side; pinch seam and ends to seal.

4. Using a sharp knife, cut roll lengthwise in half; carefully turn each half cut side up. Loosely twist strips around each other, keeping cut surfaces facing up. Shape into a coil; place on parchment. Transfer to a 6-qt. slow cooker; sprinkle with remaining 2 Tbsp. Parmesan. Let rise until doubled, about 1 hour.

5. Cook, covered, on low for 3-3½ hours or until bread is lightly browned. Remove from slow cooker and cool slightly before slicing.

1 PIECE 271 cal., 10g fat (3g sat. fat), 26mg chol., 464mg sod., 36g carb. (3g sugars, 2g fiber), 8g pro.

PANETTONE

This classic sweet bread is a must for Italian families at Christmas. Its reputation for being difficult is mostly due to multiple risings. Paper molds can be found in kitchen stores and online. If you use a metal pan instead, line it with parchment and grease to avoid it sticking.

—*Taste of Home* Test Kitchen

PREP: 30 min. + chilling • **BAKE:** 1¼ hours • **MAKES:** 12 servings

- 5 cups all-purpose flour, divided
- 1 Tbsp. quick-rise yeast
- ⅔ cup warm water (110° to 115°)
- ½ cup sugar
- 2 tsp. vanilla extract
- 1 tsp. salt
- 5 large eggs, room temperature, lightly beaten
- ¾ cup butter, softened
- ½ cup raisins
- ½ cup golden raisins
- ¼ cup chopped candied orange peel

TOPPING

- 1 large egg
- 1 Tbsp. water
- ¼ cup sliced almonds
- 1 Tbsp. coarse sugar

1. In a large bowl, combine 1 cup flour, yeast and warm water. Cover and let rise until doubled, about 30 minutes.

2. Gradually beat in remaining 4 cups of flour, sugar, vanilla and salt. Beat in eggs until blended. Switch to dough hook. Mix on medium speed for 2-3 minutes or until mixture forms a smooth stiff dough. Beat in butter, 1 Tbsp. at a time, mixing well after each addition. Beat on medium speed for 5 minutes. Stir in raisins and orange peel. Gently transfer to a greased bowl (dough will be sticky). Cover and refrigerate overnight.

3. Turn dough onto a lightly floured surface. Shape into a ball. Place in a 7-in.-wide-by-4-in.-tall paper panettone mold. Cover and let rise in a warm place until almost doubled, about 1½ hours.

4. Preheat oven to 350°. For topping, lightly beat egg with 1 Tbsp. water; gently brush over dough. Sprinkle with almonds and sugar. Bake until golden brown, 1¼-1½ hours, covering with foil after 30 minutes. Insert a metal or wood skewer horizontally through center of loaf. Allow bread to cool, upside down, by resting ends of skewer on tops of 2 large heavy cans.

1 PIECE 431 cal., 16g fat (8g sat. fat), 124mg chol., 340mg sod., 64g carb. (21g sugars, 2g fiber), 10g pro.

1

2

3

4

5

6

7

8

PEPPERONI CHEESE BREAD

As a stay-at-home mother of two little girls, I pack a lot of activity into my days. The bread machine makes it a snap for me to turn out this attractive loaf that gets its zip from cayenne pepper, pepperoni and Mexican cheese.

—Dusti Christensen, Goodridge, MN

PREP: 10 min. • **BAKE:** 4 hours • **MAKES:** 1 loaf (16 pieces)

- 1 cup water (70° to 80°)
- 1 Tbsp. butter
- 2 Tbsp. sugar
- 2 tsp. ground mustard
- ½ tsp. salt
- ½ tsp. cayenne pepper
- ¼ tsp. garlic powder
- 3 cups bread flour
- 2¼ tsp. active dry yeast
- 1½ cups shredded Mexican cheese blend
- 1 cup chopped pepperoni

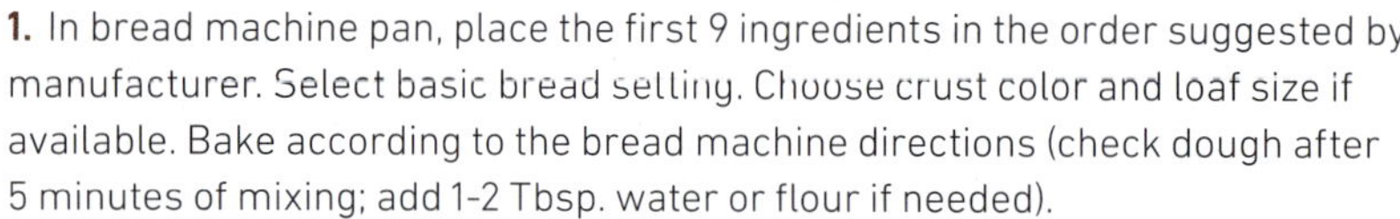

1. In bread machine pan, place the first 9 ingredients in the order suggested by manufacturer. Select basic bread setting. Choose crust color and loaf size if available. Bake according to the bread machine directions (check dough after 5 minutes of mixing; add 1-2 Tbsp. water or flour if needed).

2. Just before final kneading (your machine may audibly signal this), add cheese and pepperoni.

FREEZE OPTION Securely wrap and freeze cooled loaf in foil and place in freezer bag. To use, thaw at room temperature.

1 PIECE 177 cal., 8g fat (4g sat. fat), 19mg chol., 329mg sod., 19g carb. (2g sugars, 1g fiber), 7g pro.

"This bread is so good. It was soft and delicious. The cayenne pepper is just enough without being too hot. Thanks for sharing."

—SUSAN146, TASTEOFHOME.COM

ONION FRENCH BREAD LOAVES

Since I love variety in my cooking, I tried adding dried minced onion to my usual recipe in an attempt to copy a bread I had tasted, creating these two tasty loaves. Using the bread machine on the dough setting to make these is an easy timesaver.

—Ruth Fueller, Barmstedt, Germany

PREP: 25 min. + rising • **BAKE:** 20 min. • **MAKES:** 2 loaves (16 pieces each)

- 1 cup water (70° to 80°)
- ½ cup dried minced onion
- 1 Tbsp. sugar
- 2 tsp. salt
- 3 cups bread flour
- 2¼ tsp. active dry yeast
- 1 Tbsp. cornmeal
- 1 large egg yolk, lightly beaten

1. In bread machine pan, place first 6 ingredients in the order suggested by the manufacturer. Select dough setting (check dough after 5 minutes of mixing; add 1-2 Tbsp. water or flour if needed).

2. When cycle is completed, turn dough onto a lightly floured surface. Cover and let rest for 15 minutes. Divide dough in half. Roll each portion into a 15x10-in. rectangle. Roll up jelly-roll style, starting with a long side; pinch seams to seal. Pinch ends to seal and tuck under.

3. Sprinkle cornmeal onto a greased baking sheet. Place loaves on pan. Cover and let rise in a warm place until doubled, about 30 minutes. Brush with egg yolk. Make ¼-in.-deep cuts 2 in. apart in each loaf.

4. Bake at 375° until golden brown, 20-25 minutes. Remove from pan to a wire rack.

FREEZE OPTION Securely wrap and freeze cooled loaves in heavy-duty foil. To use, place a foil-wrapped loaf on a baking sheet and reheat in a 450° oven for 10-15 minutes. Carefully remove foil; return to the oven for a few minutes to crisp crust.

1 PIECE 46 cal., 0 fat (0 sat. fat), 7mg chol., 148mg sod., 10g carb. (1g sugars, 0 fiber), 2g pro.

PAIR IT WITH
Coconut Curry Soup, p. 77

OLIVE BREAD

You can bake this tender loaf with a colorful swirl of olives using just a few ingredients. This is a great bread to serve when you are hosting a large group at home or need something to take to a potluck.

—Ann Major, Oskaloosa, KS

PREP: 25 min. + rising • **BAKE:** 20 min. • **MAKES:** 1 loaf (30 pieces)

- 1 pkg. (¼ oz.) active dry yeast
- 1 cup warm water (110° to 115°)
- ¼ cup canola oil
- 1½ tsp. sugar
- ½ tsp. salt
- 2½ to 3 cups all-purpose flour
- ¾ cup sliced pitted kalamata or green olives

1. In a large bowl, dissolve yeast in warm water. Add oil, sugar, salt and 2 cups flour. Beat until smooth. Stir in enough remaining flour to form a firm dough.

2. Turn onto a floured surface; knead until smooth and elastic, 6-8 minutes. Place in a greased bowl, turning once to grease top. Cover and let rise in a warm place until doubled, about 1 hour.

3. Preheat oven to 375°. Spray a baking sheet with cooking spray; set aside. Punch down dough. Roll into a 16x12-in. rectangle. Sprinkle olives to within ½ in. of edges. Roll up jelly-roll style, starting with a long side; pinch seams to seal and tuck ends under. Place seam side down on prepared baking sheet. Cover and let rise until doubled, about 20 minutes.

4. Bake until golden brown, 20-25 minutes. Cool on a wire rack.

1 PIECE 62 cal., 3g fat (0 sat. fat), 0 chol., 112mg sod., 9g carb. (0 sugars, 0 fiber), 1g pro.
DIABETIC EXCHANGES ½ starch, ½ fat.

OLIVE OPTIONS

Although the recipe suggests using kalamata or green olives, any type of olive will do—as long as it's pitted and not stuffed with anything.

NO-KNEAD HARVEST BREAD

This loaf allows you to enjoy homemade bread without all the work. Fresh-baked slices are seriously irresistible.

—Christine Rukavena, Milwaukee, WI

PREP: 30 min. + rising • **BAKE:** 30 min. • **MAKES:** 1 loaf (16 pieces)

- ½ cup whole wheat flour
- ½ cup cornmeal
- ⅓ cup plus 2 Tbsp. assorted seeds, such as sesame seeds, flaxseed, sunflower kernels and poppy seeds, divided
- 1¾ tsp. salt
- ¼ tsp. active dry yeast
- 3 cups bread flour, divided
- 2¼ cups cool water (55° to 65°)
- 2 Tbsp. molasses
- Additional cornmeal

1. In a large bowl, combine whole wheat flour, cornmeal, ⅓ cup seeds, salt, yeast and 2½ cups bread flour. Stir in water and molasses until blended; dough will be wet and sticky.

2. Cover; let stand at room temperature until more than doubled in size and bubbles are present on surface, 12-18 hours. Stir in remaining bread flour.

3. Grease a baking sheet; sprinkle well with additional cornmeal. Turn the dough onto prepared pan. Using a spatula, gently shape into a 9-in. round loaf. Cover and let rise at room temperature for 2 hours or until the dough holds an indentation when gently pressed (loaf will slightly increase in size).

4. Arrange 1 oven rack at lowest rack setting; place second rack in middle of oven. Place an oven-safe skillet on bottom oven rack; preheat oven and skillet to 475°. Meanwhile, in a small saucepan, bring 2 cups water to a boil.

5. Gently press remaining seeds onto top of loaf. Wearing oven mitts, place bread on top rack. Pull the bottom rack out by 6-8 in.; add boiling water to skillet. (Work quickly and carefully, pouring water away from you. Don't worry if water is left in saucepan.) Carefully slide bottom rack back into place; quickly close door to trap steam in oven.

6. Reduce heat to 425°; bake for 10 minutes. Remove skillet from oven; bake bread 20-25 minutes longer or until deep golden brown and bread sounds hollow when center is tapped. Cool on a wire rack.

1 PIECE 134 cal., 2g fat (0 sat. fat), 0 chol., 265mg sod., 26g carb. (2g sugars, 2g fiber), 5g pro. **DIABETIC EXCHANGES** 1½ starch.

TO PREPARE IN A DUTCH OVEN After stirring in remaining bread flour, cover bowl again and let dough rise for 2 hours. Lightly oil an oven-safe 5-qt. round Dutch oven; cover and place in oven. Preheat the oven to 425°. Carefully remove hot Dutch oven. Remove lid; using a spatula, transfer dough directly from bowl into hot Dutch oven. Sprinkle remaining seeds over top. Cover and bake for 20 minutes. Uncover; bake 15-20 minutes longer or until deep golden brown and bread sounds hollow when center is tapped. Remove from pan to a wire rack. Bread may also be prepared in a clay bread baker; prepare baker according to manufacturer's directions.

BREADS

QUICK & EASY

BACON WALNUT BREAD WITH HONEY BUTTER

My savory loaf, filled with bacon bits, walnuts and blue cheese dressing, is complemented by the sweetness of honey-flavored butter. Cut yourself a thick slice, slather on the butter and enjoy!

—Pam Ivbuls, Elkhorn, NE

PREP: 25 min. • **BAKE:** 40 min. + cooling • **MAKES:** 1 loaf (16 pieces) and ¾ cup honey butter

- 2 cups all-purpose flour
- 2 tsp. baking powder
- ½ tsp. baking soda
- ¼ tsp. salt
- ¼ tsp. coarsely ground pepper
- 1 cup half-and-half cream
- ¾ cup refrigerated blue cheese salad dressing
- 2 large eggs, room temperature
- 1 Tbsp. honey
- ⅔ cup coarsely chopped walnuts
- ½ cup bacon bits

HONEY BUTTER

- ¾ cup butter, softened
- 2 Tbsp. honey

1. Preheat oven to 325°. In a large bowl, whisk the first 5 ingredients. In another bowl, whisk cream, salad dressing, eggs and honey until blended. Add to flour mixture; stir just until moistened. Fold in walnuts and bacon bits.

2. Transfer to a greased and floured 9x5-in. loaf pan. Bake until a toothpick inserted in center comes out clean, 40-50 minutes. Cool in pan for 10 minutes before removing to wire rack to cool completely.

3. For honey butter, in a small bowl, beat butter and honey. Serve with bread.

1 PIECE PLUS ABOUT 2 TSP. HONEY BUTTER 296 cal., 23g fat (9g sat. fat), 65mg chol., 350mg sod., 17g carb. (5g sugars, 1g fiber), 6g pro.

"Bursting with flavor, this bread is requested at all functions."

—BAKEOFF_QUEEN, TASTEOFHOME.COM

PAIR IT WITH
Corn Chowder with
Turkey & Bacon, p. 161

FAVORITE IRISH SODA BREAD

FAVORITE IRISH SODA BREAD

My best friend, Rita, shared this irresistible bread recipe with me. It bakes up high, with a golden brown top and a combination of sweet and savory flavors.

—Jan Alfano, Prescott, AZ

PREP: 20 min. • **BAKE:** 45 min. + cooling • **MAKES:** 1 loaf (12 wedges)

- 3 cups all-purpose flour
- ⅔ cup sugar
- 3 tsp. baking powder
- 1 tsp. salt
- 1 tsp. baking soda
- 1 cup raisins
- 2 large eggs, room temperature, beaten
- 1½ cups buttermilk
- 1 Tbsp. canola oil

1. Preheat oven to 350°. In a large bowl, combine first 5 ingredients. Stir in raisins. Set aside 1 Tbsp. beaten egg. In a bowl, combine buttermilk, oil and remaining eggs; stir into flour mixture just until moistened (dough will be sticky). Transfer dough to a greased 9-in. round baking pan; brush top with reserved egg.

2. Bake for 45-50 minutes or until a toothpick inserted in center comes out clean. Cool 10 minutes before removing from pan to a wire rack to cool. Cut into wedges.

1 WEDGE 227 cal., 3g fat (1g sat. fat), 36mg chol., 447mg sod., 46g carb. (20g sugars, 1g fiber), 6g pro.

PARMESAN HERB LOAF

This savory loaf is one of my very best quick bread recipes. I like to serve slices accompanied by individual ramekins filled with olive oil infused with herbs for dipping.

—Dianne Culley, Olive Branch, MS

PREP: 15 min. • **BAKE:** 30 min. • **MAKES:** 1 loaf (8 servings)

- 1¼ cups all-purpose flour
- 3 Tbsp. plus 1 tsp. grated Parmesan cheese, divided
- 1½ tsp. sugar
- 1½ tsp. dried minced onion
- 1¼ tsp. Italian seasoning, divided
- ½ tsp. baking powder
- ¼ tsp. baking soda
- ¼ tsp. salt
- ½ cup sour cream
- 2 Tbsp. plus 2 tsp. 2% milk
- 4½ tsp. butter, melted
- 1 large egg white, lightly beaten

1. In a small bowl, combine flour, 3 Tbsp. Parmesan cheese, sugar, onion, 1 tsp. Italian seasoning, baking powder, baking soda and salt. In another bowl, whisk sour cream, milk and butter. Stir into dry ingredients just until moistened.

2. Turn onto a floured surface; knead for 1 minute. Shape dough into a round loaf; place on a baking sheet coated with cooking spray. With kitchen scissors, cut a ¼-in.-deep cross in top of loaf. Brush with egg white. Sprinkle with the remaining 1 tsp. cheese and ¼ tsp. Italian seasoning.

3. Bake at 350° for 30-35 minutes or until golden brown. Serve warm.

1 PIECE 123 cal., 4g fat (2g sat. fat), 9mg chol., 217mg sod., 17g carb. (2g sugars, 1g fiber), 4g pro.

KETO BREAD

This keto-friendly recipe creates a toasty, golden loaf from almond flour, flaxseed, eggs and butter. It's perfect for everyday use, such as toast, sandwiches and more!

—*Taste of Home* Test Kitchen

PREP: 10 min. • **BAKE:** 45 min. • **MAKES:** 1 loaf (12 pieces)

- 2 cups almond flour
- ¼ cup ground flaxseed
- 2 tsp. baking powder
- ½ tsp. salt
- 5 large eggs, room temperature, lightly beaten
- ½ cup warm water
- ⅓ cup butter, melted

1. Preheat oven to 350°. Line an 8x4-in. loaf pan with parchment.

2. In a large bowl, whisk together flour, flaxseed, baking powder and salt. In another bowl, whisk eggs, water and butter. Stir into dry ingredients.

3. Transfer to prepared pan. Bake until a toothpick inserted in the center comes out clean, 45-50 minutes. Cool in pans for 5 minutes; remove to a wire rack to cool.

1 PIECE 194 cal., 15g fat (4g sat. fat), 91mg chol., 249mg sod., 8g carb. (1g sugars, 2g fiber), 9g pro.

HONEY BEER BREAD

It's true—this yummy bread requires only four ingredients! Simply combine self-rising flour, sugar, honey and beer, and pour the batter into the pan and bake.

—Cak Marshall, Salem, OR

PREP: 5 min. • **BAKE:** 45 min. + cooling • **MAKES:** 1 loaf (12 pieces)

- 3 cups self-rising flour
- 3 Tbsp. sugar
- ⅓ cup honey
- 1 bottle (12 oz.) beer

1. Preheat oven to 350°. In a large bowl, whisk flour and sugar. Stir in honey and beer just until moistened.

2. Transfer to a greased 8x4-in. loaf pan. Bake until a toothpick inserted in center comes out clean, 45-50 minutes. Cool in pan for 10 minutes; remove to a wire rack to cool.

1 PIECE 163 cal., 0 fat (0 sat. fat), 0 chol., 374mg sod., 35g carb. (12g sugars, 1g fiber), 3g pro.

COPYCAT STARBUCKS PUMPKIN BREAD

Skip the line and bake Starbucks pumpkin bread in your own kitchen. This copycat recipe is tops!
—*Taste of Home* Test Kitchen

PREP: 25 min. • **BAKE:** 1 hour + cooling • **MAKES:** 2 loaves (16 pieces each)

- 1 can (15 oz.) solid-pack pumpkin
- 4 large eggs, room temperature
- ¾ cup canola oil
- ⅔ cup water
- 2 cups sugar
- 1 cup honey
- 1½ tsp. vanilla extract
- 3½ cups all-purpose flour
- 2 tsp. baking soda
- 1½ tsp. salt
- 1½ tsp. ground cinnamon
- 1 tsp. ground nutmeg
- ½ tsp. ground cloves
- ½ tsp. ground ginger
- ½ cup salted pumpkin seeds or pepitas

1. Preheat oven to 350°. In a large bowl, beat pumpkin, eggs, oil, water, sugar, honey and vanilla until well blended. In another large bowl, whisk flour, baking soda, salt and spices; gradually beat into pumpkin mixture.

2. Transfer to 2 greased 9x5-in. loaf pans. Sprinkle tops with pumpkin seeds.

3. Bake 60-70 minutes or until a toothpick inserted in center comes out clean. Cool in pan for 10 minutes before removing to a wire rack to cool.

1 PIECE 202 cal., 7g fat (1g sat. fat), 23mg chol., 205mg sod., 33g carb. (22g sugars, 1g fiber), 3g pro.

PUMPKIN BREAD PARTICULARS

Why does my pumpkin bread sink in the middle? If your pumpkin bread sinks in the middle, that probably means either you let the batter stand for too long before baking or the bread is underdone.

How do you store pumpkin bread? To store pumpkin bread (and keep it ultra moist), wrap it tightly and place it in the refrigerator. It'll keep for up to 1 week. If you'd like to enjoy it for even longer, you can freeze the bread for up to 3 months.

GHOST PEPPER POPCORN CORNBREAD

I love popcorn and lots of spice and heat. I have recently been dabbling with ghost peppers and came up with this twist on classic cornbread. Try adding corn kernels for more texture.

—Allison Antalek, Cuyahoga Falls, OH

PREP: 40 min. • **BAKE:** 25 min. • **MAKES:** 8 servings

- ⅓ cup popcorn kernels
- 1 Tbsp. coconut oil or canola oil
- 1 cup all-purpose flour
- ½ cup sugar
- 2 tsp. baking powder
- ½ tsp. baking soda
- ½ tsp. salt
- ½ tsp. crushed ghost chile pepper or cayenne pepper
- 2 large eggs, room temperature
- 1½ cups 2% milk
- 4 Tbsp. melted butter, divided
- ½ cup chopped seeded jalapeno peppers

1. Preheat the oven to 400°. Heat a 10-in. cast-iron or other ovenproof skillet over medium heat. Add popcorn and coconut oil; cook until oil begins to sizzle. Cover and shake until popcorn stops popping, 3-4 minutes. Remove from heat.

2. Place popcorn in a food processor; process until ground. Transfer 2 cups ground popcorn to a large bowl (save remainder for another use). Stir in flour, sugar, baking powder, baking soda, salt and chile pepper. Add eggs, milk and 2 Tbsp. butter; beat just until moistened. Stir in jalapenos.

3. Add remaining 2 Tbsp. butter to skillet; place in oven to heat skillet. Carefully remove hot skillet from the oven. Add batter. Bake for 25-30 minutes or until top is golden brown and a toothpick inserted in center comes out clean. Cut into wedges and serve warm.

NOTE Wear disposable gloves when cutting hot peppers; the oils can burn skin. Avoid touching your face.

1 PIECE 241 cal., 10g fat (6g sat. fat), 65mg chol., 432mg sod., 34g carb. (15g sugars, 2g fiber), 6g pro.

"Easy to make and delicious too! Would recommend."

—PURPLECARROT, TASTEOFHOME.COM

ALMOND FLOUR BREAD

My almond flour bread recipe is keto-friendly. It's low in carbs with a fluffy, crumbly texture like a traditional loaf of bread.

—Caroline Baines, Spokane, WA

PREP: 10 min. • **BAKE:** 25 min. + cooling • **MAKES:** 10 servings

- 2 cups almond flour
- ¼ cup chia seeds
- 2 tsp. baking powder
- ½ tsp. salt
- 4 large eggs, room temperature
- ¼ cup unsweetened almond milk or water
- ¼ cup butter, melted or coconut oil, melted

1. Preheat the oven to 350°. In a large bowl, whisk almond flour, chia seeds, baking powder and salt. In another bowl, whisk eggs, milk and melted butter; stir into dry ingredients just until moistened. Pour into a parchment-lined 8x4-in. loaf pan.

2. Bake until a toothpick inserted in center comes out clean and top is golden brown, 25-30 minutes. Cool in pan for 10 minutes; remove to a wire rack to cool completely.

1 PIECE 219 cal., 19g fat (4g sat. fat), 87mg chol., 292mg sod., 7g carb. (1g sugars, 4g fiber), 8g pro.

ICE CREAM BREAD

Trade scoops of ice cream for slices with this two-ingredient bread. Full-fat ice cream will deliver the most flavorful, tender loaf, so now's the time to indulge.

—Katherine Kuehlman, Denver, CO

PREP: 5 min. • **BAKE:** 30 min. + cooling • **MAKES:** 1 loaf (6 pieces)

- 1 cup butter pecan ice cream, softened
- ¾ cup self-rising flour
- 1 Tbsp. sugar

In a small bowl, combine ice cream, flour and sugar. Transfer mixture to a 5¾x3x2-in. loaf pan coated with cooking spray. Bake at 350° until a toothpick inserted in the center comes out clean, 30-35 minutes. Cool 10 minutes; remove from pan to a wire rack.

1 PIECE 115 cal., 4g fat (2g sat. fat), 8mg chol., 217mg sod., 18g carb. (6g sugars, 0 fiber), 3g pro.

OLIVE QUICK BREAD

I've been baking for over 50 years, and I never get tired of trying new recipes for my family, friends and co-workers. Baking relaxes me. I feel like an artist creating a masterpiece of love. This savory loaf makes a lovely gift.

—Paula Marchesi, Lenhartsville, PA

PREP: 15 min. • **BAKE:** 45 min. + cooling • **MAKES:** 1 loaf (12 pieces)

- 1 Tbsp. canola oil
- 1 medium onion, finely chopped
- 2 cups all-purpose flour
- 1 Tbsp. minced fresh rosemary
- 1 tsp. baking soda
- ½ tsp. salt
- 2 large eggs, room temperature
- 1 cup buttermilk
- 2 Tbsp. butter, melted
- ¼ cup plus 2 Tbsp. shredded sharp cheddar cheese, divided
- ¼ cup each chopped pitted green and ripe olives

1. Preheat the oven to 350°. In a skillet, heat oil over medium-high heat. Add onion; cook and stir until tender, 2-3 minutes. Remove from heat.

2. In a large bowl, whisk flour, rosemary, baking soda and salt. In another bowl, whisk eggs, buttermilk and butter until blended. Add to flour mixture; stir just until moistened. Fold in ¼ cup cheese, olives and onion.

3. Transfer to a greased 8x4-in. loaf pan. Bake for 40 minutes. Sprinkle remaining cheese over top. Bake 5-10 minutes longer or until a toothpick inserted in the center comes out clean. Cool in pan for 10 minutes before removing to a wire rack to cool completely.

1 PIECE 150 cal., 6g fat (2g sat. fat), 41mg chol., 373mg sod., 18g carb. (1g sugars, 1g fiber), 5g pro.

"This was amazing. Huge hit. The flavors all came together, and it paired perfectly with beef stew. I will be making this recipe again."

—DEANNA783, TASTEOFHOME.COM

PAIR IT WITH

Salmon Sweet Potato Soup, p. 93

SWEET ITALIAN HOLIDAY BREAD

This is authentic ciambellotto, *a sweet loaf my great-grandmother used to bake in Italy. I still use her traditional recipe—the only update I made was for modern appliances.*

—Denise Perrin, Vancouver, WA

PREP: 15 min. • **BAKE:** 45 min. • **MAKES:** 1 loaf (20 pieces)

- 4 cups all-purpose flour
- 1 cup sugar
- 2 Tbsp. grated orange zest
- 3 tsp. baking powder
- 3 large eggs, room temperature
- ½ cup 2% milk
- ½ cup olive oil
- 1 large egg yolk, lightly beaten
- 1 Tbsp. coarse sugar

1. Preheat oven to 350°. In a large bowl, whisk flour, sugar, zest and baking powder. In another bowl, whisk eggs, milk and oil until blended. Add to flour mixture; stir just until moistened.

2. Shape into a 6-in. round loaf on a greased baking sheet. Brush top with egg yolk; sprinkle with sugar. Bake for 45-50 minutes or until a toothpick inserted in the center comes out clean. Cover top loosely with foil during the last 10 minutes if needed to prevent overbrowning. Remove from pan to a wire rack; serve warm.

1 PIECE 197 cal., 7g fat (1g sat. fat), 38mg chol., 87mg sod., 30g carb. (11g sugars, 1g fiber), 4g pro.

LAMBERTVILLE STATION COCONUT BREAD

Hearty bread made with toasted coconut is a longtime specialty at Lambertville Station in Lambertville, New Jersey. Enjoy this sweet treat the next time you crave distinctive bakery.

—Lambertville Station, Lambertville, NJ

PREP: 10 min. • **BAKE:** 40 min. + cooling • **MAKES:** 1 loaf (16 pieces)

- 3 cups all-purpose flour
- 1 cup sugar
- 3 tsp. baking powder
- ¾ tsp. salt
- 1 large egg, room temperature
- 1½ cups milk
- ¾ tsp. vanilla extract
- ¼ tsp. almond extract
- 1 cup sweetened shredded coconut, toasted

1. Preheat oven to 350°. In a large bowl, combine flour, sugar, baking powder and salt. Combine egg, milk and extracts. Stir into dry ingredients just until moistened. Fold in coconut.

2. Transfer to a greased 9x5-in. loaf pan. Bake for 40-50 minutes or until a toothpick inserted in center comes out clean. Cool for 10 minutes before removing from pan to a wire rack.

1 PIECE 182 cal., 3g fat (2g sat. fat), 14mg chol., 231mg sod., 34g carb. (16g sugars, 1g fiber), 4g pro. **DIABETIC EXCHANGES** 2 starch, ½ fat.

CARROT HONEY LOAF

As a health-care professional and busy mom, I believe my time and skills in the kitchen are among the most meaningful gifts I can give. This loaf is one I love to share for events like a housewarming or welcoming a new baby.

—Krystal Horudko, Charlottetown, PE

PREP: 20 min. • **BAKE:** 1 hour • **MAKES:** 1 loaf (16 pieces)

- 2 large eggs, room temperature
- ¾ cup canola oil
- ¾ cup honey
- 2 tsp. vanilla extract
- 1 cup all-purpose flour
- 1 cup whole wheat flour
- 2 tsp. baking powder
- 2 tsp. ground cinnamon
- 1 tsp. ground nutmeg
- ½ tsp. salt
- ¼ tsp. baking soda
- 2 cups grated carrots (about 3 large carrots)

1. Preheat the oven to 350°. In a bowl, combine eggs, oil, honey and vanilla; beat until smooth. In another bowl, whisk next 7 ingredients for 30 seconds. Stir flour mixture into egg mixture just until combined. Add carrots; mix well.

2. Pour batter into a lightly greased 9x5-in. loaf pan; bake until a toothpick inserted in the center comes out clean, about 1 hour. Cool for 10 minutes before removing to a wire rack.

1 PIECE 212 cal., 11g fat (1g sat. fat), 23mg chol., 173mg sod., 26g carb. (14g sugars, 2g fiber), 3g pro.

BEERNANA BREAD

It's simple arithmetic: Beer is good. Banana bread is good. Beernana bread is great! This recipe is a guaranteed crowd-pleaser. Even novices who don't know their way around the kitchen can pull this one off.

—Steve Cayford, Dubuque, IA

PREP: 15 min. • **BAKE:** 55 min. + cooling • **MAKES:** 1 loaf (16 pieces)

- 3 cups self-rising flour
- ¾ cup quick-cooking oats
- ½ cup packed brown sugar
- 1½ cups mashed ripe bananas (about 3 medium)
- 1 bottle (12 oz.) wheat beer
- ¼ cup maple syrup
- 2 Tbsp. olive oil
- 1 Tbsp. sesame seeds
- ¼ tsp. kosher salt

1. Preheat oven to 375°. In a large bowl, mix flour, oats and brown sugar. In another bowl, mix bananas, beer and maple syrup until blended. Add to flour mixture; stir just until moistened.

2. Transfer to a greased 9x5-in. loaf pan. Drizzle with oil; sprinkle with sesame seeds and salt. Bake for 55-60 minutes or until a toothpick inserted in the center comes out clean. Cool in pan for 10 minutes before removing to a wire rack to cool.

1 PIECE 173 cal., 2g fat (0 sat. fat), 0 chol., 304mg sod., 35g carb. (13g sugars, 1g fiber), 3g pro. **DIABETIC EXCHANGES** 2 starch, ½ fat.

CARROT HONEY LOAF

PINA COLADA ZUCCHINI BREAD

At my husband's urging, I entered this recipe at the Pennsylvania Farm Show—and won first place! You'll love the cakelike texture and tropical flavors.

—Sharon Rydbom, Tipton, PA

PREP: 25 min. • **BAKE:** 45 min. + cooling • **MAKES:** 3 loaves (12 pieces each)

- 4 cups all-purpose flour
- 3 cups sugar
- 2 tsp. baking powder
- 1½ tsp. salt
- 1 tsp. baking soda
- 4 large eggs, room temperature
- 1½ cups canola oil
- 1 tsp. each coconut, rum and vanilla extracts
- 3 cups shredded zucchini
- 1 cup canned crushed pineapple, drained
- ½ cup chopped walnuts or chopped pecans

1. Preheat oven to 350°. Line 3 greased 8x4-in. loaf pans with parchment; grease paper.

2. In a large bowl, combine flour, sugar, baking powder, salt and baking soda. In another bowl, whisk eggs, oil and extracts. Stir into dry ingredients just until moistened. Fold in zucchini, pineapple and walnuts.

3. Transfer to prepared pans. Bake for 45-55 minutes or until a toothpick inserted in center comes out clean. Cool for 10 minutes before removing from pans to wire racks. Gently remove paper.

1 PIECE 225 cal., 11g fat (1g sat. fat), 24mg chol., 165mg sod., 29g carb. (18g sugars, 1g fiber), 3g pro.

BAKING WITH ZUCCHINI

Do you have to peel zucchini before using it in zucchini bread? No, you don't! The skin is so thin and supple that it hardly adds any texture to the loaf. In fact, we love the few bright pops of green it adds to the loaf's crumb. However, if you want to hide the zucchini as much as possible, peel it beforehand.

What's the best way to grate zucchini for zucchini bread? The best way to grate zucchini is with whatever tool is fastest for the amount of zucchini you're grating. If you're just grating a few zucchini, as you would for this bread recipe, use a box grater. Any more zucchini than that should be grated with a food processor using the grating attachment.

ROASTED BUTTERNUT SQUASH BREAD

Butternut squash is so versatile, I use it to make a sweet and savory bread that's delicious for breakfast, snacking or even dessert.

—Sarah Meuser, New Milford, CT

PREP: 40 min. • **BAKE:** 55 min. + cooling • **MAKES:** 1 loaf (16 pieces)

- 3½ cups cubed peeled butternut squash (1-in. pieces)
- 2 Tbsp. olive oil
- ½ cup butter, softened
- ½ cup sugar
- ½ cup packed brown sugar
- 2 large eggs, room temperature
- 1 tsp. vanilla extract
- 1½ cups whole wheat pastry flour
- 1 tsp. baking soda
- 1 tsp. ground cinnamon
- ¾ tsp. salt
- ½ cup fat-free plain Greek yogurt
- ¼ tsp. fine sea salt

1. Preheat oven to 375°. Place squash in a greased 15x10x1-in. baking pan. Drizzle with oil and toss to coat. Roast until tender, 25-30 minutes. Reduce oven setting to 325°.

2. Transfer squash to a bowl; mash coarsely. In a large bowl, beat butter and sugars until blended. Add eggs, 1 at a time, beating well after each addition. Beat in mashed squash and vanilla. In another bowl, whisk flour, baking soda, cinnamon and salt; add to butter mixture alternately with yogurt, beating well after each addition.

3. Transfer to a greased 9x5-in. loaf pan; sprinkle with sea salt. Bake until a toothpick inserted in center comes out clean, 55-65 minutes. Cool in pan for 10 minutes before removing from pan to a wire rack to cool.

1 PIECE 179 cal., 8g fat (4g sat. fat), 39mg chol., 281mg sod., 24g carb. (14g sugars, 2g fiber), 3g pro.

"This bread is so good! It is moist and flavorful. I will make this again."

—PATTIEJEAN, TASTEOFHOME.COM

GOLDEN SWEET ONION ROUND

Put your cast-iron skillet to a new use when you bake up this hearty cornbread in it.
—*Taste of Home* Test Kitchen

PREP: 35 min. • **BAKE:** 20 min. + standing • **MAKES:** 8 servings

- 2 Tbsp. butter
- 1 large sweet onion, halved and thinly sliced
- 4 tsp. chopped seeded jalapeno pepper
- ½ tsp. chili powder, divided
- 2 Tbsp. brown sugar, divided
- 1½ cups all-purpose flour
- 1 cup yellow cornmeal
- 3 Tbsp. sugar
- 2 tsp. baking powder
- ½ tsp. kosher salt
- ½ tsp. baking soda
- 1¼ cups buttermilk
- 2 large eggs, room temperature, lightly beaten
- ¼ cup butter, melted
- ¾ cup shredded cheddar cheese
- 1 can (4 oz.) chopped green chiles

CRANBERRY BUTTER

- ½ cup whole-berry cranberry sauce
- ½ tsp. grated lime zest
- ½ cup butter, softened

1. In a 10-in. cast-iron skillet, melt 2 Tbsp. butter and tilt to coat bottom and side. Add onion, jalapeno and ¼ tsp. chili powder; cook over medium-low heat until onion is lightly browned and tender. Stir in 1 Tbsp. brown sugar until dissolved; set aside.

2. In a large bowl, combine flour, cornmeal, sugar, baking powder, salt, baking soda, and remaining chili powder and brown sugar. In a small bowl, whisk buttermilk, eggs and melted butter. Stir into dry ingredients just until moistened. Fold in cheese and chiles.

3. Pour over onion mixture in skillet. Bake at 425° for 20-25 minutes or until golden brown. Meanwhile, for cranberry butter, in a small saucepan, cook sauce and zest over low heat until heated through. Cool completely.

4. Let cornbread stand for 10 minutes. Invert onto a serving platter; cut into wedges. Pour cranberry mixture over softened butter and serve with cornbread.

NOTE Wear disposable gloves when cutting hot peppers; the oils can burn skin. Avoid touching your face.

1 PIECE WITH 1 TBSP. BUTTER AND 1 TBSP. CRANBERRY MIXTURE 468 cal., 25g fat (16g sat. fat), 118mg chol., 626mg sod., 52g carb. (17g sugars, 3g fiber), 10g pro.

AVOCADO QUICK BREAD

AVOCADO QUICK BREAD

I love to have avocados on hand, but they sometimes get too ripe before I eat them. This is a tasty, unusual way to use them. It sounds a little weird but tastes fantastic! You get all the benefits of avocado in a moist baked good. To enjoy this bread as a dessert, serve it warm with chocolate or vanilla ice cream and chocolate syrup.

—Katherine Wollgast, Troy, MO

PREP: 25 min. • **BAKE:** 1 hour + cooling • **MAKES:** 1 loaf (16 pieces)

- 2¼ cups all-purpose flour, divided
- 1¼ cups sugar, divided
- 1 Tbsp. baking cocoa
- ¼ tsp. ground cinnamon
- 3 Tbsp. butter, softened
- ¾ cup dark chocolate chips, divided
- 1 tsp. baking powder
- 1 tsp. baking soda
- ½ tsp. salt
- 2 large eggs, room temperature
- 1 cup mashed ripe avocados (about 2 medium)
- ½ cup buttermilk
- 1 tsp. vanilla extract
- ¼ cup chopped walnuts

1. Preheat the oven to 350°. For topping, in a small bowl, combine ¼ cup flour, ¼ cup sugar, cocoa and cinnamon. Cut in butter until crumbly. Stir in ¼ cup chocolate chips.

2. In a large bowl, whisk baking powder, baking soda, salt and remaining 2 cups flour and 1 cup sugar. In another bowl, whisk eggs, avocado, buttermilk and vanilla until blended. Add to flour mixture; stir just until moistened. Fold in chopped walnuts and remaining ½ cup chocolate chips.

3. Transfer to a greased 9x5-in. loaf pan; sprinkle with reserved topping. Bake for 60-70 minutes or until a toothpick inserted in center comes out clean. Cool in pan for 10 minutes before removing to a wire rack to cool completely.

1 PIECE 237 cal., 9g fat (4g sat. fat), 29mg chol., 228mg sod., 38g carb. (22g sugars, 2g fiber), 4g pro.

PULL-APART GARLIC BREAD

People go wild over this golden, garlicky loaf whenever I serve it. There's intense flavor in every bite.

—Carol Shields, Summerville, PA

PREP: 10 min. + rising • **BAKE:** 30 min. • **MAKES:** 16 servings

- ¼ cup butter, melted
- 1 Tbsp. dried parsley flakes
- 1 tsp. garlic powder
- ¼ tsp. garlic salt
- 1 loaf (1 lb.) frozen white bread dough, thawed

1. In a small bowl, combine butter, parsley, garlic powder and garlic salt. Cut dough into 1-in. pieces; dip into butter mixture. Layer in a greased 9x5-in. loaf pan. Cover and let rise until doubled, about 1 hour.

2. Bake at 350° until golden brown, about 30 minutes.

1 SERVING 104 cal., 4g fat (2g sat. fat), 8mg chol., 215mg sod., 15g carb. (1g sugars, 1g fiber), 3g pro.

GRANDMA'S ONION SQUARES

My grandma brought this recipe with her when she emigrated from Italy as a young wife and mother. It is still a family favorite.

—Janet Eddy, Stockton, CA

PREP: 40 min. • **BAKE:** 35 min. • **MAKES:** 9 servings

- 2 Tbsp. olive oil
- 2 cups sliced onion
- 1 tsp. salt, divided
- ¼ tsp. pepper
- 2 cups all-purpose flour
- 3 tsp. baking powder
- 5 Tbsp. shortening
- ⅔ cup 2% milk
- 1 large egg, room temperature
- ¾ cup sour cream

1. Preheat oven to 400°. In a large skillet, heat oil over medium heat. Add onion; cook and stir until softened, 8-10 minutes. Reduce heat to medium-low; cook until deep golden brown, 30-40 minutes, stirring occasionally. Stir in ½ tsp. salt and pepper.

2. Meanwhile, in a large bowl, combine flour, baking powder and remaining ½ tsp. salt. Cut in shortening until mixture resembles coarse crumbs. Stir in milk just until moistened. Press into a greased 9-in. square baking pan; top with onion.

3. Combine egg and sour cream; spread over onion layer. Bake until golden brown, 35-40 minutes. Cut into squares. Serve warm.

1 PIECE 256 cal., 15g fat (5g sat. fat), 27mg chol., 447mg sod., 25g carb. (3g sugars, 1g fiber), 5g pro.

PARMESAN ZUCCHINI BREAD

This loaf has a rugged, textured look that adds to its old-fashioned appeal. The mild Parmesan flavor nicely complements the zucchini, which adds bits of green color to every tender slice.

—Chris Wilson, Sellersville, PA

PREP: 10 min. • **BAKE:** 1 hour + cooling • **MAKES:** 1 loaf (16 pieces)

- 3 cups all-purpose flour
- 3 Tbsp. grated Parmesan cheese
- 1 tsp. salt
- ½ tsp. baking powder
- ½ tsp. baking soda
- 2 large eggs, room temperature
- 1 cup buttermilk
- ⅓ cup sugar
- ⅓ cup butter, melted
- 1 cup shredded peeled zucchini
- 1 Tbsp. grated onion

1. In a large bowl, combine flour, cheese, salt, baking powder and baking soda. In another bowl, whisk eggs, buttermilk, sugar and butter. Stir into dry ingredients just until moistened. Fold in zucchini and onion.

2. Pour into a greased and floured 9x5-in. loaf pan. Bake at 350° until a toothpick inserted in the center comes out clean, about 1 hour. Cool for 10 minutes before removing from pan to a wire rack.

1 PIECE 156 cal., 5g fat (3g sat. fat), 35mg chol., 288mg sod., 23g carb. (5g sugars, 1g fiber), 4g pro.

GRANDMA'S ONION SQUARES

BREADS

ROLLS, BISCUITS & MORE

HERB-CHEESE ROLLS

These low-fat rolls are flavored with garlic, dill and cheese, and they're yummy even without butter!

—Nancy Boyd, Midlothian, VA

PREP: 45 min. + rising • **BAKE:** 20 min. • **MAKES:** 2 dozen

- 4 to 4½ cups all-purpose flour
- ¼ cup sugar
- 2 Tbsp. mashed potato flakes
- 1 pkg. (¼ oz.) active dry yeast
- 2 tsp. salt
- ½ tsp. dill weed
- ¼ tsp. garlic powder
- 2 cups water
- 4½ tsp. butter
- 1 cup old-fashioned oats
- 1 large egg, room temperature
- ¾ cup shredded part-skim mozzarella cheese

TOPPING

- 2 Tbsp. fat-free milk
- 4½ tsp. grated Parmesan cheese
- ½ tsp. garlic powder
- ½ tsp. dill weed
- ½ tsp. dried basil

1. In a large bowl, combine 1½ cups flour, sugar, potato flakes, yeast, salt, dill and garlic powder. In a small saucepan, bring water and butter just to a boil.

2. In a small bowl, pour boiling liquid over oats. Let stand until mixture cools down to 120°-130°, stirring occasionally. Add to dry ingredients. Beat just until moistened. Add egg; beat until smooth. Stir in enough remaining flour to form a firm dough (dough will be sticky).

3. Turn onto a floured surface; knead until smooth and elastic, 6-8 minutes. Knead in mozzarella. Place in a large bowl coated with cooking spray, turning once to coat top. Cover and let rise in a warm place until doubled, about 1¼ hours.

4. Punch down dough. Turn onto a lightly floured surface. Divide into 24 pieces. Shape each into a ball. Place in a 13x9-in. baking pan coated with cooking spray; brush milk over rolls.

5. In a small bowl, combine remaining ingredients; sprinkle over tops. Cover and let rise until nearly doubled, about 45 minutes.

6. Preheat oven to 375°. Bake until golden brown, 20-25 minutes. Remove from pan to a wire rack. Refrigerate leftovers.

1 ROLL 119 cal., 2g fat (1g sat. fat), 13mg chol., 228mg sod., 21g carb. (3g sugars, 1g fiber), 4g pro. **DIABETIC EXCHANGES** 1½ starch.

"I made a double batch of these for Thanksgiving dinner, and the whole family argued over who would take the leftovers home. I was asked to make them again for Christmas!"

—KKRAUSERN, TASTEOFHOME.COM

PAIR IT WITH
Best Seafood Chowder,
p. 80

BAKING POWDER DROP BISCUITS

BAKING POWDER DROP BISCUITS

One day I had company coming and realized I had run out of biscuit mix. I'd never made biscuits from scratch before, but I decided to give this recipe a try. Now this is the only way I make them!

—Sharon Evans, Clear Lake, IA

TAKES: 20 min. • **MAKES:** 1 dozen

- 2 cups all-purpose flour
- 2 Tbsp. sugar
- 4 tsp. baking powder
- ½ tsp. cream of tartar
- ½ tsp. salt
- ½ cup shortening
- ⅔ cup 2% milk
- 1 large egg, room temperature

1. Preheat oven to 450°. In a large bowl, combine first 5 ingredients. Cut in shortening until mixture resembles coarse crumbs. In a small bowl, whisk milk and egg. Stir into crumb mixture just until moistened.

2. Drop by ¼ cupfuls 2 in. apart onto an ungreased baking sheet. Bake until golden brown, 10-12 minutes. Serve warm.

1 BISCUIT 170 cal., 9g fat (2g sat. fat), 17mg chol., 271mg sod., 19g carb. (3g sugars, 1g fiber), 3g pro.

HERB & SUN-DRIED TOMATO MUFFINS

Mom often served these muffins instead of bread or buns. Now I bake them to serve with soup or chili.

—Elizabeth King, Duluth, MN

PREP: 20 min. • **BAKE:** 20 min. • **MAKES:** 1 dozen

- 2 cups all-purpose flour
- 2 tsp. baking powder
- 1 tsp. snipped fresh dill or ¼ tsp. dill weed
- 1 tsp. minced fresh thyme or ¼ tsp. dried thyme
- ½ tsp. baking soda
- ½ tsp. salt
- ½ tsp. pepper
- 1 large egg, room temperature
- 1¼ cups 2% milk
- ¼ cup olive oil
- ½ cup shredded cheddar cheese
- ½ cup oil-packed sun-dried tomatoes, finely chopped

1. Preheat the oven to 375°. In a large bowl, mix first 7 ingredients. In another bowl, whisk egg, milk and oil. Add to flour mixture; stir just until moistened. Fold in cheese and tomatoes.

2. Fill 12 greased muffin cups three-fourths full. Bake until a toothpick inserted in center comes out clean, 18-20 minutes. Cool 5 minutes before removing from pan to a wire rack. Serve warm.

1 MUFFIN 161 cal., 8g fat (2g sat. fat), 25mg chol., 277mg sod., 18g carb. (2g sugars, 1g fiber), 5g pro. **DIABETIC EXCHANGES** 1½ fat, 1 starch.

EASY ONION CRESCENT ROLLS

I dress up a tube of crescent roll dough to create these golden bites. They're a nice addition to any buffet.

—Barbara Nowakowski, North Tonawanda, NY

TAKES: 20 min. • **MAKES:** 8 servings

- 1 tube (8 oz.) refrigerated crescent rolls
- 1⅓ cups french-fried onions, divided
- 1 large egg
- 1 Tbsp. water

1. Unroll crescent dough and separate into triangles. Sprinkle each with about 2 Tbsp. onions. Roll up each from the wide end; place on an ungreased foil-lined baking sheet. Curve ends down to form crescents.

2. Beat egg and water; brush over dough. Sprinkle with remaining onions. Bake at 400° until golden brown, 10-12 minutes. Serve warm.

1 ROLL 181 cal., 11g fat (3g sat. fat), 27mg chol., 311mg sod., 15g carb. (2g sugars, 0 fiber), 3g pro.

FLAKY ITALIAN BISCUITS

A biscuit mix makes it easy to stir up a batch of these tender biscuits.

—Tami Christman, Soda Springs, ID

TAKES: 30 min. • **MAKES:** 8 biscuits

- 2 cups Biscuit Baking Mix (p. 205)
- 1 tsp. Italian seasoning
- ½ cup half-and-half cream

1. In a small bowl, mix biscuit baking mix and Italian seasoning; stir in half-and-half just until moistened. Turn dough onto a lightly floured surface; knead gently 10 times. Pat or roll out to ½-in. thickness; cut with a 2½-in. biscuit cutter.

2. Place 2 in. apart on an ungreased baking sheet. Bake at 425° until golden brown, 13-16 minutes. Serve warm.

1 SERVING 179 cal., 10g fat (3g sat. fat), 8mg chol., 255mg sod., 18g carb. (1g sugars, 1g fiber), 3g pro.

GRANDMA'S YEAST ROLLS

My grandmother used to make these rolls for family get-togethers and holidays. The applesauce may be an unexpected ingredient, but it adds a lot of flavor.

—Nancy Spoth, Festus, MO

PREP: 20 min. + rising • **BAKE:** 15 min. • **MAKES:** 2 dozen

- 1 pkg. (¼ oz.) active dry yeast
- 1 cup 2% milk (110°-115°)
- ¼ cup sugar
- ¼ cup unsweetened applesauce
- 2 large egg whites, room temperature, beaten
- 1 tsp. salt
- 3½ to 4 cups all-purpose flour

1. In a large bowl, dissolve yeast in warm milk. Add sugar, applesauce, egg whites, salt and 2 cups flour; beat until smooth. Stir in enough remaining flour to form a soft dough.

2. Turn onto a lightly floured surface; knead until smooth and elastic, 6-8 minutes (dough will be slightly sticky). Place in a bowl coated with cooking spray, turning once to coat top. Cover and let rise in a warm place until doubled, about 1 hour.

3. Turn dough onto a lightly floured surface; divide into 24 pieces. Shape each piece into an 8-in. rope; tie into a knot. Place on 2 greased baking sheets.

4. Cover and let rise until doubled, about 30 minutes. Bake at 375° until golden brown, 12-16 minutes. Remove from pans to wire racks to cool.

1 ROLL 83 cal., 1g fat (1g sat. fat), 1mg chol., 109mg sod., 17g carb. (0 sugars, 1g fiber), 3g pro. **DIABETIC EXCHANGES** 1 starch.

"These are positively excellent!"

—PONGO7868, TASTEOFHOME.COM

PAIR IT WITH
Old-Fashioned Split Pea Soup with Ham Bone, p. 16

CARAWAY RYE DINNER ROLLS

Denser than most, these onion-infused buns are ideal for dipping in hearty stews. The egg wash gives them an attractive shine.

—Deborah Maki, Kamloops, BC

PREP: 35 min. + rising • **BAKE:** 15 min. • **MAKES:** 1½ dozen

- 1¼ cups rye flour
- ½ cup wheat germ
- 2 Tbsp. caraway seeds
- 1 pkg. (¼ oz.) active dry yeast
- 1 tsp. salt
- 3 cups all-purpose flour
- 1 cup 2% milk
- ½ cup water
- 3 Tbsp. butter
- 2 Tbsp. honey
- ⅓ cup finely chopped onion

EGG WASH

- 1 large egg
- 2 tsp. water

1. In a large bowl, mix first 5 ingredients and 1 cup all-purpose flour. In a small saucepan, heat milk, water, butter and honey to 120°-130°. Add to dry ingredients; beat on medium speed for 3 minutes. Stir in onion and enough remaining flour to form a soft dough (dough will be sticky).

2. Turn dough onto a floured surface; knead until smooth and elastic, 6-8 minutes. Place dough in a greased bowl, turning once to grease the top. Cover and let rise until doubled, about 1 hour.

3. Punch down dough. Turn onto a lightly floured surface. Divide and shape into 18 balls. Place 2 in. apart on greased baking sheets. Cover with a kitchen towel; let rise in a warm place until almost doubled, about 45 minutes. Preheat oven to 400°.

4. In a small bowl, whisk egg and water; brush over rolls. Bake until lightly browned, 11-14 minutes. Remove to wire racks to cool.

1 ROLL 152 cal., 3g fat (2g sat. fat), 17mg chol., 158mg sod., 26g carb. (3g sugars, 2g fiber), 5g pro.

COPYCAT TEXAS ROADHOUSE ROLLS

A touch of honey adds a bit of sweetness to these rolls. Serve them warm with honey-cinnamon butter alongside any entree, and guests will be impressed!

—*Taste of Home* Test Kitchen

PREP: 25 min. + rising • **BAKE:** 20 min. • **MAKES:** 2 dozen

- 1 pkg. (¼ oz.) active dry yeast
- 1 cup warm 2% milk (110°-115°)
- 1 large egg, room temperature
- 1 large egg yolk, room temperature
- ½ cup plus 2 Tbsp. butter, melted, divided
- 2 Tbsp. honey
- 1½ tsp. salt
- 3½ cups bread flour

1. Dissolve yeast in warm milk. In another bowl, combine egg, egg yolk, ½ cup butter, honey, salt, yeast mixture and 2 cups flour; beat on medium speed until smooth. Stir in enough remaining flour to form a soft dough (dough will be sticky).

2. Turn dough onto a floured surface; knead until smooth and elastic, 6-8 minutes. Place in a greased bowl, turning once to grease top. Cover and let rise in a warm place until doubled, about 1 hour 15 minutes.

3. Punch down dough; turn onto a lightly floured surface. Divide and shape into 24 balls; place 12 each in 2 greased 8x8-in. baking pans. Cover with kitchen towels; let rise in a warm place until doubled, about 1 hour.

4. Preheat oven to 350°. Bake until golden brown, 20-25 minutes. Brush rolls with remaining 2 Tbsp. melted butter.

1 ROLL 131 cal., 6g fat (3g sat. fat), 29mg chol., 194mg sod., 17g carb. (2g sugars, 1g fiber), 3g pro.

1

2

3

4

CHIVE PINWHEEL ROLLS

These light, pleasant-tasting dinner rolls complement almost any entree. With the chive filling swirled through a golden bread, they're suited for weeknight meals and holiday gatherings alike.

—Ann Niemela, Ely, MN

PREP: 25 min. + rising • **BAKE:** 30 min. • **MAKES:** 15 rolls

- 3½ cups all-purpose flour
- 3 Tbsp. sugar
- 1 pkg. (¼ oz.) active dry yeast
- 1½ tsp. salt
- 1 cup 2% milk
- ⅓ cup canola oil
- ¼ cup water
- ¼ cup mashed potatoes (without added milk and butter)
- 1 large egg, room temperature

CHIVE FILLING

- 1 cup sour cream
- 1 cup minced chives
- 1 large egg yolk
- Butter, melted

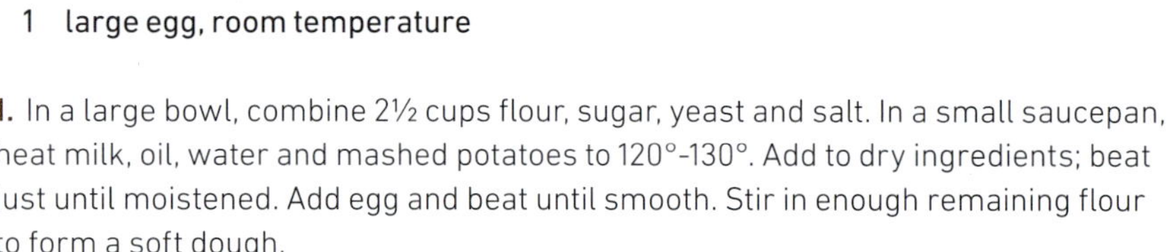

1. In a large bowl, combine 2½ cups flour, sugar, yeast and salt. In a small saucepan, heat milk, oil, water and mashed potatoes to 120°-130°. Add to dry ingredients; beat just until moistened. Add egg and beat until smooth. Stir in enough remaining flour to form a soft dough.

2. Turn onto a floured surface; knead until smooth and elastic, 6-8 minutes. Place in a greased bowl, turning once to grease top. Cover and let rise in a warm place until doubled, about 1 hour.

3. Turn dough onto a floured surface. Roll into a 15x10-in. rectangle. For filling, in a bowl, combine sour cream, chives and egg yolk. Spread over dough to within ½ in. of edges.

4. Roll up jelly-roll style, starting with a long side; pinch seam to seal. Cut into 1-in. slices. Place cut side down in a 13x9-in. baking pan. Cover and let rise until doubled, about 1 hour.

5. Bake at 350° until golden brown, 30-35 minutes. Brush with butter. Cool on a wire rack. Refrigerate leftovers.

1 ROLL 214 cal., 9g fat (3g sat. fat), 41mg chol., 258mg sod., 27g carb. (4g sugars, 1g fiber), 5g pro.

PAIR IT WITH

Hearty Homemade Chicken Noodle Soup, p. 20

HAM BISCUITS

Our Test Kitchen pros made ordinary biscuits even heartier by stirring in ground ham. These hand-held goodies taste wonderful fresh from the oven.

—*Taste of Home* Test Kitchen

PREP: 30 min. • **BAKE:** 15 min. • **MAKES:** 10 biscuits

- 1 cup cubed fully cooked ham
- 1 cup all-purpose flour
- 1 tsp. baking powder
- ¼ tsp. baking soda
- ¼ tsp. each onion powder, garlic powder and ground mustard
- 3 Tbsp. shortening
- 1 tsp. minced chives
- 6 Tbsp. buttermilk
- 1 Tbsp. butter, melted

1. Preheat oven to 450°. In a food processor, process ham until ground; set aside. In a large bowl, combine flour, baking powder, baking soda, onion powder, garlic powder and mustard. Cut in shortening until mixture is crumbly. Fold in ham and chives. Add buttermilk; stir just until dough clings together.

2. Turn dough onto a lightly floured surface; knead gently 10-12 times. Roll dough to ½-in. thickness. Cut with a floured 2½-in. biscuit cutter. Place in a large ungreased cast-iron or other ovenproof skillet. Bake until golden brown, 13-15 minutes. Brush with butter. Serve warm.

1 BISCUIT 116 cal., 6g fat (2g sat. fat), 11mg chol., 272mg sod., 10g carb. (1g sugars, 0 fiber), 4g pro.

EASY CHEESY BISCUITS

I love homemade biscuits but not the rolling and cutting that goes into making them. The drop biscuit method solves everything!

—Christy Addison, Clarksville, OH

TAKES: 30 min. • **MAKES:** 1 dozen

- 3 cups all-purpose flour
- 3 tsp. baking powder
- 1 Tbsp. sugar
- 1 tsp. salt
- ¾ tsp. cream of tartar
- ½ cup cold butter
- 1 cup shredded sharp cheddar cheese
- 1 garlic clove, minced
- ¼ to ½ tsp. crushed red pepper flakes
- 1¼ cups 2% milk

1. Preheat oven to 450°. In a large bowl, whisk flour, baking powder, sugar, salt and cream of tartar. Cut in butter until mixture resembles coarse crumbs. Stir in cheese, garlic and pepper flakes. Add milk; stir just until moistened.

2. Drop dough by heaping ¼ cupfuls 2 in. apart onto a greased baking sheet. Bake for 18-20 minutes or until golden brown. Serve warm.

1 BISCUIT 237 cal., 12g fat (7g sat. fat), 32mg chol., 429mg sod., 26g carb. (2g sugars, 1g fiber), 7g pro.

GLUTEN-FREE CORNMEAL MUFFINS

Serve these golden bites warm, with butter, honey or even salsa! Any leftovers are terrific reheated in foil in the oven.

—Laura Fall-Sutton, Buhl, ID

PREP: 20 min. • **BAKE:** 15 min. • **MAKES:** 1 dozen

- ¾ cup fat-free milk
- ¼ cup honey
- 2 Tbsp. canola oil
- 1 large egg, room temperature
- 1 large egg white, room temperature
- 1½ cups cornmeal
- ½ cup amaranth flour
- 2½ tsp. baking powder
- ½ tsp. xanthan gum
- ½ tsp. salt
- 1 cup frozen corn, thawed
- ¾ cup shredded reduced-fat Monterey Jack cheese or Mexican cheese blend

1. In a large bowl, beat first 5 ingredients until well blended. Combine cornmeal, amaranth flour, baking powder, xanthan gum and salt; gradually beat into milk mixture until blended. Stir in corn and cheese.

2. Coat 12 muffin cups with cooking spray or use foil liners; fill the cups three-fourths full with batter. Bake at 375° until a toothpick inserted in the center comes out clean, 15-18 minutes. Cool for 5 minutes before removing from pan to a wire rack.

NOTE Read all ingredient labels for possible gluten content prior to use. If you're concerned that your brand may contain gluten, contact the company.

1 MUFFIN 169 cal., 5g fat (1g sat. fat), 23mg chol., 263mg sod., 27g carb. (7g sugars, 2g fiber), 6g pro.

EASY CHEESY BISCUITS

PAIR IT WITH
Grandma's Oxtail Soup, p. 69

TENDER WHOLE WHEAT ROLLS

Even though these are whole wheat rolls they have a light texture and are soft and tender. This recipe reminds me of lots of happy meals with my family.

—Wilma Orlano, Carroll, IA

PREP: 40 min. + rising • **BAKE:** 10 min. • **MAKES:** 2 dozen

1½ cups boiling water
⅓ cup wheat bran
3 Tbsp. ground flaxseed
1½ tsp. salt
1 tsp. ground cinnamon
⅓ cup honey
¼ cup canola oil
2 pkg. (¼ oz. each) active dry yeast
¼ cup warm water (110°-115°)
2 tsp. sugar
1½ cups whole wheat flour
2½ to 3 cups bread flour

1. In a small bowl, pour boiling water over wheat bran, flaxseed, salt and cinnamon. Add honey and oil. Let stand until mixture cools to 110°-115°, stirring occasionally.

2. In a large bowl, dissolve yeast in warm water. Add sugar, whole wheat flour and wheat bran mixture. Beat on medium speed for 3 minutes. Stir in enough bread flour to form a firm dough.

3. Turn dough onto a floured surface; knead until smooth and elastic, 6-8 minutes. Place in a greased bowl, turning once to grease the top. Cover and let rise in a warm place until doubled, about 1 hour. Punch down dough.

4. Turn onto a lightly floured surface; divide dough into 24 pieces. Shape each into a roll. Place 2 in. apart on greased baking sheets. Cover and let rise until doubled, about 30 minutes.

5. Bake at 375° until golden brown, 10-15 minutes. Carefully remove from pans to wire racks.

1 ROLL 120 cal., 3g fat (0 sat. fat), 0 chol., 149mg sod., 22g carb. (4g sugars, 2g fiber), 4g pro. **DIABETIC EXCHANGES** 1½ starch, ½ fat.

"These are the most flavorful rolls. It is the best roll recipe I've found."

—ARMADATIGGER, TASTEOFHOME.COM

JUMBO PUMPKIN PECAN MUFFINS

Perk up an autumn morning with one of these hearty muffins. You'll really enjoy the pumpkin-spice flavor and crumbly nut topping—and so will everyone else!

—Janice Christofferson, Eagle River, WI

PREP: 25 min. • **BAKE:** 25 min. • **MAKES:** 6 muffins

- 2½ cups all-purpose flour
- ½ cup sugar
- ¼ cup packed brown sugar
- 2 tsp. pumpkin pie spice
- 1 tsp. baking powder
- 1 tsp. baking soda
- ½ tsp. salt
- 2 large eggs, room temperature
- 1 cup canned pumpkin
- ½ cup buttermilk
- ¼ cup canola oil
- 1 tsp. vanilla extract
- ½ cup chopped pecans

TOPPING

- ⅓ cup packed brown sugar
- ⅓ cup finely chopped pecans
- ¼ cup all-purpose flour
- ¼ cup cold butter, cubed

1. In a large bowl, combine first 7 ingredients. In another bowl, combine the eggs, pumpkin, buttermilk, oil and vanilla. Stir into dry ingredients just until moistened. Fold in pecans. Fill 6 greased or paper-lined jumbo muffin cups three-fourths full.

2. For topping, in a small bowl, combine brown sugar, pecans and flour; cut in butter until crumbly. Sprinkle over batter.

3. Bake at 375° until a toothpick inserted in center comes out clean, 25-30 minutes. Cool for 5 minutes before removing from pan to a wire rack. Serve warm.

NOTE Substitute 1 Tbsp. white vinegar or lemon juice plus enough milk to measure 1 cup for each cup of buttermilk. Stir, then let stand for 5 minutes. Or use 1 cup plain yogurt or 1¾ tsp. cream of tartar plus 1 cup milk.

1 MUFFIN 660 cal., 30g fat (7g sat. fat), 83mg chol., 619mg sod., 89g carb. (41g sugars, 4g fiber), 11g pro.

PAIR IT WITH

Pumpkin With Smoked Gouda Soup, p. 156

ICEBOX POTATO ROLLS

These tender rolls are a family favorite, and we sometimes have more than 20 people around the table. Make the dough in advance and bake when you're ready.

—Barb Linnerud, Boiling Springs, SC

PREP: 1 hour + rising • **BAKE:** 15 min. • **MAKES:** about 2½ dozen

- 1¼ lbs. potatoes, peeled and cubed (about 3½ cups)
- ¾ cup sugar
- 2 tsp. salt
- 1 pkg. (¼ oz.) active dry yeast
- 5½ to 6 cups bread flour
- 1 cup 2% milk
- ½ cup water
- ½ cup shortening
- 3 large eggs, room temperature
- ⅓ cup butter, melted

1. Place potatoes in a saucepan and add water to cover. Bring to a boil. Reduce heat; cook, uncovered, 10-15 minutes or until tender. Drain. Return to pan. Mash potatoes (you should have about 2 cups). Cool slightly.

2. In a large bowl, mix sugar, salt, yeast and 2 cups flour. In a small saucepan, heat milk, water and shortening to 120°-130°. Add to dry ingredients; beat on medium speed for 2 minutes. Add eggs and potatoes and beat on high for 2 minutes. Stir in enough remaining flour to form a soft dough (dough will be very sticky).

3. Do not knead. Place dough in a large greased bowl, turning once to grease top. Cover; refrigerate overnight.

4. Punch down dough. Using a tablespoon dipped in melted butter, drop 3 spoonfuls of dough into a greased muffin cup. Repeat, re-dipping spoon in butter.

5. Cover; let rise in a warm place until almost doubled, about 45 minutes. Preheat oven to 375°.

6. Brush tops with remaining melted butter. Bake until golden brown, 12-15 minutes. Cool in pans for 5 minutes. Remove to wire racks. Serve warm.

NOTE Dough can be made up to 3 days before baking. Prepare dough as directed, refrigerating for 1-3 days and punching down dough every 24 hours. Shape and bake rolls as directed.

1 ROLL 181 cal., 6g fat (2g sat. fat), 25mg chol., 187mg sod., 26g carb. (6g sugars, 1g fiber), 4g pro.

EASY PEASY BISCUITS

I love that I can make these biscuits and have enough left over to freeze for another meal. They are wonderful served with homemade peach preserves.

—Amanda West, Shelbyville, TN

PREP: 25 min. • **BAKE:** 10 min. • **MAKES:** 2 dozen

- 4 cups all-purpose flour
- 4 Tbsp. baking powder
- 1 Tbsp. sugar
- 1 Tbsp. ground flaxseed
- 1 tsp. sea salt
- 1 cup solid coconut oil
- 1½ cups 2% milk

1. Preheat oven to 450°. In a large bowl, whisk flour, baking powder, sugar, flaxseed and salt. Add oil and cut in with a pastry blender until mixture resembles coarse crumbs. Add milk; stir just until moistened.

2. Turn dough onto a lightly floured surface. Knead gently 8-10 times. Pat or roll the dough into a ½-in.-thick rectangle; fold dough into thirds (as you would a letter). Pat or roll dough again into a ½-in.-thick rectangle; cut with a pizza cutter or knife into 24 biscuits, each about 2½ in. square. Place 1½ in. apart on ungreased baking sheets. Bake until light brown, 8-10 minutes. Serve warm.

FREEZE OPTION Freeze cut, unbaked dough on waxed paper-lined baking sheets until firm. Transfer to airtight containers and return to the freezer. To use, bake biscuits in a preheated 350° oven until light brown, 15-20 minutes. Freeze cooled baked biscuits in airtight containers. To use, heat in a preheated 350° oven until warmed, 5-10 minutes.

1 BISCUIT 167 cal., 10g fat (8g sat. fat), 1mg chol., 328mg sod., 17g carb. (1g sugars, 1g fiber), 3g pro.

"I love cooking with coconut oil. Delicious! Thank you, Amanda, for sharing this recipe."

—ORBS, TASTEOFHOME.COM

PAIR IT WITH
Copycat Olive Garden Minestrone Soup, p. 142

HERBED ACCORDION DINNER ROLLS

To dress up everyday dinner rolls, brush herbed butter over the dough, then form accordion rolls. The aroma while baking is incredible!
—*Taste of Home* Test Kitchen

PREP: 40 min. + rising • **BAKE:** 20 min. • **MAKES:** 2 dozen

- 2 pkg. (¼ oz. each) active dry yeast
- ½ cup warm water (110°-115°)
- 1 tsp. plus ⅓ cup sugar, divided
- 1¼ cups warm 2% milk (110°-115°)
- ½ cup butter, melted
- 2 large eggs, room temperature
- 1½ tsp. salt
- 6 to 6½ cups all-purpose flour
- 3 Tbsp. butter, softened
- 1 tsp. Italian seasoning
- 1 large egg white, beaten

1. In a large bowl, dissolve yeast in warm water with 1 tsp. sugar. Add milk, melted butter, eggs, salt, 3 cups flour and remaining sugar; beat until smooth. Stir in enough remaining flour to form a soft dough.

2. Turn dough onto a floured surface; knead until smooth and elastic, 6-8 minutes. Place in a greased bowl, turning once to grease top. Cover and let rise in a warm place until doubled, about 1 hour.

3. Punch down dough; place on a lightly floured surface. Divide into 4 portions. Roll each portion into a 14x6-in. rectangle. Combine softened butter and Italian seasoning; spread over dough.

4. Score each rectangle widthwise at 2-in. intervals. Using marks as a guide, fold dough accordion-style back and forth along score lines. Cut folded dough into six 1-in. pieces. Place pieces cut side down in greased muffin cups. Cover and let rise until doubled, about 30 minutes.

5. Preheat oven to 375°. Uncover pans and let dough stand another 10 minutes before baking. Brush with egg white. Bake until golden brown, 18-22 minutes. Remove from pans to wire racks.

1 ROLL 186 cal., 6g fat (4g sat. fat), 32mg chol., 200mg sod., 28g carb. (4g sugars, 1g fiber), 5g pro.

BASIL & OREGANO DINNER ROLLS Substitute ½ tsp. each dried oregano and basil for Italian seasoning.

FRESH HERB DINNER ROLLS Substitute 1½ tsp. minced fresh parsley and ½ tsp. minced fresh thyme for Italian seasoning.

BUTTERMILK BISCUITS

These biscuits are made from a recipe that's been in our family for years. They are simple to make and smell so good when baking! The wonderful aroma takes me back to the days when Mom made this meal—it's as if I'm there in our family's kitchen again, with her busy at the stove.

—Jean Parsons, Sarver, PA

PREP: 25 min. • **BAKE:** 15 min. • **MAKES:** 1½ dozen

- 2 cups all-purpose flour
- 1 Tbsp. sugar
- 1 tsp. baking powder
- ½ tsp. salt
- ½ tsp. baking soda
- ¼ cup cold shortening
- ¾ cup buttermilk

1. Preheat oven to 450°. In a large bowl, combine flour, sugar, baking powder, salt and baking soda. Cut in shortening until mixture resembles coarse crumbs. Add buttermilk; stir just until dough clings together.

2. Turn the dough onto a lightly floured surface; knead gently 10-12 times. Roll to ½-in. thickness; cut with a floured 2-in. round biscuit cutter. Place 1 in. apart on a greased baking sheet. Bake until lightly browned, 11-12 minutes. Serve warm.

1 BISCUIT 82 cal., 3g fat (1g sat. fat), 0 chol., 147mg sod., 12g carb. (1g sugars, 0 fiber), 2g pro.

PARMESAN-RANCH PAN ROLLS

My mom taught me this easy recipe, which is perfect for feeding a crowd. There is never a crumb left over. Mom used her own bread dough, but using frozen dough is my shortcut.

—Trisha Kruse, Eagle, ID

PREP: 30 min. + rising • **BAKE:** 20 min. • **MAKES:** 1½ dozen

- 2 loaves (1 lb. each) frozen bread dough, thawed
- 1 cup grated Parmesan cheese
- ½ cup butter, melted
- 1 envelope buttermilk ranch salad dressing mix
- 1 small onion, finely chopped

1. On a lightly floured surface, divide dough into 18 portions; shape each into a ball. In a small bowl, combine cheese, butter and salad dressing mix.

2. Roll balls in cheese mixture; arrange balls in 2 greased 9-in. square baking pans. Sprinkle with onion. Cover; let rise in a warm place until doubled, about 45 minutes.

3. Meanwhile, preheat oven to 350°. Bake until golden brown, 20-25 minutes. Remove from pans to wire racks.

1 ROLL 210 cal., 8g fat (4g sat. fat), 17mg chol., 512mg sod., 26g carb. (2g sugars, 2g fiber), 7g pro.

BUTTERMILK BISCUITS

BREADS

SPECIAL & SAVORY

HERBED PUMPKIN FLATBREAD

These flatbreads benefit from the wonderful flavor and texture of pumpkin, and herbs provide an autumnal twist. They're amazing served with soup, salad or curries. The chickpea flour adds a protein boost and unique flavor.

—Kayla Capper, Ojai, CA

PREP: 20 min. + standing • **COOK:** 5 min./batch • **MAKES:** 4 servings

- 1 cup all-purpose flour
- ½ cup chickpea flour
- 1 tsp. garlic salt
- ½ tsp. dried rosemary, crushed
- ¼ tsp. baking powder
- ¼ tsp. dried thyme
- ½ cup canned pumpkin
- 1 Tbsp. plus 2 tsp. canola oil, divided
- 1 tsp. water
- Optional: Fresh thyme, fresh rosemary and tzatziki sauce

1. In a bowl, whisk first 6 ingredients. Add pumpkin, 1 Tbsp. oil and water; stir until mixture resembles coarse crumbs. Turn onto a floured surface; knead 8-10 times, forming a soft dough. Cover and let rest for 15 minutes.

2. Divide dough into 4 pieces. On a lightly floured surface, roll each piece into a 6-in. circle. Brush flatbreads on both sides with remaining 2 tsp. oil. Heat a large skillet over medium-high heat. Working in batches, cook flatbreads for 1-2 minutes on each side or until golden brown. Serve warm; if desired, top with thyme and rosemary and serve with tzatziki sauce.

TO MAKE CHICKPEA FLOUR Add dried chickpeas or garbanzo beans to a food processor. Cover and process until powdery, 2-3 minutes. Sift through a fine mesh sieve into a bowl. Add larger pieces left in the sieve to coffee or spice grinder; process until powdery.

1 FLATBREAD 231 cal., 7g fat (1g sat. fat), 0 chol., 525mg sod., 35g carb. (3g sugars, 4g fiber), 7g pro.

"I love this recipe! Great use of chickpea flour. I've also used mashed sweet potatoes instead of the pumpkin with success."

—YVONNE2154, TASTEOFHOME.COM

1
2
3
4
110
PAIR IT WITH
Copycat Olive Garden
Minestrone Soup, p. 142

5

6

7

8

COPYCAT OLIVE GARDEN BREADSTICKS

You can't think of Olive Garden without reminiscing about their endless breadsticks. Now you can have the same fresh, hot breadsticks right from your oven in just 60 minutes.

—Lauren Habermehl, Pewaukee, WI

PREP: 25 min. + rising • **BAKE:** 15 min. • **MAKES:** 12 breadsticks

- ¼ cup unsalted butter
- 1 cup whole milk
- 2 Tbsp. instant yeast
- 1 Tbsp. sugar
- 1 large egg, room temperature
- ½ tsp. salt
- 3½ cups all-purpose flour

GARLIC TOPPING

- 4 Tbsp. unsalted butter
- 1 tsp. popcorn salt or flaky sea salt
- ½ tsp. garlic powder

1. Preheat oven to 400°. Line two 15x10x1-in. baking sheets with parchment; set aside.

2. In a small saucepan, melt the butter over medium heat. Stir in milk and warm to 105°-112°.

3. Add yeast and sugar to bowl of a stand mixer fitted with a dough hook. Slowly add milk mixture; gently stir to combine. With stand mixer on lowest speed, stir in egg and salt. Add 2½ cups flour. Continue to mix, adding remaining 1 cup flour until dough clings to hook, side of bowl is clean and dough is smooth and soft. Increase mixer speed to medium-low; knead dough 3-4 minutes.

4. With lightly floured hands, divide dough into 12 equal pieces. Shape the dough into 12 breadsticks, each about 9 in. long. Place breadsticks 1 in. apart on prepared pans. Cover and let rest until breadsticks have risen slightly, 10-15 minutes.

5. Uncover breadsticks; transfer to oven. Bake until golden brown, 15-18 minutes.

6. Meanwhile, in a small saucepan, melt butter over medium heat. Add salt and garlic powder, stir to incorporate. Brush over hot breadsticks, serve warm.

1 BREADSTICK230 cal., 9g fat (5g sat. fat), 38mg chol., 274mg sod., 31g carb. (2g sugars, 2g fiber), 6g pro.

HOMEMADE FRY BREAD

Crispy, doughy and totally delicious, this fry bread is fantastic with nearly any sweet or savory toppings you can think of. We love it with a little butter, a drizzle of honey and a squeeze of lemon.

—Thelma Tyler, Dragoon, AZ

PREP: 20 min. + standing • **COOK:** 15 min. • **MAKES:** 12 servings

- 2 cups all-purpose flour
- ½ cup nonfat dry milk powder
- 3 tsp. baking powder
- ½ tsp. salt
- 4½ tsp. shortening
- ⅔ to ¾ cup water
- Oil for deep-fat frying
- Optional: Butter, honey and fresh lemon juice

1. Combine the flour, milk powder, baking powder and salt; cut in shortening until crumbly. Add water gradually, mixing to form a firm ball. Divide dough; shape into 12 balls. Let stand, covered, for 10 minutes. Roll each ball into a 6-in. circle. With a sharp knife, cut a ½-in.-diameter hole in center of each.

2. In a large cast-iron skillet, heat oil over medium-high heat. Fry dough circles, 1 at a time, until puffed and golden, about 1 minute on each side. Drain on paper towels. Serve warm, with butter, honey and fresh lemon juice if desired.

1 PIECE 124 cal., 5g fat (1g sat. fat), 1mg chol., 234mg sod., 17g carb. (2g sugars, 1g fiber), 3g pro.

CORNBREAD CROUTONS

These crunchy, savory croutons are ready to take your next soup or salad over the top.

—*Taste of Home* Test Kitchen

TAKES: 25 min. • **MAKES:** 4 cups

- 1 Tbsp. olive oil
- ½ tsp. salt
- ¼ tsp. garlic powder, optional
- 4 cups cubed cornbread

1. In a large bowl, whisk together oil, salt and, if desired, garlic powder. Add cubed cornbread and toss to coat.

2. Place mixture in a single layer on an ungreased 15x10x1-in. baking sheet. Bake at 400° for 15-20 minutes or until golden brown, stirring occasionally. Let cool; store in an airtight container.

¼ CUP 32 cal., 1g fat (0 sat. fat), 0 chol., 117mg sod., 3g carb. (0 sugars, 0 fiber), 1g pro.

QUICK JALAPENO HUSH PUPPIES

The crunchy exterior of these southern-style snacks is a nice contrast to the moist cornbread. Jalapeno peppers and hot sauce add a hint of heat.

—*Taste of Home* Test Kitchen

PREP: 15 min. • **COOK:** 5 min./batch • **MAKES:** 2½ dozen

- 1½ cups yellow cornmeal
- ½ cup all-purpose flour
- 1 tsp. baking powder
- 1 tsp. salt
- 2 large eggs, room temperature, lightly beaten
- ¾ cup 2% milk
- 2 jalapeno peppers, seeded and minced
- ¼ cup finely chopped onion
- 1 tsp. Louisiana-style hot sauce
- Oil for deep-fat frying

1. In a large bowl, combine cornmeal, flour, baking powder and salt. In another bowl, beat eggs, milk, jalapenos, onion and hot sauce. Stir into dry ingredients just until combined.

2. In a cast-iron or other heavy skillet, heat oil to 375°. Drop batter by tablespoonfuls, a few at a time, into the hot oil. Fry until golden brown on both sides, about 5 minutes. Drain on paper towels. Serve warm.

NOTE Wear disposable gloves when cutting hot peppers; the oils can burn skin. Avoid touching your face.

1 HUSH PUPPY 56 cal., 3g fat (0 sat. fat), 14mg chol., 94mg sod., 7g carb. (0 sugars, 1g fiber), 1g pro.

"Great taste! Quick and easy to make!"

—DKINSEY161, TASTEOFHOME.COM

CALZONE ROLLS

Big pizza flavor comes through in these rolls. My recipe makes two pans because you'll need 'em! It's so easy to make the dough in my bread machine.

—Barb Downie, Peterborough, ON

PREP: 20 min. + rising • **BAKE:** 20 min. • **MAKES:** 2 dozen

- 1⅔ cups water (70°-80°)
- 2 Tbsp. nonfat dry milk powder
- 2 Tbsp. sugar
- 2 Tbsp. shortening
- 1¼ tsp. salt
- 4½ cups all-purpose flour
- 2¼ tsp. active dry yeast
- ½ cup chopped onion
- ½ cup sliced fresh mushrooms
- ½ cup chopped green pepper
- ½ cup chopped sweet red pepper
- 1 Tbsp. olive oil
- ⅓ cup pizza sauce
- ½ cup diced pepperoni
- 1 cup shredded pizza cheese blend
- ¼ cup chopped ripe olives
- 2 Tbsp. grated Parmesan cheese

1. In bread machine pan, place the first 7 ingredients in order suggested by manufacturer. Select dough setting (check dough after 5 minutes of mixing; add 1-2 Tbsp. water or flour if needed).

2. In a small skillet, saute onion, mushrooms and peppers in oil until tender; cool.

3. When bread machine cycle is completed, turn dough onto a lightly floured surface; divide in half. Let rest for 5 minutes. Roll each portion into a 16x10-in. rectangle and spread with pizza sauce. Top with onion mixture, pepperoni, pizza cheese and olives. Roll up each rectangle jelly-roll style, starting with a long side; pinch seam to seal. Cut each into 12 pieces (discard end pieces).

4. Place the pieces cut side down in 2 greased 10-in. cast-iron skillets or 9-in. round baking pans. Sprinkle with Parmesan cheese. Cover and let rise until doubled, about 30 minutes.

5. Bake at 375° until golden brown, 20-30 minutes. Serve warm.

1 ROLL 144 cal., 5g fat (2g sat. fat), 7mg chol., 244mg sod., 21g carb. (2g sugars, 1g fiber), 5g pro.

NO MACHINE? NO PROBLEM!

You can prepare this dough by hand instead of using a bread machine. In a large bowl, dissolve yeast in warm water (110°-115°). Add milk powder, sugar, shortening, salt and flour to form a soft dough. Turn onto a floured surface; knead until a smooth, firm dough forms, 8-10 minutes. Cover and let rest for 10 minutes. Proceed with the recipe as directed.

PAIR IT WITH
Pumpkin & Bean
Soup, p. 109

MAPLE BUBBLE BREAD

This is my family's favorite breakfast bread. With a scrumptious topping of maple syrup and brown sugar, it's the perfect start to a special day.

—Hannah Cobb, Owings Mills, MD

PREP: 45 min. + rising • **BAKE:** 30 min. + cooling • **MAKES:** 20 servings

- 1 pkg. (¼ oz.) active dry yeast
- ¼ cup warm water (110°-115°)
- 1 cup warm 2% milk (110°-115°)
- ⅓ cup butter, melted
- ¼ cup sugar
- 1 large egg, room temperature
- 1 large egg yolk, room temperature
- ½ tsp. salt
- 5 cups all-purpose flour

TOPPING

- ⅔ cup maple syrup
- 2 Tbsp. butter
- 1 cup packed brown sugar
- ½ tsp. ground cinnamon
- 3 Tbsp. butter, melted

1. In a large bowl, dissolve yeast in warm water. Add milk, butter, sugar, egg, egg yolk, salt and 3 cups flour. Beat on medium speed for 3 minutes. Stir in enough remaining flour to form a firm dough.

2. Turn onto a floured surface; knead for 6-8 minutes or until smooth and elastic. Place in a greased bowl, turning once to grease top. Cover and let rise in a warm place until doubled, about 1 hour.

3. In a small saucepan, combine syrup and butter. Bring to a boil. Cook and stir for 3 minutes; set aside.

4. Punch down dough. Turn dough onto a lightly floured surface; divide into 20 pieces. Shape each into a roll. In a shallow bowl, combine brown sugar and cinnamon. Place the melted butter in a separate shallow bowl. Dip buns in butter, then coat in brown sugar mixture.

5. Place 8 rolls in a greased 10-in. fluted tube pan; drizzle with ⅓ cup syrup. Top with remaining rolls, syrup and brown sugar mixture. Cover and let rise until doubled, about 45 minutes.

6. Bake at 350° for 30-35 minutes or until golden brown. Cool for 10 minutes before inverting onto a serving plate. Serve warm.

1 PIECE 258 cal., 7g fat (4g sat. fat), 37mg chol., 117mg sod., 45g carb. (21g sugars, 1g fiber), 4g pro.

PARMESAN SCONES

The addition of onions gives these scones a nice bite. You can even stir in some basil or oregano if you like.

—Jolie Stinson, Marion, IN

TAKES: 25 min. • **MAKES:** 1 dozen

- 2 cups finely chopped onions
- 2 Tbsp. olive oil
- 6 garlic cloves, minced
- 4 cups all-purpose flour
- 2 cups grated Parmesan cheese
- 4 tsp. baking powder
- 1 tsp. salt
- 2 cups heavy whipping cream
- Additional grated Parmesan cheese, optional

1. In a large skillet, saute onions in oil until tender. Add garlic; saute 1 minute longer.

2. In a large bowl, combine flour, cheese, baking powder and salt. Stir in cream just until moistened. Stir in onion mixture.

3. Turn onto a floured surface; knead 10 times. Divide dough in half. Pat each portion into a 6-in. circle. Cut each circle into 6 wedges. Separate the wedges and place on a greased baking sheet.

4. Bake at 400° for 12-15 minutes or until light golden brown. If desired, sprinkle with additional cheese in last 5 minutes of baking. Serve warm.

1 SCONE 378 cal., 21g fat (12g sat. fat), 66mg chol., 551mg sod., 36g carb. (2g sugars, 2g fiber), 11g pro.

MARINA'S GOLDEN CORN FRITTERS

Just one bite of these fritters takes me back to when my kids were young.

—Marina Castle Kelley, Canyon Country, CA

TAKES: 30 min. • **MAKES:** 32 fritters

- 2½ cups all-purpose flour
- 3 tsp. baking powder
- 2 tsp. dried parsley flakes
- 1 tsp. salt
- 2 large eggs, room temperature
- ¾ cup 2% milk
- 2 Tbsp. butter, melted
- 2 tsp. grated onion
- 1 can (15¼ oz.) whole kernel corn, drained
- Oil for deep-fat frying

1. In a large bowl, whisk flour, baking powder, parsley and salt. In another bowl, whisk eggs, milk, butter and onion until blended. Add to dry ingredients, stirring just until moistened. Fold in corn.

2. In an electric skillet or deep fryer, heat oil to 375°. Drop batter by tablespoonfuls, several at a time, into hot oil. Fry for 2-3 minutes on each side or until golden brown. Drain on paper towels.

2 FRITTERS 162 cal., 8g fat (2g sat. fat), 28mg chol., 327mg sod., 18g carb. (2g sugars, 1g fiber), 4g pro.

PARMESAN SCONES

BREAD MACHINE NAAN

Chewy yeast-raised flatbread is a snap to make in a bread machine. Serve this naan with your favorite Indian dishes to soak up all the mouthwatering sauces.

—Shannon Ventresca, Middleboro, MA

PREP: 1½ hours. • **COOK:** 5 min./batch • **MAKES:** 6 servings

- ¾ cup warm 2% milk (70°-80°)
- ¾ cup plain yogurt
- 1 large egg, room temperature, beaten
- 2 Tbsp. canola oil
- 2 tsp. sugar
- 1 tsp. salt
- 1 tsp. baking powder
- 4 cups bread flour
- 2 tsp. active dry yeast
- Butter, softened, optional

1. In bread machine pan, place all ingredients in order suggested by manufacturer. Select dough setting (check dough after 5 minutes of mixing; add 1-2 Tbsp. water or flour if needed).

2. When cycle is completed, turn dough onto a lightly floured surface. Divide dough into 6 portions; shape into balls. Roll each ball into a ¼-in.-thick oval. Let rest for 5 minutes.

3. Brush tops with water. In a greased large skillet over medium-high heat, cover and cook 1 piece of dough, wet side down, for 1 minute. Turn dough; cover and cook for 30 seconds longer or until golden brown. Repeat with remaining dough. Serve with softened butter if desired.

1 NAAN 363 cal., 7g fat (2g sat. fat), 42mg chol., 502mg sod., 64g carb. (4g sugars, 2g fiber), 14g pro.

PAIR IT WITH
Matzo Ball Soup, p. 33

PASSOVER POPOVERS

Popovers have an important role at the Passover table as a substitute for bread. When puffed and golden brown, they're ready to share.

—Gloria Mezikofsky, Wakefield, MA

PREP: 25 min. • **BAKE:** 20 min. + standing • **MAKES:** 1 dozen

- 1 cup water
- ½ cup safflower oil
- ⅛ to ¼ tsp. salt
- 1 cup matzo cake meal
- 7 large eggs, room temperature

1. Preheat oven to 450°. Generously grease 12 muffin cups. In a large saucepan, bring water, oil and salt to a rolling boil. Add cake meal all at once and beat until blended. Remove from heat; let stand 5 minutes.

2. Transfer mixture to a food processor or blender. Add 2 eggs; process, covered, until blended. Continue adding eggs, 1 at a time, and processing until incorporated. Process until mixture is smooth, about 2 minutes longer.

3. Fill prepared muffin cups three-fourths full. Bake for 18-22 minutes or until puffed, very firm and golden brown. Turn off oven (do not open oven door); leave popovers in oven 10 minutes. Immediately remove popovers from pan to a wire rack. Serve hot.

NOTE This recipe was tested with Manischewitz cake meal. Look for it in the baking aisle or kosher foods section.

1 POPOVER 174 cal., 12g fat (2g sat. fat), 109mg chol., 66mg sod., 11g carb. (0 sugars, 0 fiber), 5g pro.

SHARING SECRETS

The secret to puffy popovers lies in the batter. It should be thin, so take special care not to overmix it. The key is to have a wet batter that will steam up in the hot oven, causing a good rise in the dough. Make sure your oven is fully heated to 450°. The initial blast of hot air goes a long way toward jump-starting the baking process. Keep your oven door closed during the entire baking period.

SOFT BEER PRETZEL NUGGETS

What goes together better than beer and pretzels? Not much that I can think of. That's why I put them together into one recipe. I'm always looking for new ways to combine fun flavors. I love the way this recipe turned out!

—Alyssa Wilhite, Whitehouse, TX

PREP: 1 hour + rising • **BAKE:** 10 min./batch • **MAKES:** 8 dozen

- 1 bottle (12 oz.) amber beer or nonalcoholic beer
- 1 pkg. (¼ oz.) active dry yeast
- 2 Tbsp. unsalted butter, melted
- 2 Tbsp. sugar
- 1½ tsp. salt
- 4 to 4½ cups all-purpose flour
- 10 cups water
- ⅔ cup baking soda

TOPPING

- 1 large egg yolk
- 1 Tbsp. water
- Coarse salt, optional

1. In a small saucepan, heat beer to 110°-115°; remove from heat. Stir in yeast until dissolved. In a large bowl, combine butter, sugar, salt, yeast mixture and 3 cups flour; beat on medium speed until smooth. Stir in enough remaining flour to form a soft dough (dough will be sticky).

2. Turn dough onto a floured surface; knead until smooth and elastic, 6-8 minutes. Place in a greased bowl, turning once to grease top. Cover and let rise in a warm place until doubled, about 1 hour.

3. Preheat oven to 425°. Punch down dough. Turn onto a lightly floured surface; divide and shape into 8 balls. Roll each into a 12-in. rope. Cut each rope into 1-in. pieces.

4. In a Dutch oven, bring 10 cups water and baking soda to a boil. Drop the nuggets, 12 at a time, into boiling water. Cook for 30 seconds. Remove with a slotted spoon; drain well on paper towels.

5. Place on greased baking sheets. In a small bowl, whisk egg yolk and 1 Tbsp. water; brush over pretzels. Sprinkle with coarse salt if desired. Bake 10-12 minutes or until golden brown. Remove from pans to a wire rack to cool.

FREEZE OPTION Freeze cooled pretzel nuggets in airtight containers. To use, thaw at room temperature or, if desired, microwave on high 20-30 seconds or until heated through.

6 PRETZEL NUGGETS 144 cal., 2g fat (1g sat. fat), 8mg chol., 302mg sod., 26g carb. (2g sugars, 1g fiber), 4g pro.

PRETZEL ROLLS Divide and shape dough into 8 balls; roll each into a 14-in. rope. Starting at 1 end of each rope, loosely wrap dough around itself to form a coil. Boil, top and bake as directed. You can also make traditional pretzels with the same dough.

SAVORY PARTY BREAD

SAVORY PARTY BREAD

It's impossible to stop nibbling on warm pieces of this cheesy, oniony loaf. The bread fans out for a fun presentation.

—Kay Daly, Raleigh, NC

PREP: 10 min. • **BAKE:** 25 min. • **MAKES:** 8 servings

- 1 unsliced round loaf sourdough bread (1 lb.)
- 1 lb. Monterey Jack cheese
- ½ cup butter, melted
- ½ cup chopped green onions
- 2 to 3 tsp. poppy seeds

1. Preheat oven to 350°. Cut bread widthwise into 1-in. slices to within ½ in. of bottom of loaf. Repeat cuts in opposite direction. Cut cheese into ¼-in. slices; cut slices into small pieces. Place cheese in cuts in bread.

2. In a small bowl, mix butter, green onion and poppy seeds. Drizzle over bread. Wrap in foil and place on a baking sheet. Bake for 15 minutes. Unwrap; bake until cheese is melted, about 10 minutes longer.

1 SERVING 481 cal., 31g fat (17g sat. fat), 91mg chol., 782mg sod., 32g carb. (1g sugars, 2g fiber), 17g pro.

MUSHROOM SWISS BREAD Substitute Swiss cheese and a drained 4½-oz. jar of sliced mushrooms for the Monterey Jack and green onions. Use ¼ tsp. garlic powder instead of the poppy seeds.

SAUSAGE CHEESE PUFFS

People are always surprised when I tell them there are only four ingredients in these tasty bite-sized puffs. Cheesy and spicy, the golden morsels are a fun novelty at a breakfast or brunch, and they also make yummy party appetizers.

—Della Moore, Troy, NY

TAKES: 25 min. • **MAKES:** about 4 dozen

- 1 lb. bulk Italian sausage
- 3 cups biscuit/baking mix
- 4 cups shredded cheddar cheese
- ¾ cup water

1. Preheat oven to 400°. In a large skillet, cook sausage over medium heat, until meat is no longer pink, 5-7 minutes, breaking up sausage into crumbles; drain.

2. In a large bowl, combine the biscuit mix and cheese; stir in sausage. Add water and toss with a fork until moistened. Shape into 1½-in. balls. Place 2 in. apart on ungreased baking sheets.

3. Bake until puffed and golden brown, 12-15 minutes. Cool on wire racks.

1 PUFF 89 cal., 6g fat (3g sat. fat), 14mg chol., 197mg sod., 6g carb. (0 sugars, 0 fiber), 4g pro.

YORKSHIRE PUDDING WITH BACON & SAGE

These are a nice change from traditional dinner rolls. The savory popovers are tastefully topped with crumbled bacon and fresh sage.

—Melissa Jelinek, Apple Valley, MN

PREP: 15 min. • **BAKE:** 20 min. • **MAKES:** 1 dozen

- 5 bacon strips, chopped
- 2 Tbsp. butter, melted
- 1½ cups all-purpose flour
- 3 Tbsp. minced fresh sage, divided
- ½ tsp. salt
- 1½ cups 2% milk
- 3 large eggs, room temperature

1. Preheat oven to 450°. In a large skillet, cook bacon over medium heat until crisp. Remove with a slotted spoon; drain on paper towels, reserving drippings.

2. Transfer drippings to a measuring cup; add enough melted butter to measure ¼ cup. Pour into 12 ungreased muffin cups. Place in oven until hot.

3. Meanwhile, in a bowl, combine flour, 2 Tbsp. sage and salt; beat in milk and eggs until smooth. Fold in two-thirds of bacon. Divide batter among prepared muffin cups.

4. Bake for 10 minutes. Reduce heat to 350° (do not open oven door). Bake until popovers are puffed and golden brown, 10-12 minutes longer. Sprinkle with remaining bacon and sage.

1 POPOVER 150 cal., 8g fat (3g sat. fat), 67mg chol., 224mg sod., 14g carb. (2g sugars, 0 fiber), 5g pro.

"I have made Yorkshire pudding for many years but never with sage and bacon. I love the smell and taste of sage, and who doesn't love bacon? This is definitely a keeper."

—GRANDMASCOOKING22, TASTEOFHOME.COM

PAIR IT WITH

Old-Fashioned Ham & Bean Soup, p. 106

HOMEMADE BAGELS

Instead of going to a baker, head to the kitchen and surprise your family with homemade bagels. For variation and flavor, sprinkle the tops with cinnamon-sugar instead of sesame and poppy seeds.

—Rebecca Phillips, Burlington, CT

PREP: 30 min. + rising • **BAKE:** 20 min. • **MAKES:** 1 dozen

- 1 tsp. active dry yeast
- 1¼ cups warm 2% milk (110°-115°)
- ½ cup butter, softened
- 2 Tbsp. sugar
- 1 tsp. salt
- 1 large egg yolk, room temperature
- 3¾ to 4¼ cups all-purpose flour
- Sesame or poppy seeds, optional

1. In a large bowl, dissolve yeast in warm milk. Add butter, sugar, salt and egg yolk; mix well. Stir in enough flour to form a soft dough.

2. Turn dough onto a floured surface; knead until smooth and elastic, 6-8 minutes. Place in a greased bowl, turning once to grease top. Cover and let rise in a warm place until doubled, about 1 hour.

3. Punch down dough. Shape into 12 balls. Push thumb through centers to form a 1½-in. hole. Stretch and shape dough to form an even ring. Place on a floured surface. Cover and let rest for 10 minutes; flatten bagels slightly.

4. Fill a Dutch oven two-thirds full with water; bring to a boil. Drop bagels, 2 at a time, into boiling water. Cook for 45 seconds; turn and cook 45 seconds longer. Remove with a slotted spoon; drain well on paper towels.

5. Sprinkle with sesame or poppy seeds if desired. Place 2 in. apart on greased baking sheets. Bake at 400° until golden brown, 20-25 minutes. Remove from pans to wire racks to cool.

1 BAGEL 237 cal., 9g fat (5g sat. fat), 38mg chol., 271mg sod., 33g carb. (3g sugars, 1g fiber), 5g pro.

EKCO

1

2

3

4

5

6

HERB & PARMESAN FOUGASSE

This traditional French bread, a kind of French variation of focaccia, is easy to make and so flavorful, and it looks impressive on the table. Use whatever herbs you like; try adding red pepper flakes for heat! You can also use 1 teaspoon of dried herbs in place of the fresh. It's often served with a dipping sauce, such as olive oil and garlic.

—Holly Balzer-Harz, Malone, NY

PREP: 35 min. + rising • **BAKE:** 15 min. • **MAKES:** 12 servings

- 4 cups bread flour
- 1¾ tsp. active dry yeast
- 1¾ tsp. salt
- 1½ cups warm water (110°-115°)
- 2 Tbsp. olive oil
- 2 tsp. minced fresh rosemary or 1 tsp. dried rosemary
- 2 tsp. minced fresh thyme or 1 tsp. dried thyme
- 2 tsp. minced fresh basil or 1 tsp. dried basil
- 2 tsp. chopped fresh sage or 1 tsp. dried sage leaves
- ¼ cup grated Parmesan cheese
- ½ tsp. sea salt flakes
- ½ tsp. dried basil

1. In a large bowl, mix flour, yeast and salt. Add water and oil to dry ingredients; beat on low for 2 minutes. Using a dough hook, beat on medium speed, for 5 minutes. Stir in herbs and Parmesan cheese; dough will be sticky.

2. Place in a greased bowl, turning once to grease top. Cover and let rise in a warm place until doubled, about 1 hour.

3. Preheat oven to 425°. Turn dough out onto lightly floured surface; carefully divide in half. Place each half onto parchment-lined baking sheets. With floured hands, shape into long ovals.

4. Using a sharp knife, make 1 long cut down the middle, leaving 1 in. of uncut edges on each end. Make 4 cuts on either side of the long cut, so dough resembles a leaf shape. Stretch dough as needed to emphasize cuts.

5. Cover with kitchen towels; let rise in a warm place, until almost doubled, about 20 minutes.

6. Sprinkle with salt, dried basil and additional grated Parmesan cheese. Bake until golden brown, about 15-20 minutes.

1 PIECE 194 cal., 4g fat (1g sat. fat), 1mg chol., 456mg sod., 34g carb. (0 sugars, 1g fiber), 6g pro.

SEA SALT STICKS

When my daughter was in school, her class had a recipe exchange—the kids all brought something to eat to share with the class and included the recipe. She raved about these breadsticks and wanted to make them for the family. You can even add a few tablespoons of poppy seeds to the flour before mixing.

—Marina Castle Kelley, Canyon Country, CA

PREP: 45 min. + rising • **BAKE:** 20 min. • **MAKES:** 20 servings

1 Tbsp. sugar
1 pkg. (¼ oz.) quick-rise yeast
1 tsp. sea salt
3¼ to 3¾ cups all-purpose flour
1¼ cups water
¼ cup olive oil

TOPPING

1 large egg white
1 Tbsp. water
Coarse sea salt

1. Preheat oven to 325°. In a large bowl, mix sugar, yeast, salt and 2 cups flour. In a small saucepan, heat water and oil to 120°-130°; stir into dry ingredients. Stir in enough remaining flour to form a soft dough (dough will be sticky). Turn out dough onto a floured surface; knead for 6-8 minutes or until smooth and elastic. Place in a greased bowl, turning once to grease the top. Cover and let rest 10 minutes.

2. Divide dough into 20 portions. On a lightly floured surface, roll each portion into a 14-in. rope. Place ropes 1 in. apart on greased baking sheets. Cover and let rise in a warm place until almost doubled, 15-20 minutes.

3. In a small bowl, whisk egg white with water; brush over tops of dough. Sprinkle with coarse sea salt. Bake until light brown, 20-25 minutes. Remove from pans to wire racks. Serve warm.

1 BREADSTICK 102 cal., 3g fat (0 sat. fat), 0 chol., 97mg sod., 16g carb. (1g sugars, 1g fiber), 2g pro.

"These are crazy good! They have a great salty flavor and a great crunch!"

—JELLYBUG, TASTEOFHOME.COM

PAIR IT WITH
Easy Shrimp & Scallops
Ramen Soup, p. 136

SOUPS INDEX

A

Alphabet Soup ... 23
Andouille-Shrimp Cream Soup ... 89
Avgolemono Soup ... 154

B

Balsamic Lentil Soup ... 112
Beef & Noodle Soup ... 139
Beef Barley Lentil Soup ... 27
Beef Vegetable Soup ... 18
Beefy Mushroom Soup ... 67
Best Cream of Tomato Soup ... 153
Best Seafood Chowder ... 80
Buffalo Chicken Chili ... 193
Burgoo ... 60
Butternut Squash Soup ... 39

C

Cabbage Barley Soup ... 83
Cajun Potato Soup ... 158
Carrot Soup ... 82
Cheese Chicken Soup ... 172
Cheeseburger Soup ... 166
Chicken Cassoulet Soup ... 114
Chicken Florentine Soup ... 53
Chicken Ramen Noodle Bowl ... 122
Chicken Tortilla Soup ... 42
Chinese Beef Noodle Soup ... 129
Chipotle Pumpkin Butternut Soup ... 118
Chorizo & Chickpea Soup ... 133
Clam Chowder ... 18
Coconut Curry Soup ... 77
Comforting Barley & Pumpkin Beef Stew ... 181
Copycat Olive Garden Chicken Gnocchi Soup ... 130
Copycat Olive Garden Minestrone Soup ... 142
Copycat Wendy's Chili ... 196
Corn Chowder with Turkey & Bacon ... 161
Cowboy Soup ... 54
Cream of Celery Soup ... 157
Cream of Potato Soup ... 162
Creamy Corn Crab Soup ... 172
Creamy Tuscan Chicken Soup ... 165
Creamy Vegan Cauliflower Soup ... 95

D

DIY Ramen Soup....143

E

Easy Mulligatawny Soup....103
Easy Pot Sticker Soup....135
Easy Shrimp & Scallops Ramen Soup....136
Easy White Bean Soup....115
Egg Drop Soup....27

F

Favorite Baked Potato Soup....37
Flavorful Meatball Soup....50
French Market Soup....105
French Onion Soup....31
French Onion Tortellini Soup....122
Fresh Fruit Soup....82

G

Garden Vegetable & Herb Soup....88
Gazpacho....38
Grandma's Oxtail Soup....69
Grandma's Pressure-Cooker Chicken Noodle Soup....126
Grandma's Tomato Soup....31
Green Chile Butternut Squash Soup....168
Green Chile Chicken Chili....179
Green Chile Chicken Soup....58
Grilled Watermelon Gazpacho....76

H

Hearty Homemade Chicken Noodle Soup....20
Hearty Navy Bean Soup....34
Homemade Bone Broth....9
Homemade Chicken Broth....12
Homemade Turkey Stock....11

I

Italian Sausage Bean Soup....111
Italian Sausage Pizza Soup....66
Italian Wedding Soup....41

L

Lemony Mushroom-Orzo Soup for Two....139
Loaded Broccoli-Cheese Soup....23
Lobster Bisque....30

M

Manhattan Clam Chowder....84
Matzo Ball Soup....33
Meatball Soup....145
Mexican Pork & Hominy Stew....182
Minestrone Made Easy....19

O

Old-Fashioned Ham & Bean Soup....106
Old-Fashioned Split Pea Soup with Ham Bone....16
Old-Fashioned Turkey Noodle Soup....146
Oodles of Noodles Soup....133

P

Pasta & White Bean Soup With Sun-Dried Tomatoes....125
Pork Edamame Soup....134
Potato Beer Cheese Soup....171
Potato-Beef Barley Soup....104
Pressure-Cooker Beef & Farro Stew....176
Pressure-Cooker Jalapeno Popper Chicken Chili....46
Pressure-Cooker Sonoran Chowder....91
Pressure-Cooker Spring-Thyme Chicken Stew....187
Pumpkin & Bean Soup....109
Pumpkin with Smoked Gouda Soup....156

Q

Quick Cream of Mushroom Soup 25

R

Ramen Broccoli Soup 145
Ravioli Soup 140
Ribollita 64
Roasted Garlic Soup 169

S

Salmon Sweet Potato Soup 93
Seafood Gumbo 185
Seafood Soup 92
Shrimp Bisque 96
Singapore Noodle Soup 127
Slow-Cooked Black Bean Soup 110
Slow-Cooked Pork Stew 189
Slow-Cooker Chicken Potpie 63
Smoky & Spicy Vegetable Bisque 163
Sopa Ajoblanco 150
Sopa de Camarones (Shrimp Soup) 79
Spanish Chicken Soup 70
Spinach & Sausage Lentil Soup 117
Steak Soup 49

T

The Best Beef Stew 195
The Best Ever Chili 28
Tomato Florentine Soup 126
Tortellini & Spinach Soup 100
Turkey & Noodle Tomato Soup 57
Turkey Cabbage Stew 186
Turkey Dumpling Soup 51
Turkey Sausage & Lentil Soup 59
Turkey Sausage, Butternut Squash & Kale Soup 67
Turkey Stew with Dumplings 192
Turkey-Sweet Potato Soup 57

V

Vegan Squash Soup 87
Vegetable Broth 10
Vegetarian Skillet Chili 190
Vegetarian White Bean Soup 74

W

West African Chicken Stew 180

Y

Yummy Chicken & Dumpling Soup 24

P. 281

P. 232

P. 226

BREADS INDEX

A

Almond Flour Bread....250
Avocado Quick Bread....261

B

Bacon Walnut Bread with Honey Butter....242
Baking Powder Drop Biscuits....269
Beernana Bread....254
Biscuit Baking Mix....205
Bread Machine Naan....304
Buttermilk Biscuits....288

C

Calzone Rolls....298
Caraway Bread....228
Caraway Rye Dinner Rolls....273
Carrot Honey Loaf....254
Chive Pinwheel Rolls....276
Copycat Cheesecake Factory Brown Bread....225
Copycat Olive Garden Breadsticks....295
Copycat Starbucks Pumpkin Bread....247
Copycat Texas Roadhouse Rolls....274
Cornbread Croutons....296
Country Crust Sourdough Bread....221
Crusty Homemade Bread....219

D

Dutch Oven Raisin Walnut Bread....222

E

Easy Cheesy Biscuits....278
Easy Onion Crescent Rolls....270
Easy Peasy Biscuits....284

F

Favorite Irish Soda Bread....245
Flaky Italian Biscuits....270

G

Garlic & Oregano Bread....226
Ghost Pepper Popcorn Cornbread....249
Gluten-Free Cornmeal Muffins....278
Golden Sweet Onion Round....259
Grandma's Onion Squares....262
Grandma's Yeast Rolls....271

H

Ham Biscuits....277
Herb & Parmesan Fougasse....313
Herb & Sun-Dried Tomato Muffins....269
Herb-Cheese Rolls....266
Herbed Accordion Dinner Rolls....287
Herbed Pumpkin Flatbread....292
Homemade Bagels....311
Homemade Fry Bread....296
Homemade Pumpernickel Bread....216
Honey Beer Bread....246

I

Ice Cream Bread....250
Icebox Potato Rolls....283

J

Jumbo Pumpkin Pecan Muffins....282

K

Keto Bread....246

L

Lambertville Station Coconut Bread....253

M

Maple Bubble Bread....301
Marina's Golden Corn Fritters....302

N

No-Knead Harvest Bread.... 238

O

Old-Fashioned Brown Bread....214
Olive Bread....237
Olive Quick Bread....252
Onion French Bread Loaves....235

P

Panettone....232
Parmesan Herb Loaf....245
Parmesan Scones....302
Parmesan Zucchini Bread....262
Parmesan-Ranch Pan Rolls....288
Paska Easter Bread....213
Passover Popovers....305
Pepperoni Cheese Bread....234
Pina Colada Zucchini Bread....257
Pull-Apart Garlic Bread....261

Q

Quick & Easy Bread Bowls....204
Quick Jalapeno Hush Puppies....297

R

Roasted Butternut Squash Bread....258
Rosemary Nut Bread....229

S

Sage & Gruyere Sourdough Bread....215
Sausage Cheese Puffs....309
Savory Party Bread....309
Savory Stuffing Bread....210
Sea Salt Sticks....314
Soft Beer Pretzel Nuggets....306
Sourdough Starter....206
Swedish Limpa Bread....220
Sweet Italian Holiday Bread....253
Sweet Potato & Pesto Slow-Cooker Bread....231

T

Tender Whole Wheat Rolls....281

Y

Yorkshire Pudding with Bacon & Sage....310